THE AXIOMATIC METHOD IN PHONOLOGY

THE AXIOMATIC METHOD IN PHONOLOGY

by

TADEUSZ BATÓG

LONDON
ROUTLEDGE & KEGAN PAUL LTD

First published 1967
by Routledge & Kegan Paul Limited
Broadway House, 68–74 Carter Lane
London, E.C.4

Printed in Great Britain
by Butler & Tanner Limited
Frome and London

SBN 7100 2980 2

CONTENTS

PREFACE

The present monograph is an attempt to develop a systematic and fully formalized phoneme theory based essentially on the informal ideas of Z. S. Harris. In this respect it is a continuation of my earlier articles, the first of which was published in 1961.

The exposition, though completely formalized, should be understandable to the general reader, because a particular emphasis has been laid on an informal intuitive explanation of almost all symbolic definitions and theorems. If the reader has not had some training in symbolic logic or set theory, however, he might omit the proofs of some of the theorems.

This monograph owes its very existence to Professor Geoffrey B. Keene of the University of Exeter at whose suggestion work was begun on it in 1964. I wish to express him my warmest thanks for the suggestion as well as for the revision of the manuscript.

I am also grateful to Professors S. Łuszczewska-Romahnowa and J. Giedymin, both of the University of Poznań, for their help during the preparation of this book.

TADEUSZ BATÓG

Poznań, Poland
January 1967

PART I

Logical Preliminaries

Chapter 1

AXIOMATIC METHOD AND PHONOLOGY

The problems of theoretical phonology are among the most controversial in linguistics. These problems have been discussed since the appearance of the first phonological ideas in the works of Jan Baudouin de Courtenay; however, the results of these discussions are still unsatisfactory. The general situation in present-day phonology may be characterized in the following way:

(1) At present there does not exist a phonological theory which would be accepted by all or at least by the majority of phonologists. On the contrary, it is no exaggeration to say that nowadays there are as many different phonological theories as there are phonologists. As a result of this situation the meanings of even the simplest terms of phonology differ from author to author. The same applies, also of course, to the basic term of phonology, namely, the term 'phoneme'.

(2) None of the various phonological theories constructed by linguists is satisfactory from a formal point of view: they all make use of vague and ambiguous terms, definitions are not precise and give little information, theorems often lack a clear sense. This situation makes the mutual understanding of linguists more difficult and increases the chaos prevailing in phonology.

(3) The practice of phonologists depends, as a rule, only to a limited extent on the general phonological theories assumed by them. This means that the phonologist in describing the so-called phonological system of a particular language (the stock of phonemes, their distinctive features and the principles of combination of phonemes in the flow of speech) is guided not only by the rules of the general theory he follows but also by other incidental factors which are alien to this theory. This is understandable in the light of what we have said in paragraph (2). It is also obvious that a theory which is not sufficiently clear and precise will not work in practice, and the linguist who employs such a theory will be inclined to adjust it, for instance, to those features which are peculiar to the language he is examining or to the judgments of previous investigators of that language. As a result the role of phonological theory amounts to that of a set of vague instructions only in a slight degree restricting the choice of formulations.

This is not a satisfactory situation. One of the means of improving it seems to be the application of the conceptual apparatus and the methods of mathematical logic. Obviously, logic will not cure all the weaknesses of phonology but its importance in this respect seems to be considerable.

One of the main consequences of the application of notions and methods of logic will be theoretical systematization and even axiomatization of particular phonological theories. These theories will become more definite and less vague. The shortcomings of the present theories which have been indicated above in paragraph (2) and partly those indicated in paragraph (3) will be eliminated. In fact, the axiomatic method, correctly applied, will introduce a considerable degree of exactness and clarity into phonology, which will facilitate the mutual understanding of linguists and the discovery of discrepancies between theory and its application in practice.

The axiomatic method will not, of course, remove the theoretical discrepancies between different trends of phonology. However, the very precision which the axiomatic method enforces will accentuate the essential differences between competing theories, and at the same time eliminate the apparent differences. As a result of this, a more objective comparison of particular theories will be possible. A number of theories will have to be rejected and only two or three essentially different theories of genuine scientific value will survive.

The idea of applying the axiomatic method in linguistics and especially in phonology is not new. L. Bloomfield was, of course, the first to suggest it. By 1926 under the influence of the interest in axiomatics then prevailing in logic and mathematics, Bloomfield attempted to present theoretical linguistics (and also certain problems of phonology) in the form of an axiomatic system.[1] Although at first the methodological ideas of Bloomfield aroused no interest, in the post-war period they were continued by B. Bloch. In 1948 Bloch published a paper[2] entirely devoted to theoretical phonology and in which he applied Bloomfield's method of presentation.

It should be emphasized that Bloomfield and Bloch fully realized both the significance of the axiomatic method for linguistics as well as the difficulties attaching to the axiomatization of any empirical science. Here are Bloomfield's own words on this subject:

'The method of postulates (that is, assumptions or axioms) and definitions is fully adequate to mathematics; as for other sciences, the more complex their subject-matter, the less amenable are they to this method, since, under it, every descriptive or historical fact becomes the subject of a new postulate.

[1] L. Bloomfield [5]. [2] B. Bloch [4].

'Nevertheless, the postulational method can further the study of language, because it forces us to state explicitly whatever we assume, to define our terms, and to decide what things may exist independently and what things are interdependent.

'Certain errors can be avoided or corrected by examining and formulating our (at present tacit) assumptions and defining our (often undefined) terms.

'Also, the postulational method saves discussion, because it limits our statements to a defined terminology; in particular, it cuts us off from psychological dispute. Discussion of the fundamentals of our science seems to consist one half of obvious truisms, and one half of metaphysics; this is characteristic of matters which form no real part of a subject: they should properly be disposed of by merely naming certain concepts as belonging to the domain of other sciences.' [1]

A logician will certainly agree with this opinion of the linguist, although he would formulate it in a rather different way. However, a logician will quickly notice that the realization of Bloomfield's idea is facilitated and even, in a sense, guaranteed by applying the formal methods of mathematical logic. Bloomfield and Bloch seem, however, to have overlooked or underestimated this point. This explains perhaps why the systems of these authors contain a number of shortcomings and errors which prevented them from obtaining the expected results. For instance, neither Bloomfield nor Bloch establish a list of primitive terms, that is of those terms which constitute the ultimate basis for defining all the other terms used. The definitions they actually give employ various colloquial and special linguistic expressions which are not characterized by any axioms, and hence these definitions are neither sufficiently precise nor provide a satisfactory basis for formulating and proving theorems. Thus, in spite of their intentions, they have not, because of insufficient precision, succeeded in 'saving discussion'.

During the last few years a further step was made in the field of application of the axiomatic method and of logic to phonology. Since 1959 the works of J. H. Greenberg [6], the present author [1], [3], S. Marcus [17], S. Kanger [14] have appeared successively in one-year intervals.[2] All these works were written independently of each other and each of them represents a different approach to the problems of phonology. However, they have a feature in common,

[1] L. Bloomfield [5], pp. 153–4.

[2] There are several other articles concerned with the application of logical and mathematical means, but this application is in fact so slight that there is no need to mention them here.

namely, the employment of, broadly, logical and mathematical means. In this respect they show a distinct advance on the work of Bloch. However, none of them can be recognized as a fully adequate reconstruction of a definite phonological theory. Each has its own shortcomings.[1] This does not mean, of course, that logical means are useless for the purposes of phonology. It means only that an adequate logical reconstruction of phonological theories requires much more work than has been done so far. This circumstance is, at present, widely acknowledged and it is to be expected that more detailed and more adequate works will appear shortly.

This book is intended as a further step towards an adequate logical reconstruction of phonological theories. Strictly speaking, we are mainly concerned with Z. S. Harris' structuralistic theory which is, at the present time, one of the principal phonological theories. It is this theory that we shall attempt to analyse and present in the form of an axiomatic system. Our task is not, by any means, simple. In order to obtain a tolerably complete whole we have to supply Harris' theory with a number of details; some part of this theory will have to be reinterpreted and some even changed altogether. Our strategy will be as follows: if we make some essential change in Harris' theory, we try to find a justification of this change in the works of other linguists who represent the American structuralism or related trends. In this connection we often refer to the works by D. Jones, B. Bloch, W. Jassem and H. Pilch. Of course, it is not always possible to find such a justification. We try, however, to minimize the number of changes undertaken exclusively on our own responsibility. Obviously, all changes which we decide to introduce into Harris' theory should always be 'in the spirit' of this theory and should not introduce any elements methodologically alien to it.

[1] Some shortcomings of Greenberg's theory have been indicated in [2]. Kanger's work is too superficial and employs too great simplifications. The most interesting is doubtlessly Marcus' work, which is written with a thorough knowledge of phonological problems and which analyses a theory in the spirit of Jakobson and some Russian linguists.

Chapter 2

LOGICAL APPARATUS

In developing our phonological theory it is necessary to use a certain amount of logical apparatus. That is, the theory should be based on a sufficiently well-developed system of mathematical logic.[1] Any system which provides a free usage of the basic terms of the theory of classes and relations, the theory of natural numbers, of finite sequences of sets and families of sets, and perhaps other notions of a related type, would be sufficient for our purposes. For the sake of definiteness, let us assume that our theory is based on a full system of the simple theory of types.[2]

We now present a survey of logical terms and symbols which will be used subsequently in this work.

Following the principles of the theory of types, different types of objects will be distinguished. Individuals are the simplest type of objects. They are physical things in time and space. There will be a sharp differentiation between the individuals and sets (classes) of individuals and, also, sets of sets of individuals (i.e. families of sets of individuals), etc. We will also say that the logical type of sets of individuals differs from the logical type of individuals and from the logical type of families of sets of individuals, etc.

In order to handle all these possible types it is expedient to introduce different designations for each. Let us designate, then, the logical type of individuals by $*$, the type of sets of individuals by $(*)$ and the type of families of sets of individuals by $((*))$, etc. Generally,

[1] Logic here is understood very widely. Besides propositional calculus and calculus of quantifiers we also include set theory. This is, then, as some call it, *Logica Magna* (*The Great Logic*).—The non-logical reader may learn about elements of set theory, which are indispensable for accurate understanding of all details of the present work, from K. Kuratowski [16] or P. Suppes [22] and several other handbooks. The reader who has never come across the problems of logic is advised first to read A. Tarski [24]. (This book, originally published in Polish, is now available in all main European languages). For the sake of formal training it would be useful to study if only a dozen first chapters from the first volume of the classical work *Principia Mathematica* by A. N. Whitehead and B. Russell.

[2] A very good exposition of the simple theory of types in a form especially convenient for the application in sciences other than mathematical is presented in A. Mostowski [18]. Unfortunately this book is not available in English.

we assume that if t denotes any type, then (t) denotes the type of sets the elements of which have the type t. In accordance with this principle, it is possible to construct an infinite sequence of different types, starting with the type of individuals: $*$, $(*)$, $((*))$, $(((*)))$, . . .

Moreover, besides individuals and sets of the above types various relations will be considered. Again, various types of relations will be distinguished. Thus, there are relations between individuals (binary, ternary, etc.), relations between individuals and sets of individuals etc. Logical types will be associated with relations according to the following principle: with each n-ary relation between n objects of respective types $t_1, t_2, \ldots, t_n$ we associate the type $(t_1, t_2, \ldots, t_n)$. Thus binary, ternary, quaternary etc. relations between individuals have the types: $(*,*)$, $(*,*,*)$, $(*,*,*,*)$, . . . respectively. The types $((*),(*))$, $(*,(*))$, $(*,((*)))$ correspond to binary relations between sets of individuals, between individuals and sets of individuals and between individuals and families of sets of individuals, respectively.

The letters $x, y, z, \ldots, X, Y, Z, \ldots, \mathscr{X}, \mathscr{Y}, \mathscr{Z}, \ldots$ and $R, S, \ldots$ with and without subscripts will be subsequently used as variables representing arbitrary individuals, classes (sets) of individuals, families of classes of individuals and binary relations between individuals, respectively. Occasionally we have to use variables of some other logical types; we shall use then letters of some other type faces. For the sake of greater simplicity and clarity of formulas we use the letters i, j, k, l, m, n as a special kind of variables whose range is the class of natural numbers. By natural numbers we always understand the positive integers 1, 2, 3, . . .

The symbols $\sim$, $\wedge$, $\vee$, $\rightarrow$, $\equiv$ are the usual signs for negation, conjunction, disjunction, implication and equivalence. Thus, their meanings are as follows:

$\sim$ — it is not the case that

$\wedge$ — and

$\vee$ — or

$\rightarrow$ — if . . . then . . .

$\equiv$ — if and only if

The universal quantifier *For every x* is written as $\bigwedge_x$. The existential quantifier *There is an x such that* as $\bigvee_x$. It will sometimes be convenient to write $\bigwedge_{x,\ldots,z}$ and $\bigvee_{x,\ldots,z}$ instead of $\bigwedge_x \ldots \bigwedge_z$ and $\bigvee_x \ldots \bigvee_z$, respectively. We also use the symbol $\dot{\bigvee}_x$ for *There is exactly one x such that*. The formula $\dot{\bigvee}_x A(x)$ is equivalent to the conjunction

$$\bigvee_{x} A(x) \wedge \bigwedge_{x,y} (A(x) \wedge A(y) \rightarrow x = y).$$

The unique object x, which satisfies a given condition $A(x)$, will be denoted by the symbol $(\iota x)A(x)$.

The signs: $=$ and $\neq$ have their usual meanings. The first is the sign of identity, and the second is the sign of distinctness.

If x is an object and X a set, we write $x \in X$ in order to indicate that x belongs to X. The formula $x \in X$ is read: *x belongs to X* or *x is an element of X* or *x is a member of X*. Instead of the conjunction $x_1 \in X \wedge x_2 \in X \wedge \ldots \wedge x_n \in X$ we shall write simply $x_1, x_2, \ldots, x_n \in X$. It will sometimes be convenient to write $x \notin X$ instead of $\sim(x \in X)$. The formula $x \notin X$ may be read: *x does not belong to X*.

In order to indicate that a binary relation R holds between x and y, we write $x\,R\,y$. If U is a ternary relation and U holds between x, y and z, we write briefly $U(x,y,z)$.

Every property of objects specifies a subset of the set of all objects (of a given logical type), namely, the subset of those objects which have the property in question. Thus e.g. the property of being an even number determines the set of all even numbers. It seems also reasonable in some circumstances not to distinguish between a property and the set determined by the property. This will be our position in this work. Accordingly, properties will be identified in the sequel with sets and the assertion, that the object x has the property X, will be treated as synonymous with the assertion that the object x belongs to the set X. Thus, instead of saying that e.g. x is a voiced segment, we may say that x belongs to the set of voiced segments, and vice versa.

Some properties (or sets) may be described with the help of certain sentential conditions. E.g. the property of being an even number, is described by the following condition:

$$\bigvee_{n} (k = 2n).$$

In fact, k is an even number if and only if k satisfies the above condition, i.e. if there is a number n such that $k = 2n$. If $A(x)$ is an arbitrary condition imposed on x, then the property expressed by the condition or the set of all those objects x which satisfy the condition, will be symbolized by $\{x: A(x)\}$. The symbol $\{x: A(x)\}$ is to be read: *the set of all objects x such that* $A(x)$.

Let now z be an arbitrary object. We may ask: what is the necessary and sufficient condition for z to belong to the set $\{x: A(x)\}$? The answer is quite obvious: z belongs to the set $\{x: A(x)\}$ if and only if z satisfies the condition $A(x)$, i.e. if $A(z)$ holds. Thus we have the following important logical schema:

2.1 $$z \in \{x: A(x)\} \equiv A(z)$$

Let $A(x,y)$ be a sentential condition imposed simultaneously on x and y and hence expressing a connection between them. Such a condition may be said to determine a binary relation. The relation determined by the condition $A(x,y)$ will be symbolized by $\{x,y\colon A(x,y)\}$. The symbol $\{x,y\colon A(x,y)\}$ is to be read: *the binary relation, which holds between x and y if and only if* $A(x,y)$ *holds.* We may ask once more: what is the necessary and sufficient condition for an object z to have the relation $\{x,y\colon A(x,y)\}$ to another object u? The answer is analogous to that for sets: z has the relation $\{x,y\colon A(x,y)\}$ to u if and only if $A(z,u)$ holds. Thus we have the second logical schema of great importance:

2.2 $$z\,\{x,y\colon A(x,y)\}\,u \equiv A(z,u)$$

An analogous symbolism is introduced also relatively to ternary, quaternary, . . . relations. The corresponding logical schema for ternary relations is as follows:

2.3 $$\{x,y,z\colon A(x,y,z)\}(u,v,w) \equiv A(u,v,w)$$

Notice that as we are concerned here with a ternary relation, the relation symbol is posed before the symbols of objects for which the relation is supposed to hold.

The symbols $\{x\colon A(x)\}$, $\{x,y\colon A(x,y)\}$ etc. where the conditions $A(x)$, $A(x,y)$, . . . are specified, are rather cumbersome. Hence, it is sometimes convenient to introduce certain conventional abbreviations. The fact, that we are introducing R to abbreviate e.g. the symbol $\{x,y\colon A(x,y)\}$, will be noted with the help of an equality of the form:

(1) $$R \underset{\mathrm{df}}{=} \{x,y\colon A(x,y)\}$$

Equalities of such a kind will be called *definitions*. Obviously, if we accept definition (1) we may reformulate the schema 2.2 as follows:

(2) $$z\,R\,u \equiv A(z,u)$$

It is obvious, that in every case when $A(x,y)$ is a specified condition, the symbol R introduced by (1) is not a variable but a constant name of a relation, namely of the relation $\{x,y\colon A(x,y)\}$.

All our definitions will have the form of equalities. (All equalities, which are definitions, will be marked with the subscript df). However, certain definitions will not be completely analogous to (1). There should, however, be no difficulty in understanding them.

We shall now give definitions and explanations of certain concepts taken from the logical theory of classes and relations.

2.4 $$X \cap Y \underset{\mathrm{df}}{=} \{x\colon x \in X \wedge x \in Y\}$$

2.5 $$X \cup Y \underset{\text{df}}{=} \{x: x \in X \vee x \in Y\}$$

2.6 $$X' \underset{\text{df}}{=} \{x: x \notin X\}$$

2.7 $$X - Y \underset{\text{df}}{=} \{x: x \in X \wedge x \notin Y\}$$

2.8 $$X \div Y \underset{\text{df}}{=} (X - Y) \cup (Y - X)$$

2.9 $$\Lambda \underset{\text{df}}{=} \{x: x \neq x\}$$

2.10 $$\mathrm{V} \underset{\text{df}}{=} \{x: x = x\}$$

The set $X \cap Y$ is called the *product* or *intersection* of the sets X and Y. The product $X \cap Y$ is the set of all things which belong both to X and Y. From definition 2.4 and schema 2.1 we infer the following equivalence:

$$x \in X \cap Y \equiv x \in X \wedge x \in Y.$$

Analogous equivalences may also be inferred from the other six definitions. There is no need to give them here.

The set $X \cup Y$ is called the *sum* or *union* of the sets X and Y. The sum $X \cup Y$ is the set of all things which belong to at least one of the sets X and Y. The set X' is called the *complement* of the set X. The set $X - Y$ is the *difference* of X and Y. The set $X \div Y$ is the so called *symmetric difference* of X and Y. Λ is the *empty* set; it contains no elements. V is the *universal* set; it contains as elements all individuals.

2.11 $$\bigcup \mathscr{X} \underset{\text{df}}{=} \{x: \bigvee_X (X \in \mathscr{X} \wedge x \in X)\}$$

The set $\bigcup \mathscr{X}$ is called the *sum of the family* $\mathscr{X}$. The set $\bigcup \mathscr{X}$, one might say, results from the family $\mathscr{X}$ by summing up all elements of this family. A thing x belongs to $\bigcup \mathscr{X}$ if and only if it belongs to at least one member of $\mathscr{X}$. It is clear that whenever $\mathscr{X}$ is an empty class, the sum $\bigcup \mathscr{X}$ is empty as well; in brief, $\bigcup \Lambda = \Lambda$.

Let I be an arbitrary set and assume, that with every thing x belonging to I is associated a set $F(x)$. Then the sum of all sets of the form $F(x)$, where $x \in I$, will be denoted by $\bigcup_{x \in I} F(x)$.

2.12 $$\bigcup_{x \in I} F(x) \underset{\text{df}}{=} \{y: \bigvee_x (x \in I \wedge y \in F(x))\}$$

If we assume that e.g. the letter ι is a special variable representing only elements of the set I, then the sum $\bigcup_{x \in I} F(x)$ may also be denoted by the more simple symbol $\bigcup_{\iota} F(\iota)$.

We say, that X is *included* in Y or that X is a *subset* of Y, in symbols $X \subset Y$, if and only if each element of X is also an element of Y. Formally, we have:

2.13 $$X \subset Y \equiv \bigwedge_{x}(x \in X \rightarrow x \in Y)$$

If X and Y are sets containing the same elements, then the sets are identical, and vice versa. Thus, we have:

2.14 $$\bigwedge_{x}(x \in X \equiv x \in Y) \equiv X = Y$$

The same principle is also expressed by the formula:

2.15 $$X \subset Y \wedge Y \subset X \equiv X = Y$$

It is worth remarking, that the following implication is true:

2.16 $$X \in \mathscr{X} \rightarrow X \subset \bigcup \mathscr{X}$$

The symbol $[x_1, x_2, \ldots, x_n]$ denotes the set whose only elements are $x_1, x_2, \ldots, x_n$. In particular, $[x]$ is the set consisting of a single element, namely the object x, and $[x,y]$ is the set containing x and y as its only elements. The set $[x,y]$ is called an *unordered pair*. It may not be confused with the so called *ordered pair* having x as its first and y as its second element and symbolized by $\langle x,y \rangle$. There is no need to give a definition of $\langle x,y \rangle$ here. It will be sufficient to notice that unlike the set $[x,y]$, the ordered pair $\langle x,y \rangle$ depends on the order in which the elements x and y occur in it. Thus we always have $[x,y] = [y,x]$, but $\langle x,y \rangle = \langle y,x \rangle$ if and only if $x = y$. An essential property of ordered pairs is expressed by the following equivalence:

2.17 $$\langle x,y \rangle = \langle z,u \rangle \equiv x = z \wedge y = u$$

An important role in our considerations will play the concept of a classification of a set. We say, that a family $\mathscr{X}$ is a *classification* of a given set X, in symbols: $\mathscr{X} \in \mathrm{clsf}(X)$, if and only if the following three conditions are satisfied:

$$\bigwedge_{Y}(Y \in \mathscr{X} \rightarrow Y \subset X),$$

$$\bigwedge_{x}(x \in X \rightarrow \bigvee_{Y}(Y \in \mathscr{X} \wedge x \in Y)),$$

$$\bigwedge_{Y,Z}(Y, Z \in \mathscr{X} \rightarrow Y = Z \vee Y \cap Z = \Lambda).$$

The first two of these conditions may also be combined in one short formula: $\bigcup \mathscr{X} = X$. The third states, that any two different members of a classification are disjoint sets.

The following definitions introduce some concepts and symbols from the theory of relations.

2.18 $$R^{\vee}x \underset{\mathrm{df}}{=} \{y : y\, R\, x\}$$

2.19 $$R^{\wedge}x \underset{\text{df}}{=} \{y: x\,R\,y\}$$

2.20 $$R\langle X\rangle \underset{\text{df}}{=} \{y: \bigvee_{x}(y\,R\,x \wedge x \in X)\}$$

The meaning of the symbols $R^{\vee}x$ and $R^{\wedge}x$ is easy to realize. The set $R\langle X\rangle$ is called the *image* of the set X given by the relation R. It contains those and only those things which take the relation R to at least one element of X. Notice that the following equalities hold:

2.21 $$R^{\vee}x = R\langle[x]\rangle$$

2.22 $$R\langle\Lambda\rangle = \Lambda$$

2.23 $$R\langle X \cup Y\rangle = R\langle X\rangle \cup R\langle Y\rangle$$

The last may also be generalized thus:

2.24 $$R\langle\bigcup\mathscr{X}\rangle = \bigcup_{X\in\mathscr{X}} R\langle X\rangle$$

2.25 $$\text{D}`R \underset{\text{df}}{=} \{x: \bigvee_{y}(x\,R\,y)\}$$

2.26 $$\text{Ɑ}`R \underset{\text{df}}{=} \{y: \bigvee_{x}(x\,R\,y)\}$$

2.27 $$\text{C}`R \underset{\text{df}}{=} \text{D}`R \cup \text{Ɑ}`R$$

The sets D‘R, Ɑ‘R and C‘R are called *domain*, *converse domain* and *field* of R, respectively.

2.28 $$R \mid X \underset{\text{df}}{=} \{x,y: x\,R\,y \wedge y \in X\}$$

2.29 $$X \mid R \underset{\text{df}}{=} \{x,y: x \in X \wedge x\,R\,y\}$$

$R \mid X$ is the relation R with its converse domain limited to X; $X \mid R$ is the relation R with its domain limited to X.

The following definitions introduce some operations on binary relations. The first three operations (product, sum, complement) correspond to some operations on sets.

2.30 $$R \cap S \underset{\text{df}}{=} \{x,y: x\,R\,y \wedge x\,S\,y\}$$

2.31 $$R \cup S \underset{\text{df}}{=} \{x,y: x\,R\,y \vee x\,S\,y\}$$

2.32 $$R' \underset{\text{df}}{=} \{x,y: \sim x\,R\,y\}$$

2.33 $$\breve{R} \underset{\text{df}}{=} \{x,y: y\,R\,x\}$$

2.34 $$R/S \underset{\text{df}}{=} \{x,y: \bigvee_{z}(x\,R\,z \wedge z\,S\,y)\}$$

$\breve{R}$ is the *converse* of R. R/S is called the *relative product* of R and S.

We say, that a relation R is *included* in a relation S, in symbols: $R \subset S$, if and only if $x\,R\,y$ always implies $x\,S\,y$. Thus, we have:

2.35 $$R \subset S \equiv \bigwedge_{x,y} (x\,R\,y \rightarrow x\,S\,y)$$

Notice, that the following two theorems hold:

2.36 $$R \subset S \rightarrow R/T \subset S/T$$

2.37 $$R \subset S \rightarrow T/R \subset T/S$$

If for every x in X, we have $x\,R\,x$, then we say that the relation R is *reflexive in* X and write: $R \in \text{refl}(X)$. The class $\text{refl}(X)$ of all reflexive relations in X may be formally defined as follows:

2.38 $$\text{refl}(X) \underset{\text{df}}{=} \{R\colon \bigwedge_{x}(x \in X \rightarrow x\,R\,x)\}$$

In a similar way we formulate definitions of *symmetric*, *asymmetric*, *antisymmetric*, *transitive*, *connected* and *compact* relations in X.

2.39 $$\text{sym}(X) \underset{\text{df}}{=} \{R\colon \bigwedge_{x,y} (x, y \in X \wedge x\,R\,y \rightarrow y\,R\,x)\}$$

2.40 $$\text{asym}(X) \underset{\text{df}}{=} \{R\colon \bigwedge_{x,y} (x, y \in X \wedge x\,R\,y \rightarrow y\,R'\,x)\}$$

2.41 $$\text{ansym}(X) \underset{\text{df}}{=} \{R\colon \bigwedge_{x,y} (x,y \in X \wedge x \neq y \wedge x\,R\,y \rightarrow y\,R'\,x)\}$$

2.42 $$\text{trans}(X) \underset{\text{df}}{=} \{R\colon \bigwedge_{x,y,z} (x, y, z \in X \wedge x\,R\,y \wedge y\,R\,z \rightarrow x\,R\,z)\}$$

2.43 $$\text{con}(X) \underset{\text{df}}{=} \{R\colon \bigwedge_{x,y} (x, y \in X \rightarrow x\,R\,y \vee y\,R\,x)\}$$

2.44 $$\text{comp}(X) \underset{\text{df}}{=} \{R\colon \bigwedge_{x,y} (x, y \in X \wedge x\,R\,y \rightarrow \bigvee_{z}(z \in X \wedge \wedge\, x\,R\,z \wedge z\,R\,y))\}$$

Instead of refl(V), sym(V) etc., we shall write simply refl, sym, etc.

If a relation R is at the same time reflexive, symmetric and transitive in a set X, then we say that R is an *equivalence relation in* X. The class of all equivalence relations in X we denote by $\text{eq}(X)$.

2.45 $$\text{eq}(X) \underset{\text{df}}{=} \text{refl}(X) \cap \text{sym}(X) \cap \text{trans}(X)$$

The importance of equivalence relations is connected with the so called abstraction principle. This principle states that for any relation R the property of R being an equivalence relation in X and the property consisting in the existence of such a classification $\mathscr{X}$ of X that two elements of X belong to the same number of $\mathscr{X}$ if and only if they have the relation R to each other, are equivalent. If $R \in \text{eq}(X)$, then such a classification is the so called *family of R-equivalence classes in X*. The family will be here denoted by the symbol $\mathfrak{A}(R,X)$ and defined formally thus:

$$2.46 \quad \mathfrak{A}(R,X) \underset{\text{df}}{=} \{Y: \bigvee_{x}(x \in X \wedge \bigwedge_{y}(y \in Y \equiv y \in X \wedge y\, R\, x))\}$$

According to this definition, a set Y belongs to the family of R-equivalence classes in X (or Y is simply an *R-equivalence class in X*) if and only if there exists an object x in X such that Y results by gathering into one set all those elements of X, which belong to X and have the relation R to x. The abstraction principle, mentioned above, may now be exactly formulated in the form of the following three logical theorems:

$$2.47 \quad R \in \text{eq}(X) \rightarrow \mathfrak{A}(R,X) \in \text{clsf}(X)$$

$$2.48 \quad R \in \text{eq}(X) \wedge x,y \in X \rightarrow (x\, R\, y \equiv \bigvee_{Y}(Y \in \mathfrak{A}(R,X) \wedge x,y \in Y))$$

$$2.49 \quad \mathscr{X} \in \text{clsf}(X) \wedge \bigwedge_{x,y}(x,y \in X \rightarrow (x\, R\, y \equiv \bigvee_{Y}(Y \in \mathscr{X} \wedge x,y \in Y))) \rightarrow \\ \rightarrow R \in \text{eq}(X)$$

If a relation R is at the same time reflexive, antisymmetric, transitive and connected in X, then we say that R is an *ordering in X*; if, moreover, the condition

$$\bigwedge_{Y}(Y \subset X \wedge Y \neq \Lambda \rightarrow \bigvee_{y}(y \in Y \wedge \bigwedge_{z}(z \in Y \rightarrow y\, R\, z))),$$

is fulfilled, then we say that R is a *well-ordering in X* and write $R \in \text{word}(X)$. The above symbolic condition states that every non-empty subset of X has an R-first element.

Another very common kind of relations is represented by the so called *functions*. The class of all functions we denote by the symbol fnc and define formally as follows:

$$2.50 \quad \text{fnc} \underset{\text{df}}{=} \{R: \bigwedge_{x,y,z} (x\, R\, z \wedge y\, R\, z \rightarrow x = y)\}$$

If $R \in \text{fnc}$ and $\breve{R} \in \text{fnc}$, then we say that R is an *one-one correspondence* and write: $R \in \text{crs}$. If $R \in \text{fnc}$ and $X = \text{Cl}`R$, then we say that $R$ is a function defined on the set $X$. Notice, that if $R$ is a function defined on $X$, then for every $x$ in $X$ there is exactly one $y$ such that $y\, R\, x$; this unique $y$ will be denoted by the symbol $R`x$.

$$2.51 \quad R`x \underset{\text{df}}{=} (\imath y)(y\, R\, x)$$

It is worth remembering that the following equivalence is true:

$$2.52 \quad y = R`x \equiv \dot{\bigvee_{z}}(z\, R\, x) \wedge y\, R\, x$$

A function R defined on the set $\{i: i \leqslant n\}$ is said to be a (finite) *sequence of n terms*. The value $R'i$ (for a given sequence R) is called the i-th *term* of the sequence R.

If X and Y are sets such that there is an one-one correspondence between the elements of X and of Y (i.e. such a correspondence R that $X = \mathrm{D}'R$ and $Y = \mathrm{Ɑ}'R$), then we say that the two sets are *equinumerous*. It is obvious that two sets are equinumerous if and only if they have the same number of elements. The number of elements of a given set X will be denoted by $\overline{\overline{X}}$. It is well known, that there are sets containing infinitely many elements. E.g. the set of all natural numbers [1, 2, 3, . . .] is infinite; the number of its elements will be denoted by the symbol $\aleph_0$. The number $\aleph_0$ is the smallest number among all infinite numbers. Hence, the inequality $\overline{\overline{X}} < \aleph_0$ means always that the set X is finite. An example of a number greater than $\aleph_0$ is $2^{\aleph_0}$, i.e. the number of elements of the set of all real numbers. The sets containing $\aleph_0$ or $2^{\aleph_0}$ elements are said to be denumerable or sets of the power of the continuum, respectively.

An essential part in our considerations will be played by the notion of an ordinal correlator (isomorphism) of relations. We say that R is an *ordinal correlator* of S and T if and only if the following conditions are satisfied:

$$R \in \mathrm{crs}, \quad \mathrm{D}'R = \mathrm{C}'S, \quad \mathrm{Ɑ}'R = \mathrm{C}'T,$$

$$\bigwedge_{x,y,z,u} (x\,R\,y \wedge z\,R\,u \rightarrow (x\,S\,z \equiv y\,T\,u)).$$

It is worth remembering, that if S and T are orderings in their fields, respectively, and, moreover,

$$\overline{\overline{\mathrm{C}'S}} = \overline{\overline{\mathrm{C}'T}} < \aleph_0,$$

then there is exactly one ordinal correlator of S and T.

Chapter 3

ELEMENTS OF MEREOLOGY

Apart from purely logical concepts discussed in the previous chapter, a considerable part, in this book, will be played by the concepts: '*part of*', '*precedence in time*', and other related ones. In order to clarify the necessity of introducing these concepts into the field of phonology (and to linguistics, in general) it will be useful to discuss the following simple example. Let us assume that a certain person *A* uttered the following sentence:

(s) *Warsaw is situated on the Vistula*

in a certain definite time *t*. As a result of this act of speech we have a certain concrete sound-event, a certain concrete utterance. Let us denote this utterance by (u). It is clear from the intuitive point of view, that the utterance (u) is something absolutely individual and unique, it is something that has its definite and unique time of duration and together with this time, belongs to the irretrievable past. The same holds for every instance of spoken language—that is of the language which is the main object of interest of linguists (written language, in linguistics, is treated as, in a sense, a secondary phenomenon in relation to spoken language). Hence, other utterances of sentence (s) by other persons in the same time *t*, or by the same person *A* in different times t_1, t_2, . . . are not the same as the utterance (u): they are phonetically equivalent but they are not identical.

The utterances of the (u) type are generally considered in linguistics to be sequences (possibly finite) of certain concrete speech-sounds (segments). Of course, it is possible to accept this way of speaking, but it is necessary to realize that the word 'sequence' is used here in a non-mathematical sense. In logic and mathematics, sequences are always understood as certain abstract entities which cannot be perceived by senses (e.g. by ear as in the case of utterances) and it would be absurd to ascribe a duration to them. Therefore, the statement that the utterance (u) is a sequence of sounds must and should be understood as the statement that (u) is a whole composed of a certain number of sounds which are ordered by the relation of precedence in time. These sounds are contained in the utterance (u) as parts of it and not as terms of a sequence in the mathematical sense. They are of the same type as the utterance (u) and, thus, like (u) they are individuals.

Clearly then, the concepts: '*part*', '*precedence in time*', '*whole*' and perhaps other similar concepts belong to the basic part of the conceptual apparatus of linguistics. Thus our axiomatic phonological theory should be equipped with these concepts together with certain axioms which specify their properties. In this connection we shall base our discussion on Tarski's article [23] which gives a unified theory of the concepts in question. We shall refer to Tarski's theory as extended mereology or simply mereology.[1] Some elements of mereology will now be presented.

The primitive symbols in mereology are: **P** and **T**; denoting certain binary relations between individuals. The expression $x \mathbf{P} y$ means that the thing x is a *part* of the thing y; the expression $x \mathbf{T} y$ means either that the whole thing x precedes the whole thing y in time, or that the last time slice of x coincides in time with the first time slice of y.

Following Tarski we use in the axioms of extended mereology besides primitive notions also certain notions introduced by definition. This enables us to express the axioms more clearly. At first, we will assume the following three definitions:

3.1 $\mathbf{S} \underset{\text{df}}{=} \{y,X\colon X \subset \mathbf{P}^{\vee}y \wedge \bigwedge_{z}(z \mathbf{P} y \rightarrow \mathbf{P}\langle X\rangle \cap \mathbf{P}^{\vee}z \neq \Lambda)\}$

3.2 $\mathbf{pn} \underset{\text{df}}{=} \{x\colon \mathbf{P}^{\vee}x = [x]\}$

3.3 $\mathbf{mo} \underset{\text{df}}{=} \{x\colon x \mathbf{T} x\}$

The definition 3.1 introduces the notion of the *mereological sum* of the set of things. We read the formula $y \mathbf{S} X$ as follows: y is the (mereological) sum of the set X, or: y is the whole composed of all and only of the elements of the set X. From 3.1 by schema 2.2 results the following equivalence:

$$y \mathbf{S} X \equiv X \subset \mathbf{P}^{\vee}y \wedge \bigwedge_{z}(z \mathbf{P} y \rightarrow \mathbf{P}\langle X\rangle \cap \mathbf{P}^{\vee}z \neq \Lambda).$$

So, y is the sum of the set X if and only if all the elements of X are parts of the thing y and if every part of the thing y overlaps some element of the set X.

It is important to be clear about the logical types of the relations

[1] As it is known 'mereology' is the term used by S. Leśniewski for his theory of the relation of being a part; this theory was worked out as early as in 1916. Tarski's system is more extensive than Leśniewski's mereology (which is included in it) since it embraces also the problems of time relations.

P and **S** and the differences in this respect between them and the relations $\in$ and $\subset$. The types of these relations are as follows:

$$\mathbf{P} - (*,*)$$
$$\mathbf{S} - (*,(*))$$
$$\in - (*,(*))$$
$$\subset - ((*),(*))$$

The definition 3.2 introduces the notion of point. The symbol **pn** denotes the set of all *points*. From 3.2, according to the schema 2.1, we have:

$$x \in \mathbf{pn} \equiv \mathbf{P}^{\vee}x = [x].$$

So, x belongs to the set of points (or simply x is a point), if and only if x is the only part of itself (or if x is not composed of any smaller parts).

The definition 3.3 introduces the notion of a momentary thing. The symbol **mo** denotes the set of all *momentary things*. According to the schema 2.1, the definition 3.3 may be expanded as follows:

$$x \in \mathbf{mo} \equiv x \,\mathbf{T}\, x.$$

According to the above explanation of the relation **T** the formula $x \,\mathbf{T}\, x$ means either that the whole thing x is preceded in time by the whole thing x, or that the last slice of x coincides in time with the first slice of x. However, the first alternative cannot hold (since it is impossible for any object to precede itself in time), therefore, the formula $x \,\mathbf{T}\, x$ states the second alternative. Thus x is an element of the set of momentary things (or x is a momentary thing) if and only if its beginning coincides in time with its end. The accordance of the definition 3.3 with the current intuitive concept of momentarity should not arouse any doubts.

The following propositions 3.4–3.14 are the axioms of extended mereology:

3.4 $\quad \mathbf{P} \in \mathrm{trans}$

3.5 $\quad x \,\mathbf{S}\, [y] \rightarrow x = y$

3.6 $\quad X \neq \Lambda \rightarrow \mathbf{S}^{\vee}X \neq \Lambda$

3.7 $\quad \mathbf{pn} \cap \mathbf{P}^{\vee}x \neq \Lambda$

3.8 $\quad \mathbf{T} \in \mathrm{trans}$

3.9 $\quad \mathbf{T} \in \mathrm{comp}$

3.10 $\quad \bigwedge_{x} \bigvee_{y,z} (y \,\mathbf{T}'\, x \wedge x \,\mathbf{T}'\, z)$

3.11 $\quad x,y \in \mathbf{mo} \rightarrow x \,\mathbf{T}\, y \vee y \,\mathbf{T}\, x$

3.12 $$\bigvee_{X}(X \subset \mathbf{mo} \wedge \overline{\overline{X}} = \aleph_0 \wedge \mathbf{T}' \subset (\mathbf{T}' \mid X)/\mathbf{T}')$$

3.13 $$x\,\mathbf{T}\,y \equiv \bigwedge_{u,v}(u \in \mathbf{mo} \cap \mathbf{P}^{\vee}x \wedge v \in \mathbf{mo} \cap \mathbf{P}^{\vee}y \rightarrow u\,\mathbf{T}\,v)$$

3.14 $$x \in \mathbf{pn} \rightarrow \overline{\overline{\mathbf{pn} \cap \mathbf{T}^{\vee}x \cap \mathbf{T}^{\wedge}x}} = 2^{\aleph_0}$$

The first eight axioms and also the axiom 3.13 are quite clear. The axiom 3.14 says that the set of all points simultaneous with a given point has the power of the continuum. Before explaining the axiom 3.12 let us consider the following property of the set of real numbers: between any two different real numbers there is at least one rational number. Assuming that X is the set of all rational numbers and the variables x, y, z stand for real numbers, the above property may be expressed as follows:

(1) $$\bigwedge_{x,y}(x < y \rightarrow \bigvee_{z}(z \in X \wedge x < z \wedge z < y)).$$

This property is sometimes expressed in the following way: the set of rational numbers (which is denumerable) is a denumerable median class for the relation $<$ between real numbers. Now it is evident that the inclusion $\mathbf{T}' \subset (\mathbf{T}' \mid X)/\mathbf{T}'$ which is seen in 3.12 is equivalent to the following formula:

$$\bigwedge_{x,y}(x\,\mathbf{T}'\,y \rightarrow \bigvee_{z}(z \in X \wedge x\,\mathbf{T}'\,z \wedge z\,\mathbf{T}'\,y)).$$

This formula is analogous to (1). Therefore, it states that the set X is a median class for the relation $\mathbf{T}'$. The content of the axiom 3.12 may now be expressed as follows: there exists a denumerable set of momentary things which is a median class for the relation $\mathbf{T}'$. The accordance of the above assumption with a standard view on time is rather obvious; it is enough to notice that $x\,\mathbf{T}'\,y$ means that the beginning of the thing y precedes in time the end of the thing x.

Not all of the above axioms of mereology are of equal significance for our further considerations. From this point of view some of them could be omitted (e.g. 3.14), and some, at least weakened. We do not however introduce these modifications. Without discussing the details of this matter we may briefly state that we omit them since in this work we apply only the so-called informal (material) axiomatics. Thus we assume that the concepts with which the above axioms are concerned are not defined by these axioms but are known prior to the axioms from the external experience. In this case, it seems desirable to give a thorough characterization of the primitive terms, irrespective of the fact that not all of the properties stated in the axioms will be further applied. Let us add, by the way, that the above axiom-system gives, in a sense, as thorough a characterization of the relations **P** and **T** as possible; for, it is a categorical system (in the classic, Veblenan sense of the term).[1]

We now present several mereological theorems and go on to define various concepts which will be useful in our later discussion of the linguistic problems.

3.15 $x = \mathbf{S}`[x]$

3.16 $x = y \rightarrow x\,\mathbf{P}\,y$

3.17 $x\,\mathbf{P}\,y \wedge y\,\mathbf{P}\,x \rightarrow x = y$

3.18 $\bigwedge_z(z\,\mathbf{P}\,y \rightarrow \mathbf{P}^{\vee}x \cap \mathbf{P}^{\vee}z \neq \Lambda) \rightarrow y\,\mathbf{P}\,x$

3.19 $\mathbf{S} \in \mathrm{fnc}$

3.20 $X \neq \Lambda \rightarrow \dot{\bigvee_y}(y\,\mathbf{S}\,X)$

3.21 $X \neq \Lambda \wedge X \subset \mathbf{P}^{\vee}x \rightarrow \mathbf{S}`X \in \mathbf{P}^{\vee}x$

3.22 $X \neq \Lambda \rightarrow X \subset \mathbf{P}^{\vee}\mathbf{S}`X$

3.23 $X \subset Y \wedge X \neq \Lambda \rightarrow \mathbf{S}`X \in \mathbf{P}^{\vee}\mathbf{S}`Y$

3.24 $x = \mathbf{S}`(\mathbf{pn} \cap \mathbf{P}^{\vee}x)$

The next two formulas are definitions. They introduce in due order the notions of (mereological) *sum* and *product* of two things. The product $x \dot{\cap} y$ is the common part of the thing x and of the thing y.

3.25 $x \dot{\cup} y \underset{\mathrm{df}}{=} \mathbf{S}`[x,y]$

3.26 $x \dot{\cap} y \underset{\mathrm{df}}{=} \mathbf{S}`(\mathbf{P}^{\vee}x \cap \mathbf{P}^{\vee}y)$

The general properties of these two operations are completely analogous to the properties of usual set-theoretical operations $\cup$ and $\cap$. The more useful properties are the following:

3.27 $y,z \in \mathbf{P}^{\vee}(y \dot{\cup} z)$

3.28 $\mathbf{P}^{\vee}y \cup \mathbf{P}^{\vee}z \subset \mathbf{P}^{\vee}(y \dot{\cup} z)$

3.29 $\mathbf{P}^{\vee}y \cap \mathbf{P}^{\vee}z \neq \Lambda \rightarrow y \dot{\cap} z \in \mathbf{P}^{\vee}(y \dot{\cup} z)$

3.30 $\mathbf{P}^{\vee}y \cap \mathbf{P}^{\vee}z \neq \Lambda \rightarrow y \dot{\cap} z \in \mathbf{P}^{\vee}y \cap \mathbf{P}^{\vee}z$

3.31 $\mathbf{P}^{\vee}y \cap \mathbf{P}^{\vee}z \neq \Lambda \rightarrow \mathbf{P}^{\vee}y \cap \mathbf{P}^{\vee}z = \mathbf{P}^{\vee}(y \dot{\cap} z)$

3.32 $X \neq \Lambda \wedge Y \neq \Lambda \rightarrow \mathbf{S}`X \dot{\cup} \mathbf{S}`Y = \mathbf{S}`(X \cup Y)$

3.33 $\mathbf{pn} \cap \mathbf{P}^{\vee}(y \dot{\cup} z) \subset \mathbf{P}^{\vee}y \cup \mathbf{P}^{\vee}z$

[1] For the notion of categoriticity of an axiomatic system and the differentiation between informal (material) and formal axiomatics, see S. C. Kleene [15], particularly § 8.

The following three theorems deal with the momentary things.

3.34 $$x \in \mathbf{mo} \equiv \mathbf{P}^{\vee}x \subset \mathbf{mo}$$

3.35 $$\mathbf{mo} \cap \mathbf{P}^{\vee}x \neq \Lambda$$

3.36 $$\mathbf{pn} \subset \mathbf{mo}$$

3.37 $$\mathbf{C} \underset{\mathrm{df}}{=} \mathbf{T} \cap \breve{\mathbf{T}}$$

The above definition introduces the relation of coincidence in time between momentary things (it may be proved that $\mathbf{C}\text{‘}\mathbf{C} = \mathbf{mo}$). The formula $x\ \mathbf{C}\ y$ may be read: the momentary things x and y are *coincident* in time.

3.38 $$x\,\mathbf{C}\,y \equiv x\,\mathbf{T}\,y \wedge y\,\mathbf{T}\,x$$

3.39 $$\mathbf{C} \in \mathrm{refl}(\mathbf{mo}) \cap \mathrm{sym} \cap \mathrm{trans}$$

3.40 $$\mathbf{T_c} \underset{\mathrm{df}}{=} (\breve{\mathbf{P}}/\breve{\mathbf{T}}/\mathbf{P})'$$

This definition introduces the relation of a complete precedence in time. The formula $x\ \mathbf{T_c}\ y$ may be read: the thing x *completely precedes* the thing y in time.

3.41 $$x\,\mathbf{T_c}\,y \equiv \bigwedge_{z,u}(z\,\mathbf{P}\,x \wedge u\,\mathbf{P}\,y \rightarrow u\,\mathbf{T}'\,z)$$

3.42 $$\mathbf{T_c} \subset \breve{\mathbf{T}}' \cap \mathbf{T}$$

3.43 $$\mathbf{T_c} \in \mathrm{asym} \cap \mathrm{trans}$$

3.44 $$x\,\mathbf{T_c}\,y \equiv \bigwedge_{u,v}(u \in \mathbf{mo} \cap \mathbf{P}^{\vee}x \wedge v \in \mathbf{mo} \cap \mathbf{P}^{\vee}y \rightarrow u\,\mathbf{T_c}\,v)$$

3.45 $$\mathbf{P}/\mathbf{T_c}/\breve{\mathbf{P}} = \mathbf{P}/\mathbf{T_c} = \mathbf{T_c}/\breve{\mathbf{P}} = \mathbf{T_c}$$

3.46 $$x, y \in \mathbf{mo} \rightarrow x\,\mathbf{C}\,y \vee x\,\mathbf{T_c}\,y \vee x\,\breve{\mathbf{T}}_\mathbf{c}\,y$$

3.47a $$\mathbf{C}/\mathbf{T_c} \subset \mathbf{T_c}$$

3.47b $$\mathbf{T_c}/\mathbf{C} \subset \mathbf{T_c}$$

3.48 $$x\,\mathbf{T_c}\,y \rightarrow \mathbf{P}^{\vee}x \cap \mathbf{P}^{\vee}y = \Lambda$$

3.49 $$(\mathbf{S}\text{‘}X)\,\mathbf{T_c}\,y \equiv X \neq \Lambda \wedge X \subset \mathbf{T_c}^{\vee}y$$

3.50 $$x\,\mathbf{T_c}\,(\mathbf{S}\text{‘}Y) \equiv Y \neq \Lambda \wedge Y \subset \mathbf{T_c}^{\wedge}x$$

The next two formulas are again definitions. The first introduces the relation $\mathbf{T_e}$ such, that $x\ \mathbf{T_e}\ y$ holds if and only if either $x\ \mathbf{T_c}\ y$ holds or x is identical with y. The second definition introduces the relation of *immediate precedence* in time.

3.51 $$\mathbf{T_e} \underset{\mathrm{df}}{=} \{x, y : x\,\mathbf{T_c}\,y \vee x = y\}$$

3.52 $$\mathbf{T_i} \underset{\mathrm{df}}{=} \mathbf{T_c} \cap (\mathbf{T_c}/\mathbf{T_c})'$$

3.53 $X \subset \mathbf{T}_c{}^{\vee}x \wedge x\,\mathbf{T}_i\,y \rightarrow \mathbf{S}`(X \cup [x])\,\mathbf{T}_i\,y$

3.54 $X \subset \mathbf{T}_c{}^{\wedge}y \wedge x\,\mathbf{T}_i\,y \rightarrow x\,\mathbf{T}_i\,\mathbf{S}`(X \cup [y])$

3.55 $X \subset \mathbf{T}_c{}^{\vee}x \wedge \mathbf{S}`(X \cup [x])\,\mathbf{T}_i\,y \rightarrow x\,\mathbf{T}_i\,y$

3.56 $X \subset \mathbf{T}_c{}^{\wedge}y \wedge x\,\mathbf{T}_i\,\mathbf{S}`(X \cup [y]) \rightarrow x\,\mathbf{T}_i\,y$

3.57 $\mathbf{ms} \underset{\mathrm{df}}{=} \mathbf{mo} \cap \{x: \mathbf{C}^{\vee}x \subset \mathbf{P}^{\vee}x\}$

The elements of the set **ms** defined here will be called *momentary world-sections* or simply *moments*. According to the above definition x is a momentary world-section, i.e. $x \in \mathbf{ms}$, if and only if x is a momentary thing and every momentary thing which coincides with x in time is a part of x.

3.58 $x \in \mathbf{mo} \rightarrow \mathbf{S}`\mathbf{C}^{\vee}x = (\imath y)(y \in \mathbf{ms} \cap \mathbf{C}^{\vee}x) = (\imath y)(y \in \mathbf{ms} \cap \mathbf{P}^{\wedge}x)$

3.59 $\mathbf{T}_c \in \mathrm{con}(\mathbf{ms}) \cap \mathrm{comp}(\mathbf{ms})$

The next definition introduces the notion of a *linear object*.[1] Namely, we say that x is a linear object, in symbols: $x \in \mathbf{ln}$, if and only if the common part of x and of any moment which neither precedes x nor is preceded by x in time is a point. Roughly speaking, x is a linear object if it is continuous in time and not extensive in space.

3.60 $\mathbf{ln} \underset{\mathrm{df}}{=} \{x: \bigwedge_{y}(y \in \mathbf{ms} \wedge x\,\mathbf{T}_c'\,y \wedge y\,\mathbf{T}_c'\,x \rightarrow y \dot{\cap} x \in \mathbf{pn})\}$

It may be proved that $\mathbf{pn} \subset \mathbf{ln}$. But the converse inclusion is not true. Thus, the class **ln** is more comprehensive than **pn**. Moreover, the following theorems hold:

3.61 $u \in \mathbf{ln} \wedge x \in \mathbf{pn} \cap \mathbf{P}^{\vee}u \rightarrow \dot{\bigvee_{v}}(v \in \mathbf{ms} \wedge x = u \dot{\cap} v)$

3.62 $u \in \mathbf{ln} \wedge x,y \in \mathbf{pn} \cap \mathbf{P}^{\vee}u \rightarrow (x\,\mathbf{C}\,y \equiv x = y)$

3.63 $u \in \mathbf{ln} \rightarrow \mathbf{T}_e \in \mathrm{con}(\mathbf{pn} \cap \mathbf{P}^{\vee}u)$

The last theorem shows (in view of 3.43), that $\mathbf{T}_e$ is an ordering in $\mathbf{pn} \cap \mathbf{P}^{\vee}u$, for every $u \in \mathbf{ln}$. It may be also proved that this ordering is compact and even continuous. Hence, the relation $\mathbf{T}_e$ in $\mathbf{pn} \cap \mathbf{P}^{\vee}u$ (for $u \in \mathbf{ln}$) is similar to the relation $\leqslant$ in the field of real numbers, excepting that the set $\mathbf{pn} \cap \mathbf{P}^{\vee}u$ may contain the first and the last element with respect to $\mathbf{T}_e$. The proofs of these facts are rather involved and there is no need to give them here.

[1] This notion does not appear in the existing works on mereology. It is introduced here since we consider its usefulness for the purposes of theoretical linguistics.

PART II

Axiomatic System of Phonology

Chapter 1

PRIMITIVE NOTIONS

Besides logical and mereological terms and symbols the language of our phonological theory will contain certain terms and symbols peculiar to linguistics. First we shall discuss the terms and symbols which are not defined in our system. In order to justify our choice of these primitive terms we will start with some remarks on the procedures of phonological analysis of language (dialect).

A structural linguist who intends to establish the phonemic system of a particular dialect in a purely descriptive way and without recourse to any semantic means chooses, first of all, a sample of this dialect. To this end he takes some competent informants speaking this dialect and records (e.g. on the magnetic tape) a certain amount of their speech. The sample of the dialect is the totality of the recorded utterances. These utterances are, of course, individual entities and, strictly speaking, can be perceived (by ear) only once, viz. in the moment when they are actually uttered by the speaker.[1] The corpus of data thus obtained is the appropriate and sole object of phonetic and phonemic investigations. Obviously, this does not mean that such a corpus of data has to be completed before any analysis is undertaken. The choice (the recording) of the linguistic material and its, at least partial, analysis may be performed simultaneously. This is a purely practical matter without any theoretical significance. The only essential point is that the results of linguistic analysis and especially all the general and existential statements do refer, strictly speaking, exclusively to this corpus of data and are relativized to it. The extension of these results to the whole of the dialect will always be an extrapolation and requires a special justification. For, although the linguist intends to examine the whole dialect, he does, in fact, examine only a certain limited number of concrete utterances, that is, as we will consequently call it, a certain *idiolect*.

The term 'idiolect' is taken from B. Bloch [4] but we endow it with a slightly different meaning. By an idiolect, in the most compre-

[1] For practical reasons the linguist considers the tape-recorded speech as if it were identical with the original speech of the informant. Without such identification he would be completely helpless.

hensive sense, we mean any set of concrete utterances. It is, of course, evident that the majority of such idiolects will be, from the point of view of linguistics, of no interest whatever. For, if any specific idiolect is to have a linguistic value it should fulfil certain indispensable requirements. First of all it must be linguistically uniform, i.e. all utterances which are the elements of a given idiolect should be uttered by members of the same speech community, that is, they should belong to the same dialect. Moreover, an idiolect should be a sufficiently representative sample of a dialect. Therefore, it should be sufficiently ample and internally differentiated.[1] Finally, it is not irrelevant whether the utterances are pronounced carefully, naturally, not too vehemently and if they are representative of the same style of speech etc.[2] To meet all these requirements is not an easy task, especially when the linguist does not know the language he examines. However, we will not discuss the problem of practical methods which the linguist should follow in order to obtain a sufficiently 'good' idiolect since these problems are irrelevant from the point of view of theoretical linguistics. The basic procedures of our phonological system will refer to any idiolect, no matter whether it meets the above requirements. In this respect our attitude does not differ from that of Harris who in his introductory methodological remarks states: 'The procedures discussed below are applied to a corpus of material without regard to the adequacy of the corpus as a sample of the language.'[3]

It is worth remarking that in accordance with the above explanations the set of all utterances (past and future) of all members of a specific speech community, that is, the set of all utterances pronounced in a specific dialect, is an idiolect in our understanding of the term. It is obvious that such an idiolect, although ideal in theory, will never be a corpus of data for a linguist. From the theoretical point of view, however, nothing stands in the way of considering and discussing such 'maximal' idiolects. What is more, it seems that the phonological theory discussed below is most comprehensible and natural if by idiolect we mean the 'maximal idiolect' of the kind we have been discussing.

In our axiomatic system of phonology *idiolect* is one of the primitive (undefined) terms. The above remarks concerning our understanding of this term cannot, by any means, be considered to be its definition. The class of all idiolects we denote by **I**. Since particular idiolects are sets of individuals, that is objects of the type (∗), **I** is a set (family) of sets that is, **I** is an object of the type ((∗)). We may

[1] Cf. Z. S. Harris [7], pp. 12–13.
[2] Cf. D. Jones [13], p. 9, and Z. S. Harris [7], pp. 9–11.
[3] Z. S. Harris [7], p. 13.

read the formula $X \in \mathbf{I}$ as follows: the set X belongs to the class of idiolects, or briefly, the set X is an idiolect.

It should be pointed out that in our system the class **I** represents, in a sense, the whole of human speech. Since each utterance is an element of, at least one idiolect, the sum $\mathbf{UI}$ is the set of all (past and future) human utterances. This point plays a considerable part in the linguistic interpretation of many notions which will be introduced in the sequel.

The first step in a linguistic examination of a given speech sample (corpus of data, idiolect) is the distinction of so-called *segments* within the utterances which belong to this sample. It should be pointed out, however, that the term 'segment' is ambiguous and has often various meanings in linguistics. Definitions of the term 'segment' vary with different authors and, as a rule, they are not very precise. Nevertheless, the particular conceptions of 'segment' appear to be sufficiently clear. Therefore, the necessity and justification of using such or another concept of segment is rather generally accepted in linguistics. D. Jones seems to render the matter most distinctly; having stated that from the purely physical point of view segments do not exist, he further explains:

'Nevertheless, the conception of the chain of speech-sounds is indispensable in all linguistic investigations. It is, moreover, justified by the means by which speech is produced. Speech is the result of certain actions performed by the articulatory mechanism. The lips, tongue, etc., take up various positions or make various movements successively, and these positions and movements can be described and classified. The conception would appear to be also justifiable on psychological grounds: when we speak, we think we utter successions of sounds most of which are held for an appreciable time; and when we listen to speech, we think we hear similar successions of sounds. The effect is so definite to us that we have as a rule no particular difficulty in saying what the sounds in words are, or in assigning letters to them in alphabetic writing.'[1]

Subsequently we are going to use the term 'segment' in two meanings. In order to avoid ambiguity we shall introduce an appropriate differentiation in the terminology. We shall namely speak about *elementary segments* and about *unit-length segments*.

By elementary segment we mean what Pike, Bloch and Jassem call, simply, a segment. For the sake of clarity we shall quote the definitions given by the above authors. Pike's definition: 'A single sound

[1] D. Jones [13], § 4. Let us indicate that Jones uses the term 'speech-sound' instead of 'segment'.

caused by the movement of a single articulator (or the synchronous movement of several articulators) may be called a sound segment.'[1] Bloch's definition: 'A fraction of an utterance between any two immediately successive change-points is a segment.'[2] Jassem defines segments as 'such minimal elements the impressions of which cannot be further divided by the ear.'[3] The accordance of Pike's and Bloch's definitions seems rather obvious. The accordance of the two and Jassem's definition is less evident, since the latter is confined exclusively to perception and does not consider articulatory aspects. However the identity of the class of segments in Jassem's sense with the class of segments in the sense of Pike and Bloch seems to be justifiable on phonetic grounds.

The term 'unit-length segment' will be precisely defined in a later part of this work and therefore we shall not discuss it here. Let us remark only that in formulating our definition of the term 'unit-length segment' we intend to define precisely the corresponding term employed by Harris.[4] Moreover, our term 'unit-length segment' seems to be synonymous with the term 'phonemic segment' (*phonematisches Segment*) used by Pilch[5] and with the term 'concrete speech-sound' employed by Jones.[6]

The term 'elementary segment' is one of the basic terms in our axiomatic system of phonology. It will not be a primitive term of the system. Nevertheless, regarding the intuitive understanding of this term its only basis is formed by the explanations of the linguists quoted above. For, our definition of 'elementary segment', or, strictly speaking, of 'the set of elementary segments' will be stated in terms of another, much more complicated concept, the intuitive understanding of which is not possible if the concept of elementary segment is not first understood. This definition will be only a purely formal reduction of the number of primitive notions and it will not provide any clue for the intuitive understanding of the term elementary segment.

In order to avoid possible misunderstandings as regards the term 'segment', let us emphasize another important point which seems to be not always clearly realized by the linguists. The point is that segments (both elementary and unit-length) are parts of concrete utterances and, as such, are concrete, individual and non-repeatable sounds. Hence, they are physical things uttered in a definite time and by a definite speaker. Thus, in our approach both utterances and segments are individuals and therefore the relation between a segment and the utterance comprising it is the relation of a part to the

[1] K. L. Pike [19], p. 11.
[2] B. Bloch [4], p. 12.
[3] W. Jassem [10], p. 15.
[4] Z. S. Harris [7], Chapter 5.
[5] H. Pilch [20], pp. 88–91.
[6] D. Jones [13], §§ 2–7 and 20.

corresponding whole (i.e. the mereological relation **P**) and not, for instance, the membership relation (i.e. the set theoretical relation $\in$). The second consequence of our approach is that no two segments of a concrete utterance can be identical; they can be, at most, phonetically equivalent. Thus, for example, in every standard pronunciation of the Polish word *szafa* [ʃafa] we have 4 different elementary segments, the second and the fourth being phonetically equivalent. Similarly, in any standard pronunciation of the English *an analysis* [ən ənælisis] we have 10 different elementary segments, the first and the third and also the second and the fourth being phonetically equivalent.

The second main step in the linguistic analysis of a given speech sample (after performing the segmentation) is the determination of *phonetic features* and an appropriate classification of all distinguished elementary segments. Of course not each property of an elementary segment is a phonetic feature. For instance, the fact that a given segment was uttered at such and such a moment or by such and such a speaker is certainly not a phonetic feature of this segment. Also the properties which account for the individual colouring of the speaker's voice are not phonetic features. By phonetic features we mean such and only such articulatory and acoustic features which according to phoneticians account for the fact that some two elementary segments are or are not phonetically equivalent (that is 'identical', in phoneticians' wording). We are perfectly aware that the above 'explanation' explains very little. However, we think that the notion of phonetic feature considered here is sufficiently clear for the phoneticians. Therefore for theoretical purposes we assume that every phonetician has at his disposal, so to say, from the start the general set (stock) of phonetic features. Moreover, we also assume that he is also given such a classification of all phonetic features in *kinds*, that two features are of the same kind if and only if they are homogeneous, that means if they are features 'in the same respect'. (Examples of homogeneous features are e.g. voiced, voiceless; discontinuous, continuant. Examples of non-homogeneous features are e.g. nasal, continuant; voiced, discontinuous).

Of course, neither all phonetical features nor all kinds of these features will be listed here. It is only in practical description of definite languages that such lists are needed. For the purposes of pure theory of phonology it is quite sufficient to know that such lists do exist. Let us note that different linguists may assume different lists of this kind. Our theory, therefore, will be developed quite independently of any particular such list.

The class of all kinds (in the above meaning) of phonetic features will be denoted by **K**. Therefore, the elements of the class **K** are particular kinds (and hence sets) of phonetic features. It is, also, obvious that each phonetic feature belongs to a certain kind of features, that is to a certain element of **K**. It follows then that the set-theoretical sum of all elements of **K** is identical with the set of all phonetic features. Therefore we may put down the following equations:

(1) $\mathbf{K}$ = the class of all kinds of phonetic features;

(2) $\bigcup\mathbf{K}$ = the class of all phonetic features.

Let us consider for a moment the notion of a phonetic feature of an elementary segment. In accordance with what has been stated in chapter I.2, features (properties) of objects are treated extensionally and are identified with certain sets of these objects. Thus, phonetic features are simply some sets of elementary segments. For example, voiceness is the set of all voiced elementary segments, nasalization, the set of all nasal elementary segments, etc. Of course, each elementary segment has at least one phonetic feature, that is it belongs to at least one element of the class $\bigcup\mathbf{K}$. Thus by summing all elements of the class $\bigcup\mathbf{K}$ we obtain the set of all elementary segments. Therefore

(3) $\bigcup\bigcup\mathbf{K}$ = the class of all elementary segments.

The notions of phonetic feature and of the kind of phonetic features, just as the notion of segment, will play a major role in our axiomatic system of phonology. As it is seen from the equations (1)–(3) it suffices to assume only one of these notions, that is the notion of kind of feature, to be a primitive term and the remaining two will be definable. This is what we are going to do. Thus the symbol **K** will be the second (besides **I**) primitive symbol of our system. It is easily seen, that the class **K** is of the type $(((*)))$. In fact, elementary segments as individuals are of the type $*$, phonetic features as sets of segments are of the type $(*)$, kinds of features as sets of features are of the type $((*))$, and, ultimately, the class **K** as the set of kinds of features must be of the type $(((*)))$. Thus, in accordance with the assumed designations, the following formulas: $x \in \bigcup\bigcup\mathbf{K}$, $X \in \bigcup\mathbf{K}$, $\mathscr{X} \in \mathbf{K}$ may be read: x is an elementary segment, X is a phonetic feature, $\mathscr{X}$ is a kind of phonetic features, respectively.

The third (and last) primitive term of our system is the term *pause*. Pauses are, simply, moments of silence dividing utterances. They are easily discernible in any flow of speech. The notion of pause plays a very significant role in linguistics, and especially, in phonological discussions. It is quite common in phonetics to speak of sounds standing before or after a pause.

In our subsequent discussion pauses will also be called *elementary zero segments*. And therefore in order to avoid misunderstandings the elements of $\bigcup\bigcup\mathbf{K}$ will be called *proper segments*.

The set of all pauses (zero segments) we shall denote by $\mathbf{0}$. It is the third (besides $\mathbf{I}$ and $\mathbf{K}$) primitive symbol of our system. Similarly to proper segments pauses are considered as individuals; the set $\mathbf{0}$ is, then, of the type $(*)$. The formula $x \in \mathbf{0}$ may be read as follows: x is a zero segment, or, x is a pause.

Chapter 2

AXIOMS

The primitive symbols (**I**, **K**, **0**) will preserve in the sequel the intuitive sense explained in the previous chapter. The properties of the entities denoted by these symbols which are important from the linguistic point of view or indispensable in developing the formal system of theoretical phonology will be specified by means of the axioms of the system.

As axioms of our system we assume the following propositions[1] A1–A14:

A1. $\mathbf{I} \neq \Lambda$

A2. $X \in \mathbf{I} \rightarrow 0 < \overline{\overline{X}} < \aleph_0$

A3. $\mathsf{U}\mathbf{I} \subset \mathbf{ln}$

A4. $u \in \mathsf{U}\mathbf{I} \wedge x\, \mathbf{P}\, u \rightarrow \mathbf{P}^{\vee}x \cap \mathbf{P}\langle \mathbf{P}^{\vee}u \cap (\mathsf{UU}\mathbf{K} \cup \mathbf{0})\rangle \neq \Lambda$

A5. $u \in \mathsf{U}\mathbf{I} \rightarrow \mathbf{P}^{\vee}u \cap \mathbf{P}\langle \mathsf{UU}\mathbf{K}\rangle \neq \Lambda$

A6. $u \in \mathsf{U}\mathbf{I} \rightarrow \bigvee_{x,y}(x,y \in \mathbf{pn} \cap \mathbf{P}^{\vee}u \wedge$
$\wedge (\mathbf{pn} \cap \mathbf{P}^{\vee}u \cap \mathbf{T}^{\vee}x) \cup (\mathbf{pn} \cap \mathbf{P}^{\vee}u \cap \mathbf{T}^{\wedge}y) \subset \mathbf{P}\langle \mathbf{0}\rangle)$

A7. $u \in \mathsf{U}\mathbf{I} \rightarrow \mathbf{T}_{e} \in \mathrm{con}(\mathbf{P}^{\vee}u \cap (\mathsf{UU}\mathbf{K} \cup \mathbf{0}))$

A8. $u \in \mathsf{U}\mathbf{I} \wedge X \neq \Lambda \wedge X \subset \mathbf{P}^{\vee}u \cap (\mathsf{UU}\mathbf{K} \cup \mathbf{0}) \rightarrow \bigvee_{x}(x \in X \wedge$
$\wedge \bigwedge_{y}(y \in X \rightarrow x\, \mathbf{T}_{e}\, y)) \wedge \bigvee_{v}(v \in X \wedge \bigwedge_{z}(z \in X \rightarrow z\, \mathbf{T}_{e}\, v))$

A9. $u_1, u_2 \in \mathsf{U}\mathbf{I} \wedge \mathbf{P}^{\vee}u_1 \cap \mathbf{P}^{\vee}u_2 \cap \mathbf{P}\langle \mathsf{UU}\mathbf{K}\rangle \neq \Lambda \rightarrow$
$\rightarrow u_1 \dot{\cup} u_2 \in \mathbf{P}\langle \mathsf{U}\mathbf{I}\rangle$

A10. $\mathsf{UU}\mathbf{K} \cup \mathbf{0} \subset \mathbf{mo}' \cap \mathbf{P}\langle \mathsf{U}\mathbf{I}\rangle$

A11. $\mathbf{P}\langle \mathsf{UU}\mathbf{K}\rangle \cap \mathbf{P}\langle \mathbf{0}\rangle = \Lambda$

A12. $\mathscr{X}, \mathscr{Y} \in \mathbf{K} \rightarrow \mathscr{X} \cap \mathscr{Y} = \Lambda \vee \mathscr{X} = \mathscr{Y}$

A13. $\mathscr{X} \in \mathbf{K} \rightarrow \mathsf{UU}\mathbf{K} \subset \mathsf{U}\mathscr{X}$

A14. $\mathscr{X} \in \mathbf{K} \wedge X, Y \in \mathscr{X} \rightarrow X \cap Y = \Lambda \vee X = Y$

[1] In one of following chapters we shall assume one additional axiom.

The intuitive sense of the above axioms will now be explained. Of course, these explanations should not be considered to be the 'official' statement of our assumptions. They are given in order to facilitate the understanding of the above exact, symbolic formulations.

Axiom A1 states that the set of idiolects is non-empty or, to put it more freely, that there exists at least one set of linguistically homogeneous utterances. This axiom does not decide, however, whether this set of utterances is non-empty. This is done by the second axiom which says that the number of the utterances which are the elements of an idiolect is always more than 0 and at the same time that it is finite. Thus, both these axioms, taken together, state, among other things, that there is at least one non-empty set of linguistically homogeneous utterances. From the intuitive point of view it is possible to see here an implicit assumption stating the existence of some speech communities and consequently some connection between these axioms and certain postulates of Bloomfield and Bloch.[1]

Axiom A3 states that all elements of idiolects are linear objects. This axiom is a precisation of the well-known principle of linearity of utterances formulated by F. de Saussure: 'Le signifiant, étant de nature auditive, se déroule dans le temps seul et a les caractères qu'il emprunte au temps: (*a*) il représente une étendue, et (*b*) cette étendue est mesurable dans une seule dimension: c'est une ligne. [. . .] Par opposition aux signifiants visuels (signaux maritimes, etc.), qui peuvent offrir des complications simultanées sur plusieurs dimensions, les signifiants acoustiques ne disposent que de la ligne du temps; leurs éléments se présentent l'un après l'autre; ils forment une chaine.'[2] As will be shown in the following chapter (theorem 3.26) from A3 and some other axioms of our system results that all segments are linear. The above corollary seems to be in accordance with de Saussure.

The fourth axiom may be explained as follows: Let u be an element of an idiolect and x an arbitrary part of the utterance u. Then, there is an elementary (not necessarily proper) segment y which is a part of u and, moreover, has a certain part in common with x. In other words, any part of an utterance overlaps at least one elementary segment (proper or not) completely contained in this utterance.

It follows from A4 that each utterance which is an element of an idiolect comprises at least one elementary segment. A4 does not guarantee, however, that among elementary segments which are

[1] L. Bloomfield [5], p. 154, B. Bloch [4], p. 6.

[2] F. de Saussure [21], p. 105. The term 'le signifiant' used by de Saussure may be understood simply as 'utterance' or 'expression'. In connection with the point (*a*) of de Saussure's principle, see also the theorem 3.10 in the next chapter.

parts of an utterance there is at least one proper segment, that is, that the utterance is not composed exclusively of pauses. This guarantee is provided by the fifth axiom. True enough, this axiom only says that if u is an element of any idiolect, then at least one proper elementary segment overlaps u. But this together with A4 and A10 enables us to prove that each utterance comprises at least one entire proper segment. (See the following chapter, theorem 3.15).

The content of the sixth axiom may be explained as follows: Let us assume that u is an utterance in a specific idiolect. Then, there exist two points x,y which are parts of u, so that (*a*) all points which are parts of u and which precede or coincide in time with x are parts of certain zero segments, and similarly (*b*) all points which are parts of u and follow or coincide in time with y are parts of certain zero segments. In other words, all initial points of an utterance up to a certain moment and all final points coming after a certain moment are, so to say, of 'pausal' nature. Hence, an utterance which is an element of an idiolect begins and ends always with a pause. Let us notice that these initial and final pauses are considered to be parts of the utterance itself. This approach is perhaps slightly artificial, but it is theoretically convenient in view of the role which is played by pauses in phonetic and phonological analyses.

A7 states the connectedness of the relation of total precedence in time in the set of all elementary segments of any utterance. Thus, if $u \in \mathsf{U}\mathbf{I}$ and x and y are any two different elementary segments of the utterance u, then one of these segments is completely preceded in time by the other, that is, either $x\ \mathbf{T}_c\ y$ or $y\ \mathbf{T}_c\ x$.

The eighth axiom says that each non-empty set of elementary segments of a given utterance contains the earliest and the latest segment.

According to the ninth axiom any two utterances which have even a fragment of a proper elementary segment in common are parts of one longer utterance.

A10 says that each elementary segment is a non-momentary part of an element of an idiolect. Thus elementary segments exist only as parts of certain utterances. This axiom seems also to imply that the totality of human speech is divided into idiolects and is entirely comprised in them. This is in harmony with our statement in the previous chapter that the set **I** of all idiolects represents the whole of human speech.

According to the eleventh axiom no proper elementary segment has a part in common with any zero segment. Therefore it is evident that the sets: $\mathsf{U}\mathbf{K}$ and $\mathbf{0}$ are disjoint, i.e. that no proper segment is a pause.

The last three axioms characterize (rather weakly) the notions of a phonetic feature and kind of phonetic feature. In particular, A12 says that any two different kinds of features are disjoint. Hence, no feature 'in some respect' is at the same time a feature in another respect. Similarly A14 states that every two different features of the same kind are disjoint. From this follows the truism that no segment can have two different features in the same respect.

A13 says that each proper elementary segment is characterized in all respects interesting from the phonetic point of view, i.e. that it has at least one (and as is seen from A14 at most one) feature of every kind (see the following chapter, theorem 3.3). This assumption requires explanation. Quite often phoneticians concern themselves with features which make sense only for a specific category (class) of segments and not for all elementary proper segments. For instance, in a certain respect all segments are divided into two classes X, X', then again, in another respect which is determined only for the elements of the class X, the class X is divided into sub-classes X_1, X_2, X_3. Should we consider the families: $[X, X']$ and $[X_1, X_2, X_3]$ as separate kinds of phonetic features this would violate our axiom A13, for the segments belonging to X' are not characterized with respect to $[X_1, X_2, X_3]$. Therefore from our point of view, only one kind of features, namely $[X_1, X_2, X_3, X']$ should be considered instead of the two: $[X, X']$ and $[X_1, X_2, X_3]$. Similarly in any other —even more complicated—case it is possible to find such a set of kinds of features which satisfies A13 and is, in a sense, equivalent to the initial system of kinds.

Chapter 3

IMMEDIATE CONSEQUENCES OF AXIOMS

In the preceding two chapters we have described the foundations of our axiomatic system in the frame of which the principles of theoretical phonology will be formulated. Of course, we shall be mainly concerned with analysing and precisely defining the term 'phoneme'. Therefore, definitions will play the principal role in our further considerations. At the same time, of course, we shall formulate various theorems. These however will be from the intuitive point of view rather obvious. The main aim of our formulating these theorems will be to point out that various simple and 'obvious' properties of intuitive phonological concepts pertain (may be deduced from the axioms and definitions) also to their precisely defined counterparts. Our second aim is to state various simple relations holding between different concepts in order to facilitate a more profound understanding of our definitions.

Before we start a systematic development of the conceptual apparatus of theoretical phonology we shall put down here a certain number of simple corollaries resulting immediately from the assumed axioms. They may help to elucidate the content of the axioms themselves.

3.1 $$\mathscr{X} \in \mathbf{K} \rightarrow \mathsf{U}\mathscr{X} = \mathsf{UU}\mathbf{K}$$

Proof. If $\mathscr{X} \in \mathbf{K}$, then $\mathscr{X} \subset \mathsf{U}\mathbf{K}$, whence $\mathsf{U}\mathscr{X} \subset \mathsf{UU}\mathbf{K}$, and thus by virtue of A13 $\mathsf{U}\mathscr{X} = \mathsf{UU}\mathbf{K}$.

3.2 $$\mathscr{X},\mathscr{Y} \in \mathbf{K} \rightarrow \mathsf{U}\mathscr{X} = \mathsf{U}\mathscr{Y}$$

Proof. If $\mathscr{X},\mathscr{Y} \in \mathbf{K}$ then by 3.1 $\mathsf{U}\mathscr{X} = \mathsf{UU}\mathbf{K}$ and $\mathsf{U}\mathscr{Y} = \mathsf{UU}\mathbf{K}$, whence $\mathsf{U}\mathscr{X} = \mathsf{U}\mathscr{Y}$.

3.3 $$x \in \mathsf{UU}\mathbf{K} \wedge \mathscr{X} \in \mathbf{K} \rightarrow \dot{\bigvee_{X}}(X \in \mathscr{X} \wedge x \in X)$$

Proof. Let $x \in \mathsf{UU}\mathbf{K}$ and $\mathscr{X} \in \mathbf{K}$. Then by 3.1 $x \in \mathsf{U}\mathscr{X}$, whence by virtue of the definition of sum it follows that there exists an X such that $X \in \mathscr{X}$ and $x \in X$. The uniqueness of X follows from A14.

According to 3.3 every elementary proper segment has exactly one feature of each kind or—in other words—is uniquely characterized in each phonetically essential respect.

3.4 $$\mathsf{U}\mathbf{I} \neq \Lambda$$

Proof. This theorem is an immediate consequence of A1 and A2, since the sum of any non-empty family of non-empty sets is non-empty.

3.5 $$\mathsf{U}\mathsf{U}\mathbf{K} \neq \Lambda$$

Proof. By virtue of 3.4 there is an u such that $u \in \mathsf{U}\mathbf{I}$. Then by A5 $\mathbf{P}^{\vee}u \cap \mathbf{P}\langle \mathsf{U}\mathsf{U}\mathbf{K}\rangle \neq \Lambda$, whence $\mathbf{P}\langle \mathsf{U}\mathsf{U}\mathbf{K}\rangle \neq \Lambda$ and thus by I.2.22 $\mathsf{U}\mathsf{U}\mathbf{K} \neq \Lambda$.

3.6 $$\mathsf{U}\mathbf{K} \neq \Lambda \qquad \text{(by 3.5)}$$

3.7 $$\mathbf{K} \neq \Lambda \qquad \text{(by 3.6)}$$

3.8 $$\mathscr{X} \in \mathbf{K} \rightarrow \mathscr{X} \neq \Lambda$$

Proof. If $\mathscr{X} \in \mathbf{K}$, then by 3.1 and 3.5 $\mathsf{U}\mathscr{X} \neq \Lambda$, whence $\mathscr{X} \neq \Lambda$.

3.9 $$\mathbf{0} \neq \Lambda$$

Proof. By 3.4 there is an u such, that $u \in \mathsf{U}\mathbf{I}$. Then by A6 there is an x such that $x \in \mathbf{pn} \cap \mathbf{P}^{\vee}u$ and

(1) $$\mathbf{pn} \cap \mathbf{P}^{\vee}u \cap \mathbf{T}^{\vee}x \subset \mathbf{P}\langle \mathbf{0}\rangle$$

But since $x \in \mathbf{pn}$, hence by I.3.36 $x \in \mathbf{mo}$, and thus by I.3.3 $x \in \mathbf{T}^{\vee}x$. Thus, we have $x \in \mathbf{pn} \cap \mathbf{P}^{\vee}u \cap \mathbf{T}^{\vee}x$, whence by (1) $x \in \mathbf{P}\langle \mathbf{0}\rangle$, so that $\mathbf{P}\langle \mathbf{0}\rangle \neq \Lambda$ and so $\mathbf{0} \neq \Lambda$.

3.10 $$u \in \mathsf{U}\mathbf{I} \rightarrow \mathbf{P}^{\vee}u \cap (\mathsf{U}\mathsf{U}\mathbf{K} \cup \mathbf{0}) \neq \Lambda$$

Proof. Let $u \in \mathsf{U}\mathbf{I}$. Since $u\,\mathbf{P}\,u$, it follows by A4 that

$$\mathbf{P}\langle \mathbf{P}^{\vee}u \cap (\mathsf{U}\mathsf{U}\mathbf{K} \cup \mathbf{0})\rangle \neq \Lambda$$

whence $$\mathbf{P}^{\vee}u \cap (\mathsf{U}\mathsf{U}\mathbf{K} \cup \mathbf{0}) \neq \Lambda$$

3.11 $$\mathsf{U}\mathbf{I} \subset \mathbf{mo}'$$

Proof. Let $u \in \mathsf{U}\mathbf{I}$. Then by 3.10 there is a z such that

(2) $$z \in \mathbf{P}^{\vee}u$$

and

(3) $$z \in \mathsf{U}\mathsf{U}\mathbf{K} \cup \mathbf{0}.$$

From (3) by A10 we derive $z \notin \mathbf{mo}$, whence by (2) and I.3.34 $u \notin \mathbf{mo}$.

3.12 $$\mathsf{U}\mathsf{U}\mathbf{K} \cap \mathbf{0} = \Lambda \qquad \text{(by A10, I.3.16)}$$

3.13 $$u \in \mathsf{U}\mathbf{I} \rightarrow u = \mathbf{S}`(\mathbf{P}^{\vee}u \cap (\mathsf{U}\mathsf{U}\mathbf{K} \cup \mathbf{0}))$$

Proof. Let $u \in \mathsf{U}\mathbf{I}$. Since $\mathbf{P}^{\vee}u \cap (\mathsf{U}\mathsf{U}\mathbf{K} \cup \mathbf{0}) \subset \mathbf{P}^{\vee}u$, it follows by A4 and I.3.1 that $u\,\mathbf{S}(\mathbf{P}^{\vee}u \cap (\mathsf{U}\mathsf{U}\mathbf{K} \cup \mathbf{0}))$. But then by virtue of 3.10 and I.3.20 $u = \mathbf{S}`(\mathbf{P}^{\vee}u \cap (\mathsf{U}\mathsf{U}\mathbf{K} \cup \mathbf{0}))$.

3.14 $$u \in \mathsf{U}\mathbf{I} \wedge x,y \in \mathbf{P}^{\vee}u \cap (\mathsf{U}\mathsf{U}\mathbf{K} \cup \mathbf{0}) \rightarrow x = y \vee \mathbf{P}^{\vee}x \cap \mathbf{P}^{\vee}y = \Lambda$$

Proof. If $x \neq y$, then by hypothesis and A7 either $x\,\mathbf{T_c}\,y$ or $y\,\mathbf{T_c}\,x$. In both cases, however, by I.3.48 we have $\mathbf{P}^{\vee}x \cap \mathbf{P}^{\vee}y = \Lambda$.

3.15 $$x,y \in \mathsf{U}\mathsf{U}\mathbf{K} \rightarrow x = y \vee \mathbf{P}^{\vee}x \cap \mathbf{P}^{\vee}y = \Lambda$$

Proof. Assume that $x,y \in \mathsf{U}\mathbf{UK}$ and $\mathbf{P}^{\vee}x \cap \mathbf{P}^{\vee}y \neq \Lambda$. Then by A10 there must be utterances u_1, u_2 such that u_1, $u_2 \in \mathsf{U}\mathbf{I}$, $x \in \mathbf{P}^{\vee}u_1$ and $y \in \mathbf{P}^{\vee}u_2$. Then obviously

$$\mathbf{P}^{\vee}u_1 \cap \mathbf{P}^{\vee}u_2 \cap \mathbf{P}\langle \mathsf{U}\mathbf{UK}\rangle \neq \Lambda$$

whence by A9 $u_1 \dot{\cup} u_2 \in \mathbf{P}\langle \mathsf{U}\mathbf{I}\rangle$, that is, there is a $u \in \mathsf{U}\mathbf{I}$ such that $u_1 \dot{\cup} u_2 \in \mathbf{P}^{\vee}u$. Since $x \in \mathbf{P}^{\vee}u_1$ and $y \in \mathbf{P}^{\vee}u_2$, it follows that $x,y \in \mathbf{P}^{\vee}u$. From this by 3.14 we derive $x = y$.

The above theorem states that any two different elementary proper segments are external to each other, i.e. do not overlap. It is worth noting that the theorem is true only for proper segments. This seems to be in accordance with linguists' intuitions, which neither ascribe to pauses any definite length nor exclude the possibility of partial overlapping of certain pauses in utterances produced by different speakers.

3.16 $\quad u \in \mathsf{U}\mathbf{I} \wedge x \in \mathbf{pn} \cap \mathbf{P}^{\vee}u \rightarrow \dot{\bigvee_{y}}(x\,\mathbf{P}\,y \wedge y \in \mathbf{P}^{\vee}u \cap (\mathsf{U}\mathbf{UK} \cup \mathbf{0}))$

Proof. From hypothesis by A4 we infer that

$$\mathbf{P}^{\vee}x \cap \mathbf{P}\langle \mathbf{P}^{\vee}u \cap (\mathsf{U}\mathbf{UK} \cup \mathbf{0})\rangle \neq \Lambda$$

Since $x \in \mathbf{pn}$, therefore $\mathbf{P}^{\vee}x = [x]$ so that

$$x \in \mathbf{P}\langle \mathbf{P}^{\vee}u \cap (\mathsf{U}\mathbf{UK} \cup \mathbf{0})\rangle$$

Thus, there is a y such that $x\,\mathbf{P}\,y$ and $y \in \mathbf{P}^{\vee}u \cap (\mathsf{U}\mathbf{UK} \cup \mathbf{0})$. The uniqueness of y follows from 3.14.

3.17 $\quad u \in \mathsf{U}\mathbf{I} \rightarrow \mathbf{P}^{\vee}u \cap \mathsf{U}\mathbf{UK} \neq \Lambda$

Proof. From the hypothesis by virtue of A5 we infer that there is an x and a z such that $x\,\mathbf{P}\,u$, $x\,\mathbf{P}\,z$ and $z \in \mathsf{U}\mathbf{UK}$. On account of I.3.7 and I.3.1 we may assume that $x \in \mathbf{pn}$. Then by 3.16 there is a y such that $x\,\mathbf{P}\,y$ and $y \in \mathbf{P}^{\vee}u \cap (\mathsf{U}\mathbf{UK} \cup \mathbf{0})$. Now suppose that $y \in \mathbf{0}$. Then $x\,\mathbf{P}\,z$, where $z \in \mathsf{U}\mathbf{UK}$, and $x\,\mathbf{P}\,y$, where $y \in \mathbf{0}$, contrary to A11. Hence $y \notin \mathbf{0}$, that is $y \in \mathbf{P}^{\vee}u \cap \mathsf{U}\mathbf{UK}$, which completes the proof.

3.18 $\quad u \in \mathsf{U}\mathbf{I} \wedge x \in \mathbf{pn} \cap \mathbf{P}^{\vee}u \rightarrow \dot{\bigvee_{v}}(v \in \mathbf{ms} \wedge x = u \dot{\cap} v)$

3.19 $\quad u \in \mathsf{U}\mathbf{I} \wedge x,y \in \mathbf{pn} \cap \mathbf{P}^{\vee}u \rightarrow (x\,\mathbf{C}\,y \equiv x = y)$

3.20 $\quad u \in \mathsf{U}\mathbf{I} \rightarrow \mathbf{T}_e \in \mathrm{con}(\mathbf{pn} \cap \mathbf{P}^{\vee}u)$

The theorems 3.18–3.20 are immediate consequences of A3 and the theorems I.3.61–I.3.63. Thus, the relation $\mathbf{T}_e$ is an ordering in the set of points of any utterance. In accordance with our comment to I.3.63, it may be proved that the ordering is compact and continuous. But this is of small importance for phonology. In view of A7 $\mathbf{T}_e$ is also an ordering in the set of segments of any utterance, i.e.

in the set $\mathbf{P}^{\vee}u \cap (\mathsf{U}\mathsf{U}\mathbf{K} \cup \mathbf{0})$, for every $u \in \mathsf{U}\mathbf{I}$. However, this is an ordering of a different kind. Namely, a well-ordering of a finite type, since in view of A8 every non-empty subset of $\mathbf{P}^{\vee}u \cap (\mathsf{U}\mathsf{U}\mathbf{K} \cup \mathbf{0})$ contains the first and the last element. It follows from the above statement, that the number of elementary segments contained in an utterance is finite and greater than 0. And since by virtue of A2 idiolects are finite sets of utterances, therefore the number of elementary segments in an idiolect is finite as well. Thus, we have the following corollaries:

3.21 $$u \in \mathsf{U}\mathbf{I} \rightarrow 0 < \overline{\overline{\mathbf{P}^{\vee}u \cap (\mathsf{U}\mathsf{U}\mathbf{K} \cup \mathbf{0})}} < \aleph_0$$

3.22 $$X \in \mathbf{I} \rightarrow 0 < \overline{\overline{\mathbf{P}\langle X\rangle \cap (\mathsf{U}\mathsf{U}\mathbf{K} \cup \mathbf{0})}} < \aleph_0$$

We shall now prove that the first elementary segment in any utterance is a pause.

3.23 $$u \in \mathsf{U}\mathbf{I} \wedge x \in \mathbf{P}^{\vee}u \cap (\mathsf{U}\mathsf{U}\mathbf{K} \cup \mathbf{0}) \wedge \bigwedge_{y}(y \in \mathbf{P}^{\vee}u \cap (\mathsf{U}\mathsf{U}\mathbf{K} \cup \mathbf{0}) \rightarrow$$
$$\rightarrow x\,\mathbf{T}_e\,y) \rightarrow x \in \mathbf{0}$$

Proof. Assume that x satisfies the hypothesis of the theorem and $x \notin \mathbf{0}$. Then $x \in \mathsf{U}\mathsf{U}\mathbf{K}$. Let $z \in \mathbf{pn} \cap \mathbf{P}^{\vee}x$ (the existence of such a point is guaranteed by I.3.7). We shall prove that

(4) $$\mathbf{pn} \cap \mathbf{P}^{\vee}u \cap \mathbf{T}^{\vee}z \subset \mathbf{P}^{\vee}x.$$

Let us suppose that $v \in \mathbf{pn} \cap \mathbf{P}^{\vee}u \cap \mathbf{T}^{\vee}z$. Then by 3.16 v is a part of a segment y such that $y \in \mathbf{P}^{\vee}u \cap (\mathsf{U}\mathsf{U}\mathbf{K} \cup \mathbf{0})$, whence by hypothesis $x\,\mathbf{T}_e\,y$, that is either $x = y$ or $x\,\mathbf{T}_c\,y$. But the second alternative may not be true. For, if $x\,\mathbf{T}_c\,y$, then $z\,\mathbf{P}\,x \wedge x\,\mathbf{T}_c\,y \wedge y\,\breve{\mathbf{P}}\,v$ and so by I.3.45 $z\,\mathbf{T}_c\,v$, whence by I.3.42 $v\,\mathbf{T}'\,z$, contrary to our supposition that $v \in \mathbf{T}^{\vee}z$. Thus $x = y$, so that $v \in \mathbf{P}^{\vee}x$ and (4) is established.

On the other hand, we infer from A6 that there is a w such that

(5) $$w \in \mathbf{pn} \cap \mathbf{P}^{\vee}u \wedge \mathbf{pn} \cap \mathbf{P}^{\vee}u \cap \mathbf{T}^{\vee}w \subset \mathbf{P}\langle\mathbf{0}\rangle.$$

From this and I.3.36 and I.3.3 follows

(6) $$w \in \mathbf{P}\langle\mathbf{0}\rangle.$$

By 3.20 either $w\,\mathbf{T}_c\,z$ or $z\,\mathbf{T}_c\,w$ or $z = w$. But, if $w\,\mathbf{T}_c\,z$ holds, then by (4) $w \in \mathbf{P}^{\vee}x$, where $x \in \mathsf{U}\mathsf{U}\mathbf{K}$, which combined with (6) contradicts the axiom A11. Now suppose that $z\,\mathbf{T}_c\,w$. Then by (5) $z \in \mathbf{P}\langle\mathbf{0}\rangle$, and this, combined with the assumption that $z \in \mathbf{P}^{\vee}x$, where $x \in \mathsf{U}\mathsf{U}\mathbf{K}$, contradicts the axiom A11. A similar contradiction is also derived in the case when $z = w$.

Thus we have proved that the assumption that the hypothesis is, but the thesis is not satisfied, yields a contradiction. And thus the proof is completed.

The next theorem states that the last elementary segment in any utterance is a pause. The proof is quite analogous to that of 3.23, therefore it is omitted.

3.24 $$u \in \mathsf{U}\mathbf{I} \wedge x \in \mathbf{P}^{\vee}u \cap (\mathsf{UU}\mathbf{K} \cup \mathbf{0}) \wedge \bigwedge_{y}(y \in \mathbf{P}^{\vee}u \cap (\mathsf{UU}\mathbf{K} \cup \mathbf{0}) \rightarrow \rightarrow y\, \mathbf{T}_{\mathrm{c}}\, x) \rightarrow x \in \mathbf{0}$$

According to 3.16 every utterance contains at least one proper segment. Such a segment, by virtue of 3.23 and 3.24 is neither the first nor the last segment of the utterance, so that it must be situated between the first and the last segment. From this it follows that every utterance contains at least three different elementary segments, among them at least two pauses and at least one proper segment. Thus, we have the following corollaries:

3.25 $$u \in \mathsf{U}\mathbf{I} \rightarrow \overline{\overline{\mathbf{P}^{\vee}u \cap \mathbf{0}}} \geqslant 2$$

3.26 $$u \in \mathsf{U}\mathbf{I} \rightarrow \overline{\overline{\mathbf{P}^{\vee}u \cap (\mathsf{UU}\mathbf{K} \cup \mathbf{0})}} \geqslant 3$$

Finally, we conclude this chapter by showing that every elementary segment is a linear object.

3.27 $$\mathsf{UU}\mathbf{K} \cup \mathbf{0} \subset \mathbf{ln}$$

Proof. Suppose $x \in \mathsf{UU}\mathbf{K} \cup \mathbf{0}$ and $x \notin \mathbf{ln}$. Then by A10 there is a $u \in \mathsf{U}\mathbf{I}$ such that $x \in \mathbf{P}^{\vee}u$, and by I.3.60 there is a $y \in \mathbf{ms}$ such that $x\, \mathbf{T}'_{\mathrm{c}}\, y$ and $y\, \mathbf{T}'_{\mathrm{c}}\, x$, but at the same time either the product $y \dot{\cap} x$ does not exist or it exists but it is not a point. Then it is easily proved that $u\, \mathbf{T}'_{\mathrm{c}}\, y$ and $y\, \mathbf{T}'_{\mathrm{c}}\, u$.

(*a*) Suppose the product $y \dot{\cap} x$ does not exist. In this case there also does not exist the product $y \dot{\cap} u$. For, if $y \dot{\cap} u$ does exist, then by making use of 3.16, it may be proved that there is a segment v such that $v \neq x$, $v\, \mathbf{T}'_{\mathrm{c}}\, x$ and $x\, \mathbf{T}'_{\mathrm{c}}\, v$, which contradicts A7. Thus $y \dot{\cap} u$ does not exist, whence $u \notin \mathbf{ln}$, contrary to A3.

(*b*) Suppose the product $y \dot{\cap} x$ does exist but it is not a point. Then there are two different points z, v such that $z \in \mathbf{P}^{\vee}(y \dot{\cap} x)$ and $v \in \mathbf{P}^{\vee}(y \dot{\cap} x)$. Since $y \in \mathbf{ms}$, therefore $z\, \mathbf{C}\, v$ and at the same time $z \neq v$ and $z, v \in \mathbf{pn} \cap \mathbf{P}^{\vee}u$, which contradicts 3.19.

In both cases we have a contradiction and thus the proof is completed.

Chapter 4

PHONETIC CHAINS

In this chapter we are concerned with the notion of a phonetic chain (sequence).

For the sake of clarity and simplicity of formulas, we use, when writing down theorems and definitions in symbolic form, the letters ι, ι_1, ι_2, . . . as a special kind of set variables. They take as their values only idiolects, i.e. arbitrary elements of the class **I**. Thus, for instance, instead of

$$\bigwedge_X (X \in \mathbf{I} \rightarrow \mathrm{A}(X)) \quad \text{and} \quad \bigvee_X (X \in \mathbf{I} \wedge \mathrm{A}(X))$$

we shall write $\bigwedge_\iota \mathrm{A}(\iota)$ and $\bigvee_\iota \mathrm{A}(\iota)$, respectively.

We begin with two auxiliary definitions. The first introduces the symbol **esg** for the class of elementary segments. The second defines the *relation of being an elementary segment in*.

4.1 $$\mathbf{esg} \underset{\mathrm{df}}{=} \bigcup\bigcup \mathbf{K} \cup \mathbf{0}$$

4.2 $$\mathbf{Esg} \underset{\mathrm{df}}{=} \{x,y\colon x \, \mathbf{P} \, y \wedge x \in \mathbf{esg}\}$$

Thus, x is an elementary segment in y, in symbols: $x \, \mathbf{Esg} \, y$, if and only if x is a part of y and x is an elementary segment.

4.3 $\mathbf{Esg}^{\vee}y = \mathbf{P}^{\vee}y \cap \mathbf{esg}$

4.4 $\mathbf{Esg}\,\langle\iota\rangle = \{x\colon \bigvee_u (u \in \iota \wedge x \, \mathbf{Esg} \, u)\} = \bigcup_{u \in \iota} \mathbf{Esg}^{\vee}u$

4.5 $\mathbf{esg} = \mathbf{Esg}\,\langle \bigcup \mathbf{I} \rangle = \bigcup_\iota \mathbf{Esg}\,\langle\iota\rangle$ (by A10)

4.6 $x \in \mathbf{esg} \rightarrow \mathbf{Esg}^{\vee}x = [x]$

Proof. Under the assumption $x \in \mathbf{esg}$, the inclusion $[x] \subset \mathbf{Esg}^{\vee}x$ is obvious. Hence we need only to prove the converse inclusion. To this end we now suppose that $y \in \mathbf{Esg}^{\vee}x$. From A10 follows that there is a $u \in \bigcup \mathbf{I}$ such that $x,y \in \mathbf{P}^{\vee}u \cap \mathbf{esg}$. From this and 3.14 we infer that either $x = y$ or $\mathbf{P}^{\vee}x \cap \mathbf{P}^{\vee}y = \Lambda$. But $y \in \mathbf{P}^{\vee}x \cap \mathbf{P}^{\vee}y$, and so the second alternative may not hold. Hence $x = y$, so that $y \in [x]$ and the inclusion $\mathbf{Esg}^{\vee}x \subset [x]$ is established.

4.7 $\mathbf{P}^{\vee}y \cap \mathbf{P}^{\vee}z \neq \Lambda \rightarrow \mathbf{Esg}^{\vee}(y \dot{\cap} z) = \mathbf{Esg}^{\vee}y \cap \mathbf{Esg}^{\vee}z$

Proof. From the hypothesis follows that the product $y \dot{\cap} z$ does exist. Moreover, by 4.3 and I.3.31 we have the equalities:

$$\begin{aligned} \mathbf{Esg}^{\vee}(y \dot{\cap} z) &= \mathbf{P}^{\vee}(y \dot{\cap} z) \cap \mathbf{esg} \\ &= \mathbf{P}^{\vee}y \cap \mathbf{P}^{\vee}z \cap \mathbf{esg} \\ &= (\mathbf{P}^{\vee}y \cap \mathbf{esg}) \cap (\mathbf{P}^{\vee}z \cap \mathbf{esg}) \\ &= \mathbf{Esg}^{\vee}y \cap \mathbf{Esg}^{\vee}z. \end{aligned}$$

We now define the term *phonetic chain.* We use the term 'phonetic chain' instead of the term 'sequence' used in American linguistic publications, because the latter will be subsequently used in a different viz. mathematical meaning.

The definitions of the *relation of being a phonetic chain in* an utterance (**Ch**) and of the set of all *phonetic chains* (**ch**) are as follows.

4.8 $$\mathbf{Ch} \underset{\mathrm{df}}{=} \{x,u: u \in \mathsf{U}\mathbf{I} \wedge x\, \mathbf{P}\, u \wedge x = \mathbf{S}\text{‘}\mathbf{Esg}^{\vee}x \wedge \wedge (\mathbf{Esg}^{\vee}u \cap \breve{\mathbf{T}}_c\langle \mathbf{Esg}^{\vee}x\rangle \cap \mathbf{T}_c\langle \mathbf{Esg}^{\vee}x\rangle \subset \mathbf{P}^{\vee}x)\}$$

4.9 $$\mathbf{ch} \underset{\mathrm{df}}{=} \mathbf{Ch}\langle \mathsf{U}\mathbf{I}\rangle$$

The above definitions seem to render precisely the intentions of Bloch who defines the term 'phonetic chain' (i.e. sequence, in his own terminology) in the following way: 'An uninterrupted succession of two or more segments is a sequence.'[1] However, our definitions are slightly more general, since the phonetic chain is not required to contain at least two segments.

In accordance with definition 4.8 x is a phonetic chain in u if and only if u is an element of an idiolect, x is a part of u and at the same time (*a*) x is the mereological sum of the set of elementary segments which are parts of x and (*b*) every elementary segment which is a part of the utterance u and which is comprised between any two segments (that is, follows one segment and precedes another) which are parts of x is itself also a part of x. The condition (*b*) guarantees that x is an 'uninterrupted succession'. The condition (*a*), on the other hand, guarantees that x is a succession of whole segments, and therefore x cannot, for example, begin or end in the middle of an elementary segment.

The symbols introduced here enable to form easily the names of various special sets of phonetic chains. And thus, for instance, if u is an utterance in a certain idiolect, i.e. $u \in \mathsf{U}\mathbf{I}$, then $\mathbf{Ch}^{\vee}u$ is the set of all chains contained in u. If y is not a whole utterance in a certain idiolect but is, for instance, a fragment of an utterance, the set of phonetic chains contained in y may be defined as $\mathbf{ch} \cap \mathbf{P}^{\vee}y$. The set of all phonetic chains in a given idiolect ι may be defined as $\mathbf{Ch}\langle\iota\rangle$.

[1] B. Bloch [4], p. 13.

We shall now prove several theorems which show a number of properties of phonetic chains. The first two theorems are simple corollaries of 4.8, nevertheless we have put them down for the sake of reference.

4.10 $x \, \mathbf{Ch} \, u \rightarrow x = \mathbf{S}\text{‘}\mathbf{Esg}^{\vee} x$

4.11 $x \, \mathbf{Ch} \, u \rightarrow \mathbf{Esg}^{\vee} u \cap \breve{\mathbf{T}}_c \langle \mathbf{Esg}^{\vee} x \rangle \cap \mathbf{T}_c \langle \mathbf{Esg}^{\vee} x \rangle \subset \mathbf{P}^{\vee} x$

4.12 $u \in \mathsf{UI} \rightarrow u \, \mathbf{Ch} \, u$ (by 4.8, 3.13)

4.13 $\mathsf{UI} \subset \mathbf{ch}$ (by 4.12)

4.14 $\iota \subset \mathbf{Ch} \langle \iota \rangle$ (by 4.12)

4.15 $\mathbf{esg} \subset \mathbf{ch}$ (by A10, 4.6, I.3.15, I.3.43)

4.16 $\mathbf{Esg} \langle \iota \rangle \subset \mathbf{Ch} \langle \iota \rangle$ (by 4.6, I.3.15, 3.43)

4.17 $x \in \mathbf{ch} \rightarrow \mathbf{Esg}^{\vee} x \neq \Lambda$ (by 4.10)

4.18 $\mathbf{ch} \subset \mathbf{ln} \cap \mathbf{mo}'$

Proof. Suppose that $x \in \mathbf{ch}$ and $x \notin \mathbf{ln}$. Then by 4.8 and 4.9 there is a $u \in \mathsf{UI}$ such that $x \, \mathbf{Ch} \, u$. Moreover, by virtue of I.3.60, there is a $y \in \mathbf{ms}$ such that $x \, \mathbf{T}'_c \, y$ and $y \, \mathbf{T}'_c \, x$, but at the same time either the product $y \mathbin{\dot\cap} x$ does not exist or it exists but it is not a point. Clearly $x \, \mathbf{P} \, u$, so it is easily proved that $u \, \mathbf{T}'_c \, y$ and $y \, \mathbf{T}'_c \, u$. But since $u \in \mathsf{UI}$, therefore by A3 $u \in \mathbf{ln}$, whence $y \mathbin{\dot\cap} u \in \mathbf{pn}$. From this follows that $y \mathbin{\dot\cap} x$ does not exist. Let z be the only segment such that $z \, \mathbf{P} \, u$ and $y \mathbin{\dot\cap} u \in \mathbf{P}^{\vee} z$ (cf. 3.16). Clearly, $\sim z \, \mathbf{P} \, x$. From this by 4.11 we infer that either z completely precedes all segments contained in x or z is completely preceded in time by all segments contained in x. Thus either $y \mathbin{\dot\cap} u$ completely precedes all segments contained in x or $y \mathbin{\dot\cap} u$ is completely preceded by all segments contained in x. Hence by I.3.49 and I.3.50 either $y \mathbin{\dot\cap} u \, \mathbf{T}_c \, x$ or $x \, \mathbf{T}_c \, y \mathbin{\dot\cap} u$, whence $y \, \mathbf{T}_c \, x$ or $x \, \mathbf{T}_c \, y$, contrary to our supposition. Thus the inclusion $\mathbf{ch} \subset \mathbf{ln}$ is established. The inclusion $\mathbf{ch} \subset \mathbf{mo}'$ follows immediately from A10 and 4.17.

4.19 $v \in \mathbf{ch} \wedge x \, \mathbf{P} \, v \rightarrow \mathbf{P}^{\vee} x \cap \mathbf{P} \langle \mathbf{Esg}^{\vee} v \rangle \neq \Lambda$

Proof. If $v \in \mathbf{ch}$, then by 4.10 $v = \mathbf{S}\text{‘}\mathbf{Esg}^{\vee} v$. Therefore, if $x \, \mathbf{P} \, v$, then by I.3.1 $\mathbf{P}^{\vee} x \cap \mathbf{P} \langle \mathbf{Esg}^{\vee} v \rangle \neq \Lambda$.

4.20 $v \in \mathbf{ch} \rightarrow \mathbf{T}_c \in \mathrm{con}(\mathbf{Esg}^{\vee} v)$

Proof. If $v \in \mathbf{ch}$, then for some $u \in \mathsf{UI}$ we have $v \, \mathbf{P} \, u$. Hence $\mathbf{Esg}^{\vee} v \subset \mathbf{Esg}^{\vee} u$, whence by A7 $\mathbf{T}_c \in \mathrm{con}(\mathbf{Esg}^{\vee} v)$.

4.21 $v \in \mathbf{ch} \wedge x, y \in \mathbf{Esg}^{\vee} v \rightarrow x = y \vee \mathbf{P}^{\vee} x \cap \mathbf{P}^{\vee} y = \Lambda$

Proof. If $x \neq y$, then by hypothesis and 4.20 either $x \, \mathbf{T}_c \, y$ or $y \, \mathbf{T}_c \, x$. In both cases we have $\mathbf{P}^{\vee} x \cap \mathbf{P}^{\vee} y = \Lambda$ by I.3.48.

4.22 $v \in \mathbf{ch} \wedge x \in \mathbf{pn} \cap \mathbf{P}^{\vee} v \rightarrow \dot{\bigvee}_{y} (x \, \mathbf{P} \, y \wedge y \in \mathbf{Esg}^{\vee} v)$

Proof. From hypothesis by 4.19 we infer that $\mathbf{P}^{\vee}x \cap \mathbf{P}\langle \mathbf{Esg}^{\vee}v\rangle \neq \Lambda$. Since $x \in \mathbf{pn}$, therefore $\mathbf{P}^{\vee}x = [x]$, whence $x \in \mathbf{P}\langle \mathbf{Esg}^{\vee}v\rangle$. Hence, for some y we have $x \mathbf{P} y$ and $y \in \mathbf{Esg}^{\vee}v$. The uniqueness of y follows from 4.21.

4.23 $$v \in \mathbf{ch} \wedge x \in \mathbf{pn} \cap \mathbf{P}^{\vee}v \rightarrow \dot{\bigvee_{w}}(w \in \mathbf{ms} \wedge x = v \dot{\cap} w)$$

4.24 $$v \in \mathbf{ch} \wedge x,y \in \mathbf{pn} \cap \mathbf{P}^{\vee}v \rightarrow (x \mathbf{C} y \equiv x = y)$$

4.25 $$v \in \mathbf{ch} \rightarrow \mathbf{T}_c \in \mathrm{con}(\mathbf{pn} \cap \mathbf{P}^{\vee}v)$$

The theorems 4.23–4.25 are immediate consequences of I.3.61–I.3.63 and 4.18.

4.26 $$v \in \mathbf{ch} \wedge X \neq \Lambda \wedge X \subset \mathbf{Esg}^{\vee}v \rightarrow \bigvee_{x}(x \in X \wedge \bigwedge_{y}(y \in X \rightarrow$$
$$\rightarrow x \mathbf{T}_e y)) \wedge \bigvee_{z}(z \in X \wedge \bigwedge_{w}(w \in X \rightarrow w \mathbf{T}_e z))$$

Proof. If $v \in \mathbf{ch}$, then there is a $u \in \mathbf{UI}$ such that $v \mathbf{P} u$. Hence $\mathbf{Esg}^{\vee}v \subset \mathbf{Esg}^{\vee}u$. From this the thesis of our theorem follows by A8.

It is easy to see that theorems 4.17–4.26 are generalizations of certain previously given axioms and theorems which were concerned with those utterances which are elements of **UI**. The above theorems show that the time ordering of elementary segments and points in phonetic chains is analogous to the time ordering of elementary segments and points in whole utterances (i.e. in elements of **UI**), excepting that the first and the last segment of a chain must not be a pause.

4.27 $$v \in \mathbf{ch} \wedge x,y \in \mathbf{Esg}^{\vee}v \rightarrow (x \mathbf{T}_i y \equiv x \mathbf{T}_c y \wedge$$
$$\wedge \sim \bigvee_{z}(z \in \mathbf{Esg}^{\vee}v \wedge x \mathbf{T}_c z \wedge z \mathbf{T}_c y))$$

Proof. Since the implication

(1) $$x \mathbf{T}_i y \rightarrow x \mathbf{T}_c y \wedge \sim \bigvee_{z}(z \in \mathbf{Esg}^{\vee}v \wedge x \mathbf{T}_c z \wedge z \mathbf{T}_c y)$$

is obvious, it is sufficient to prove only the converse implication. To this end we now suppose that the hypothesis of the theorem and the consequent of (1) are true. Suppose also, for reductio ad absurdum, that $x \mathbf{T}_i' y$. From this follows that there is a u such that $x \mathbf{T}_c u$ and $u \mathbf{T}_c y$. On account of I.3.35 and I.3.43 we may assume that $u \in \mathbf{mo}$. Then by I.3.58 $\mathbf{S}`\mathbf{C}^{\vee}u \in \mathbf{ms} \cap \mathbf{C}^{\vee}u$. Thus by I.3.47 $x \mathbf{T}_c \mathbf{S}`\mathbf{C}^{\vee}u$ and $\mathbf{S}`\mathbf{C}^{\vee}u \mathbf{T}_c y$. But $x,y \in \mathbf{P}^{\vee}v$ so that by I.3.45 and I.3.43 $v \mathbf{T}_c' \mathbf{S}`\mathbf{C}^{\vee}u$ and $\mathbf{S}`\mathbf{C}^{\vee}u \mathbf{T}_c' v$. Since, however, $v \in \mathbf{ch}$, therefore by 4.18 $v \in \mathbf{ln}$ and consequently $(\mathbf{S}`\mathbf{C}^{\vee}u) \dot{\cap} v \in \mathbf{pn}$. Obviously $(\mathbf{S}`\mathbf{C}^{\vee}u) \dot{\cap} v \in \mathbf{P}^{\vee}v$. Hence, by 4.22, there is a $w \in \mathbf{Esg}^{\vee}v$ such that $(\mathbf{S}`\mathbf{C}^{\vee}u) \dot{\cap} v \in \mathbf{P}^{\vee}w$. Clearly $x \mathbf{T}_c (\mathbf{S}`\mathbf{C}^{\vee}u) \dot{\cap} v$ and $(\mathbf{S}`\mathbf{C}^{\vee}u) \dot{\cap} v \mathbf{T}_c y$, whence by I.3.48

$(\mathbf{S}`\mathbf{C}^{\vee}u) \dot{\cap} v \notin \mathbf{P}^{\vee}x$ and $(\mathbf{S}`\mathbf{C}^{\vee}u) \dot{\cap} v \notin \mathbf{P}^{\vee}y$. Thus $w \neq x$ and $w \neq y$. Obviously $w \mathbf{T}'_c x$, since in the opposite case it would be $(\mathbf{S}`\mathbf{C}^{\vee}u) \dot{\cap} v \mathbf{T}_c x$ which is impossible on account of asymmetry of $\mathbf{T}_c$. From this we conclude by 4.20 that $x \mathbf{T}_c w$. In a similar way it is pointed out that $y \mathbf{T}'_c w$ and $w \mathbf{T}_c y$. Hence there is a z (e.g. $z = w$) such that $x \mathbf{T}_c z$ and $z \mathbf{T}_c y$, contrary to our assumption that the consequent of (1) is true.

The above theorem shows, that if two different segments in a given chain are not separated by a third segment, then they are not separated by anything.

The next six theorems are stated here without proofs.

4.28 $x \mathbf{Ch}\, u \wedge y \in \mathbf{ch} \cap \mathbf{P}^{\vee}x \rightarrow y \mathbf{Ch}\, u$

4.29 $u \in \mathsf{UI} \rightarrow \mathbf{Ch}^{\vee}u = \mathbf{ch} \cap \mathbf{P}^{\vee}u$

4.30 $y,z \in \mathbf{ch} \wedge \mathbf{P}^{\vee}y \cap \mathbf{P}^{\vee}z \cap \mathbf{P}\langle\mathsf{UUK}\rangle \neq \Lambda \rightarrow$
$$\rightarrow \bigvee_u (u \in \mathsf{UI} \wedge y,z \in \mathbf{P}^{\vee}u)$$

4.31 $y,z \in \mathbf{ch} \wedge \mathbf{P}^{\vee}y \cap \mathbf{P}\langle\mathbf{0}\rangle = \Lambda \rightarrow \mathbf{Esg}^{\vee}(y \dot{\cup} z) = \mathbf{Esg}^{\vee}y \cup \mathbf{Esg}^{\vee}z$

4.32 $x \in \mathbf{ch} \wedge y,z \in \mathbf{ch} \cap \mathbf{P}^{\vee}x \rightarrow \mathbf{Esg}^{\vee}(y \dot{\cup} z) = \mathbf{Esg}^{\vee}y \cup \mathbf{Esg}^{\vee}z$

4.33 $y, z \in \mathbf{ch} \wedge \mathbf{P}^{\vee}y \cap \mathbf{P}^{\vee}z \cap \mathbf{P}\langle\mathsf{UUK}\rangle \neq \Lambda \rightarrow$
$$\rightarrow \mathbf{Esg}^{\vee}y \cap \mathbf{Esg}^{\vee}z \cap \mathsf{UUK} \neq \Lambda$$

4.34 $x \in \mathbf{Ch}\langle\iota\rangle \wedge y,z \in \mathbf{ch} \cap \mathbf{P}^{\vee}x \wedge y \mathbf{T}_i z \rightarrow y \dot{\cup} z \in \mathbf{Ch}\langle\iota\rangle$

Proof. By hypothesis $x \in \mathbf{Ch}\langle\iota\rangle$, hence there is a u such that

(2) $$u \in \iota$$

and $x \mathbf{Ch}\, u$. Then $x \mathbf{P}\, u$ and since $y,z \in \mathbf{P}^{\vee}x$

(3) $$y \dot{\cup} z \in \mathbf{P}^{\vee}u.$$

By hypothesis $y,z \in \mathbf{ch}$, therefore $y = \mathbf{S}`\mathbf{Esg}^{\vee}y$ and $z = \mathbf{S}`\mathbf{Esg}^{\vee}z$. From this and the assumption that $x \in \mathbf{Ch}\langle\iota\rangle$ and $y,z \in \mathbf{P}^{\vee}x$ we infer by 4.32 that $\mathbf{Esg}^{\vee}(y \dot{\cup} z) = \mathbf{Esg}^{\vee}y \cup \mathbf{Esg}^{\vee}z$. Thus, using I.3.32, we have

(4) $$y \dot{\cup} z = \mathbf{S}`\mathbf{Esg}^{\vee}y \dot{\cup} \mathbf{S}`\mathbf{Esg}^{\vee}z = \mathbf{S}`(\mathbf{Esg}^{\vee}y \cup \mathbf{Esg}^{\vee}z) = = \mathbf{S}`\mathbf{Esg}^{\vee}(y \dot{\cup} z).$$

Suppose now that $v \in \mathbf{Esg}^{\vee}u$ and
$$v \in \breve{\mathbf{T}}_c\langle\mathbf{Esg}^{\vee}(y \dot{\cup} z)\rangle \cap \mathbf{T}_c\langle\mathbf{Esg}^{\vee}(y \dot{\cup} z)\rangle.$$

Then there are $w_1,w_2 \in \mathbf{Esg}^{\vee}(y \dot{\cup} z)$ such that

(5) $$w_1 \mathbf{T}_c v \wedge v \mathbf{T}_c w_2.$$

On account of equality $\mathbf{Esg}^{\vee}(y \dot{\cup} z) = \mathbf{Esg}^{\vee}y \cup \mathbf{Esg}^{\vee}z$, there are four possible cases:

$$(a) \quad w_1 \in \mathbf{Esg}^{\vee}y, \quad w_2 \in \mathbf{Esg}^{\vee}y$$

(*b*) $w_1 \in \mathbf{Esg}^{\vee}y, \quad w_2 \in \mathbf{Esg}^{\vee}z$
(*c*) $w_1 \in \mathbf{Esg}^{\vee}z, \quad w_2 \in \mathbf{Esg}^{\vee}y$
(*d*) $w_1 \in \mathbf{Esg}^{\vee}z, \quad w_2 \in \mathbf{Esg}^{\vee}z$

Let us consider them successively.

(*a*) In this case $v \in \breve{\mathbf{T}}_c\langle \mathbf{Esg}^{\vee}y\rangle \cap \mathbf{T}_c\langle \mathbf{Esg}^{\vee}y\rangle$, and since by 4.28 $y\ \mathbf{Ch}\ u$, therefore by 4.11 $v \in \mathbf{P}^{\vee}y$ and so $v \in \mathbf{P}^{\vee}(y \cup z)$.

(*b*) Let s be the last segment in the set $\mathbf{Esg}^{\vee}y$, and p the first segment in the set $\mathbf{Esg}^{\vee}z$. (The existence of such segments is guaranteed by 4.17 and 4.26). Since by hypothesis $y\ \mathbf{T}_i\ z$, therefore by I.3.35 $s\ \mathbf{T}_i\ z$, whence by I.3.36 $s\ \mathbf{T}_i\ p$. From this and (5) it follows that either $w_1 \neq s$, or $w_2 \neq p$, whence either $w_1\ \mathbf{T}_c\ s$ or $p\ \mathbf{T}_c\ w_2$. Now, if $v\ \mathbf{T}_c\ s$, then $w_1\ \mathbf{T}_c\ v \wedge v\ \mathbf{T}_c\ s$ which yields by 4.11 $v \in \mathbf{P}^{\vee}y$. If $v = s$, then also $v \in \mathbf{P}^{\vee}y$. If, finally, $v\ \breve{\mathbf{T}}_c\ s$, then either $v = p$ or $p\ \mathbf{T}_c\ v$, since $v\ \mathbf{T}_c\ p$ is impossible. In both cases we have $v \in \mathbf{P}^{\vee}z$, since by 4.28 $z\ \mathbf{Ch}\ u$. (When distinguishing the above cases we are using A7 applied to u as the utterance and w_1, s, p, w_2, v as its segments). Thus we always have $v \in \mathbf{P}^{\vee}y \cup \mathbf{P}^{\vee}z$, whence $v \in \mathbf{P}^{\vee}(y \cup z)$.

(*c*) This case is impossible, since from the assumption that $y\ \mathbf{T}_i\ z$ follows that $w_2\ \mathbf{T}_c\ w_1$ and, on the other hand, from (5)—that $w_1\ \mathbf{T}_c\ w_2$; this, however, contradicts the asymmetry of $\mathbf{T}_c$.

(*d*) In this case $v \in \breve{\mathbf{T}}_c\langle \mathbf{Esg}^{\vee}z\rangle \cap \mathbf{T}_c\langle \mathbf{Esg}^{\vee}z\rangle$ and on account of that $z\ \mathbf{Ch}\ u$, we have $v \in \mathbf{P}^{\vee}z$, whence $v \in \mathbf{P}^{\vee}(y \cup z)$.

Thus we have proved that

(6) $\mathbf{Esg}^{\vee}u \cap \breve{\mathbf{T}}_c\langle \mathbf{Esg}^{\vee}(y \cup z)\rangle \cap \mathbf{T}_c\langle \mathbf{Esg}^{\vee}(y \cup z)\rangle \subset \mathbf{P}^{\vee}(y \cup z)$.

From (2), (3), (4) and (6) we infer by 4.8 that $y \cup z \in \mathbf{Ch}\langle \iota\rangle$.

The proofs of the following theorems are rather tedious and are omitted.

4.35 $y,z \in \mathbf{ch} \wedge \mathbf{P}^{\vee}y \cap \mathbf{P}^{\vee}z \cap \mathbf{P}\langle \mathsf{UUK}\rangle \neq \Lambda \rightarrow y \cup z \in \mathbf{ch}$

4.36 $x \in \mathbf{Ch}\langle \iota\rangle \wedge y,z \in \mathbf{ch} \cap \mathbf{P}^{\vee}x \wedge \mathbf{P}^{\vee}y \cap \mathbf{P}^{\vee}z \neq \Lambda \rightarrow$
$\rightarrow y \dot{\cap} z \in \mathbf{Ch}\langle \iota\rangle$

4.37 $y,z \in \mathbf{ch} \wedge \mathbf{P}^{\vee}y \cap \mathbf{P}^{\vee}z \cap \mathbf{P}\langle \mathsf{UUK}\rangle \neq \Lambda \rightarrow y \dot{\cap} z \in \mathbf{ch}$

Chapter 5

PREDECESSOR, SUCCESSOR AND SEGMENTING FUNCTION

We say that y *is a predecessor of* x, in symbols: $y\ \mathbf{p}\ x$, if and only if y is an elementary segment immediately preceding x in time and forming together with x a phonetic chain. Formally:

5.1 $$\mathbf{p} \underset{\mathrm{df}}{=} \{y, x : y \in \mathbf{esg} \wedge y\ \mathbf{T_i}\ x \wedge y \cup x \in \mathbf{ch}\}$$

The condition $y \cup x \in \mathbf{ch}$ is included into the above definition in order to guarantee that y and x are taken from the same utterance.

5.2 $$y\ \mathbf{p}\ x \rightarrow x \in \mathbf{ch}$$

Proof. If $y\ \mathbf{p}\ x$, then by 5.1 $y \in \mathbf{esg}$, $y\ \mathbf{T_i}\ x$ and $y \cup x \in \mathbf{ch}$. From the last property follows that there is a u such that

(1) $$u \in \mathsf{UI}$$

and $y \cup x \in \mathbf{Ch}^{\vee}u$. It is clear that

(2) $$x \in \mathbf{P}^{\vee}u.$$

Now suppose that $z \in \mathbf{Esg}^{\vee}(y \cup x)$ and $z \neq y$. If, moreover, $v \in \mathbf{pn} \cap \mathbf{P}^{\vee}z$, then by I.3.25 either $v\ \mathbf{P}\ y$ or $v\ \mathbf{P}\ x$. But $\sim v\ \mathbf{P}\ y$, since $v\ \mathbf{P}\ z$ and by 4.21 $\mathbf{P}^{\vee}y \cap \mathbf{P}^{\vee}z = \Lambda$. Thus $v\ \mathbf{P}\ x$, which establishes the inclusion

$$\mathbf{pn} \cap \mathbf{P}^{\vee}z \subset \mathbf{pn} \cap \mathbf{P}^{\vee}x.$$

From this by I.3.23 follows $\mathbf{S}‘(\mathbf{pn} \cap \mathbf{P}^{\vee}z) \in \mathbf{P}^{\vee}\mathbf{S}‘(\mathbf{pn} \cap \mathbf{P}^{\vee}x)$, that is, by I.3.24 $z \in \mathbf{P}^{\vee}x$. Thus we have proved the inclusion

(3) $$\mathbf{Esg}^{\vee}(y \cup x) - [y] \subset \mathbf{Esg}^{\vee}x.$$

Next, suppose $v \in \mathbf{pn} \cap \mathbf{P}^{\vee}x$. Then $v \in \mathbf{pn} \cap \mathbf{P}^{\vee}(y \cup x)$, and, since $y \cup x \in \mathbf{ch}$, we infer by 4.22 that there is a z such that $z \in \mathbf{Esg}^{\vee}(y \cup x)$ and $v\ \mathbf{P}\ z$. But $y\ \mathbf{T_i}\ x$, hence it is easy to prove that $z \neq y$. From this by (3) follows that $z \in \mathbf{Esg}^{\vee}x$. Therefore, by I.3.22, $z \in \mathbf{P}^{\vee}\mathbf{S}‘\mathbf{Esg}^{\vee}x$ and consequently $v \in \mathbf{pn} \cap \mathbf{P}^{\vee}\mathbf{S}‘\mathbf{Esg}^{\vee}x$. Thus we have proved the inclusion

$$\mathbf{pn} \cap \mathbf{P}^{\vee}x \subset \mathbf{pn} \cap \mathbf{P}^{\vee}\mathbf{S}‘\mathbf{Esg}^{\vee}x.$$

It is easy to verify that the converse inclusion holds as well. We conclude that

$$\mathbf{pn} \cap \mathbf{P}^{\vee}x = \mathbf{pn} \cap \mathbf{P}^{\vee}\mathbf{S}‘\mathbf{Esg}^{\vee}x.$$

Since $\mathbf{pn} \cap \mathbf{P}^{\vee}x \neq \Lambda$,

$$\mathbf{S}`(\mathbf{pn} \cap \mathbf{P}^{\vee}x) = \mathbf{S}`(\mathbf{pn} \cap \mathbf{P}^{\vee}\mathbf{S}`\mathbf{Esg}^{\vee}x),$$

whence by I.3.24

(4) $$x = \mathbf{S}`\mathbf{Esg}^{\vee}x.$$

Finally, suppose that $v \in \mathbf{Esg}^{\vee}u$ and there are $w_1, w_2 \in \mathbf{Esg}^{\vee}x$ such that $w_1\ \mathbf{T}_c\ v \wedge v\ \mathbf{T}_c\ w_2$. Then $w_1, w_2 \in \mathbf{Esg}^{\vee}(y \cup x)$ and, since $y \cup x \in \mathbf{Ch}^{\vee}u$, 4.11 gives $v \in \mathbf{Esg}^{\vee}(y \cup x)$. But $y\ \mathbf{T}_i\ x$, and so $y\ \mathbf{T}_c\ w_1$, whence $y\ \mathbf{T}_c\ v$. Thus $v \neq y$. Hence by (3) $v \in \mathbf{Esg}^{\vee}x$, whence $v \in \mathbf{P}^{\vee}x$. Thus we have proved the inclusion

(5) $$\mathbf{Esg}^{\vee}u \cap \breve{\mathbf{T}}_c\langle\mathbf{Esg}^{\vee}x\rangle \cap \mathbf{T}_c\langle\mathbf{Esg}^{\vee}x\rangle \subset \mathbf{P}^{\vee}x.$$

From (1), (2), (4) and (5) follows the thesis of our theorem.

5.3 $$y\ \mathbf{p}\ x \wedge z\ \mathbf{p}\ x \wedge \mathbf{P}\langle\mathsf{UUK}\rangle \cap \mathbf{P}^{\vee}x \neq \Lambda \rightarrow y = z$$

Proof. It follows from the hypothesis that

(6) $$y \in \mathbf{esg} \wedge y\ \mathbf{T}_i\ x \wedge y \cup x \in \mathbf{ch}$$

and

(7) $$z \in \mathbf{esg} \wedge z\ \mathbf{T}_i\ x \wedge z \cup x \in \mathbf{ch}.$$

Therefore, for some $u_1, u_2 \in \mathsf{UI}$, $y \cup x\ \mathbf{Ch}\ u_1$ and $z \cup x\ \mathbf{Ch}\ u_2$, whence $y \cup x \in \mathbf{P}^{\vee}u_1$ and $z \cup x \in \mathbf{P}^{\vee}u_2$. But $\mathbf{P}\langle\mathsf{UUK}\rangle \cap \mathbf{P}^{\vee}x \neq \Lambda$, and so $\mathbf{P}^{\vee}u_1 \cap \mathbf{P}^{\vee}u_2 \cap \mathbf{P}\langle\mathsf{UUK}\rangle \neq \Lambda$, whence by A9 $u_1 \cup u_2 \in \mathbf{P}\langle\mathsf{UI}\rangle$. Thus there is a $u \in \mathsf{UI}$ such that $y \cup x \in \mathbf{P}^{\vee}u$ and $z \cup x \in \mathbf{P}^{\vee}u$. Hence $y,z \in \mathbf{Esg}^{\vee}u$. By A7 either $y\ \mathbf{T}_c\ z$ or $z\ \mathbf{T}_c\ y$ or $y = z$. The first two alternatives are excluded by (6) and (7), and thus $y = z$.

5.4 $$x \in \mathbf{ch} \wedge \mathbf{0} \cap \mathbf{Esg}^{\vee}x = \Lambda \rightarrow \dot{\bigvee_{y}}(y\ \mathbf{p}\ x)$$

Proof. By hypothesis there is a $u \in \mathsf{UI}$ such that $x\ \mathbf{Ch}\ u$. Moreover, the first segment of u (which is a pause) does not belong to $\mathbf{Esg}^{\vee}x$. Let z be the first segment in the chain x, and y—the last among those segments of u which completely precede z in time. In accordance with 4.27 $y\ \mathbf{T}_i\ z$, and using I.3.54 it is easy to prove that $y\ \mathbf{T}_i\ x$. Moreover, it follows by virtue of 4.13, 4.15 and 4.34 that $y \cup z \in \mathbf{ch}$. Hence $y\ \mathbf{p}\ x$. Thus we need show only that y is the unique predecessor of x. Now, if $x \in \mathbf{ch}$, then by 4.17 $\mathbf{Esg}^{\vee}x \neq \Lambda$. On account of the assumption $\mathbf{0} \cap \mathbf{Esg}^{\vee}x = \Lambda$, we infer from this that $\mathbf{Esg}^{\vee}x \subset \mathsf{UUK}$, whence $\mathsf{UUK} \cap \mathbf{P}^{\vee}x \neq \Lambda$. The uniqueness of y follows now from theorem 5.3.

The theorem 5.4 may be also rewritten as follows.

5.5 $$x \in \mathbf{ch} \wedge \mathbf{0} \cap \mathbf{Esg}^{\vee}x = \Lambda \rightarrow \bigvee_{y}(y = \mathbf{p}`x)$$

5.6 $$x \in \mathsf{UUK} \rightarrow \bigvee_{y}(y = \mathbf{p}`x)$$

Proof. If $x \in \mathsf{UUK}$, then by 4.15 $x \in \mathbf{ch}$, and by 3.12 and 4.6 $x \notin \mathbf{0}$ and $\mathbf{Esg}^{\vee}x = [x]$, whence $\mathbf{0} \cap \mathbf{Esg}^{\vee}x = \Lambda$. From this by 5.5 we infer the thesis of the theorem.

5.7 $$x\ \mathbf{Ch}\ u \wedge \mathbf{0} \cap \mathbf{Esg}^{\vee}x = \Lambda \rightarrow \mathbf{p}'x \in \mathbf{Esg}^{\vee}u$$

Proof. If $x\ \mathbf{Ch}\ u$, then $u \in \mathsf{UI}$ and $x\ \mathbf{P}\ u$. From the assumption that $\mathbf{0} \cap \mathbf{Esg}^{\vee}x = \Lambda$ it follows that the first segment of u does not belong to $\mathbf{Esg}^{\vee}x$. Let z be the first segment of x, and y—the last among those segments of u which completely precede z. Using an argument similar to that employed in the proof of 5.4 it is easy to prove that $y\ \mathbf{p}\ x$. From this by virtue of 5.4 we obtain $y = \mathbf{p}'x$. Since $y \in \mathbf{Esg}^{\vee}u$, therefore $\mathbf{p}'x \in \mathbf{Esg}^{\vee}u$.

5.8 $$x \in \mathbf{Ch}\langle\iota\rangle \wedge \mathbf{0} \cap \mathbf{Esg}^{\vee}x = \Lambda \rightarrow \mathbf{p}'x \in \mathbf{Esg}\langle\iota\rangle \qquad \text{(by 5.7)}$$

5.9 $$x \in \mathbf{ch} \wedge y,z \in \mathbf{Esg}^{\vee}x \rightarrow (y\ \mathbf{p}\ z \equiv y\ \mathbf{T}_{\mathrm{i}}\ z)$$

Proof. Suppose $y\ \mathbf{T}_{\mathrm{i}}\ z$. Then by 4.15, 4.34 and the hypothesis we have $y \mathbin{\dot\cup} z \in \mathbf{ch}$, whence $y\ \mathbf{p}\ z$. Thus we have the implication

$$y\ \mathbf{T}_{\mathrm{i}}\ z \rightarrow y\ \mathbf{p}\ z.$$

The converse implication follows from 5.1 and is true independently of the hypothesis of our theorem.

5.10 $$x \in \mathbf{ch} \wedge y,z \in \mathbf{Esg}^{\vee}x \wedge z \notin \mathbf{0} \rightarrow (y = \mathbf{p}'z \equiv y\ \mathbf{T}_{\mathrm{i}}\ z)$$

Proof. It follows from the hypothesis that $z \in \mathsf{UUK}$ and so by 5.6

$$y\ \mathbf{p}\ z \equiv y = \mathbf{p}'z.$$

From this by 5.9 we infer the thesis of our theorem.

5.11 $$u \in \mathsf{UI} \wedge x \in \mathsf{UUK} \cap \mathbf{P}^{\vee}u \rightarrow (y = \mathbf{p}'x \equiv y \in \mathbf{Esg}^{\vee}u \wedge y\ \mathbf{T}_{\mathrm{i}}\ x)$$

Proof. It follows from the hypothesis that $x\ \mathbf{Ch}\ u$ and

$$\mathbf{0} \cap \mathbf{Esg}^{\vee}x = \Lambda.$$

Therefore, the implication

$$y = \mathbf{p}'x \rightarrow y \in \mathbf{Esg}^{\vee}u \wedge y\ \mathbf{T}_{\mathrm{i}}\ x$$

follows by 5.7 and 5.1. The converse implication follows from 4.13 and 5.10.

We now introduce the notion of a *successor*. It is quite similar to that of predecessor. We say, that y is a successor of x, in symbols $y\ \mathbf{s}\ x$, if and only if y is an elementary segment immediately preceded by x and forming together with x a phonetic chain.

5.12 $$\mathbf{s} \underset{\mathrm{df}}{=} \{y,x : y \in \mathbf{esg} \wedge x\ \mathbf{T}_{\mathrm{i}}\ y \wedge x \mathbin{\dot\cup} y \in \mathbf{ch}\}$$

We omit proofs of the following ten theorems dealing with the notion of successor.

5.13 $$y\ \mathbf{s}\ x \rightarrow x \in \mathbf{ch}$$

5.14 $y \mathbf{s} x \wedge z \mathbf{s} x \wedge \mathbf{P}\langle \mathsf{UUK}\rangle \cap \mathbf{P}^{\vee}x \neq \Lambda \rightarrow y = z$

5.15 $x \in \mathbf{ch} \wedge \mathbf{0} \cap \mathbf{Esg}^{\vee}x = \Lambda \rightarrow \dot{\bigvee}_{y}(y \mathbf{s} x)$

5.16 $x \in \mathbf{ch} \wedge \mathbf{0} \cap \mathbf{Esg}^{\vee}x = \Lambda \rightarrow \bigvee_{y}(y = \mathbf{s}`x)$

5.17 $x \in \mathsf{UUK} \rightarrow \bigvee_{y}(y = \mathbf{s}`x)$

5.18 $x \mathbf{Ch}\, u \wedge \mathbf{0} \cap \mathbf{Esg}^{\vee}x = \Lambda \rightarrow \mathbf{s}`x \in \mathbf{Esg}^{\vee}u$

5.19 $x \in \mathbf{Ch}\langle \iota\rangle \wedge \mathbf{0} \cap \mathbf{Esg}^{\vee}x = \Lambda \rightarrow \mathbf{s}`x \in \mathbf{Esg}\langle \iota\rangle$

5.20 $x \in \mathbf{ch} \wedge y,z \in \mathbf{Esg}^{\vee}x \rightarrow (y \mathbf{s} z \equiv z \mathbf{T}_{\mathrm{i}}\, y)$

5.21 $x \in \mathbf{ch} \wedge y,z \in \mathbf{Esg}^{\vee}x \wedge z \notin \mathbf{0} \rightarrow (y = \mathbf{s}`z \equiv z \mathbf{T}_{\mathrm{i}}\, y)$

5.22 $u \in \mathsf{UI} \wedge x \in \mathsf{UUK} \cap \mathbf{P}^{\vee}u \rightarrow (y = \mathbf{s}`x \equiv y \in \mathbf{Esg}^{\vee}u \wedge x \mathbf{T}_{\mathrm{i}}\, y)$

The next theorem establishes a simple connection between the notion of a predecessor and that of successor.

5.23 $y,z \in \mathbf{esg} \rightarrow (y \mathbf{p} z \equiv z \mathbf{s} y)$ (by 5.1, 5.12)

It should not be inferred from this theorem that **s** is the converse of **p**. For, if $y \mathbf{p} z$ and $z \notin \mathbf{esg}$, then $\sim z \mathbf{s} y$.

The next definition introduces the notion of the *length* of a phonetic chain. By the length of x (in symbols: λ_x) we mean the number of elementary segments contained in x. (The symbol λ_x is meaningful also when x is not a phonetic chain, but it will be practically applied to chains exclusively).

5.24 $\lambda_x \underset{\mathrm{df}}{=} \overline{\overline{\mathbf{Esg}^{\vee}x}}$

As an illustration of the notion, if x is an elementary segment, then $\lambda_x = 1$; if x is only a fragment of a segment, then $\lambda_x = 0$.

5.25 $x \in \mathbf{ch} \rightarrow 1 \leqslant \lambda_x < \aleph_0$ (by 4.17, 3.21)

It follows from 4.20, 4.26 and 5.25 that, if $x \in \mathbf{ch}$, then there is an ordinal correlator (isomorphism) of $\mathbf{T}_{\mathrm{e}}$ with its field limited to $\mathbf{Esg}^{\vee}x$ and $\leqslant$ with its field limited to the set of natural numbers $[1, 2, \ldots, \lambda_x]$. (Both these relations are well-orderings: the first in $\mathbf{Esg}^{\vee}x$ and the second in $[1, 2, \ldots, \lambda_x]$ and, moreover, the sets $\mathbf{Esg}^{\vee}x$ and $[1, 2, \ldots, \lambda_x]$ are finite and equinumerous). It may also be pointed out that there is but one ordinal correlator of this kind (comp. the end of chapter 1, part I). The unique ordinal correlator will be symbolized by $\vartheta(x)$. The parameter x appears here for the sake of marking that the ordinal correlator depends on the phonetic chain x and changes when we pass to another chain y.

A formal definition of $\vartheta(x)$ will not be given here in symbolic form. We shall limit ourselves to stating it once more in words.

5.26 $\vartheta(x)$ is the unique ordinal correlator of $\mathbf{T}_e$ with its field limited to $\mathbf{Esg}^{\vee}x$ and $\leqslant$ with its field limited to the set $[1, 2, \ldots, \lambda_x]$.

From this by the definition of the term 'ordinal correlator' we have the following corollary:

5.27 $$x \in \mathbf{ch} \rightarrow \vartheta(x) \in \mathrm{crs} \wedge \mathrm{D}`\vartheta(x) = \mathbf{Esg}^{\vee}x \wedge \mathrm{G}`\vartheta(x) = \{n : n \leqslant \lambda_x\} \wedge \bigwedge_{y,z} \bigwedge_{n,m} (y\,\vartheta(x)\,n \wedge z\,\vartheta(x)\,m \rightarrow (y\,\mathbf{T}_e\,z \equiv n \leqslant m))$$

(The hypothesis $x \in \mathbf{ch}$ appears here on account of the fact that in the case when $x \notin \mathbf{ch}$ the corresponding ordinal correlator must not exist.)

According to 5.27 $\vartheta(x)$ is a function defined on the set $[1, 2, \ldots, \lambda_x]$. This enables us to use the symbol $\vartheta(x)`n$ in every case when $x \in \mathbf{ch}$ and $n \in [1,2, \ldots, \lambda_x]$. The symbol $\vartheta(x)`n$ will be, however, abbreviated as follows:

5.28 $$\vartheta_n(x) \underset{\mathrm{df}}{=} \vartheta(x)`n$$

From the intuitive point of view, if $x \in \mathbf{ch}$, then $\vartheta(x)$ is a finite sequence (with λ_x terms) of elementary segments contained in x. Moreover, the order of the terms of the sequence mirrors the time order of segments in the chain x. In other words, the sequence $\vartheta(x)$ is simply a numbering of consecutive segments in x with the help of natural numbers $1, 2, \ldots, \lambda_x$. Thus, the successive terms $\vartheta_1(x)$, $\vartheta_2(x), \ldots, \vartheta_n(x), \ldots, \vartheta_{\lambda_x}(x)$ represent simply the first, the second, ..., the n-th, ..., the last elementary segment in the chain x.

As we have mentioned above, the sequence $\vartheta(x)$ strictly depends on the choice of the chain x. This dependence is functional and, in fact, we should have defined the function ϑ itself as a function associating with every phonetic chain $x, y, \ldots$ the corresponding sequences $\vartheta(x)$, $\vartheta(y), \ldots$ However, such a complication is not necessary here. Let us note only, that the function ϑ may be called the *segmenting function*. In fact, the assigning of the sequence $\vartheta(x)$ to the chain x consists, as it were, in 'cutting' this chain into separate elementary segments.

We now state some theorems concerning the segmenting function.

5.29 $x \in \mathbf{ch} \wedge y \in \mathbf{Esg}^{\vee}x \rightarrow \bigvee_n (n \leqslant \lambda_x \wedge y = \vartheta_n(x))$ (by 5.27, 5.28)

5.30 $x \in \mathbf{ch} \wedge n \leqslant \lambda_x \rightarrow \vartheta_n(x) \in \mathbf{Esg}^{\vee}x$ (by 5.27, 5.28)

5.31 $x \in \mathbf{ch} \wedge n,m \leqslant \lambda_x \rightarrow (\vartheta_n(x)\,\mathbf{T}_e\,\vartheta_m(x) \equiv n \leqslant m)$

Proof. It follows from the hypothesis that the segments $\vartheta_n(x)$ and $\vartheta_m(x)$ do exist. Clearly, $\vartheta_n(x)$ bears the relation $\vartheta(x)$ to n, and $\vartheta_m(x)$ bears the relation $\vartheta(x)$ to m. From this by the last part of 5.27 we infer the thesis of our theorem.

5.32 $\quad x \in \mathbf{ch} \wedge n,m \leqslant \lambda_x \rightarrow (\vartheta_n(x)\ \mathbf{T_c}\ \vartheta_m(x) \equiv n < m)$

Proof. This theorem follows from 5.32 and the fact that according to 5.27 $\vartheta(x) \in \text{crs}$.

5.33 $\quad x \in \mathbf{ch} \wedge n < \lambda_x \rightarrow \vartheta_n(x)\ \mathbf{T_i}\ \vartheta_{n+1}(x)$

Proof. From the hypothesis by 5.30 and 5.32 we infer that $\vartheta_n(x) \in \mathbf{Esg}^{\vee}x$, $\vartheta_{n+1}(x) \in \mathbf{Esg}^{\vee}x$ and $\vartheta_n(x)\ \mathbf{T_c}\ \vartheta_{n+1}(x)$. But assume that $\vartheta_n(x)\ \mathbf{T_i'}\ \vartheta_{n+1}(x)$. Then by 4.24 there is a segment z such that $z \in \mathbf{Esg}^{\vee}x$, $\vartheta_n(x)\ \mathbf{T_c}\ z$ and $z\ \mathbf{T_c}\ \vartheta_{n+1}(x)$. According to 5.29 there is an i such that $z = \vartheta_i(x)$. Thus $\vartheta_n(x)\ \mathbf{T_c}\ \vartheta_i(x)$ and $\vartheta_i(x)\ \mathbf{T_c}\ \vartheta_{n+1}(x)$. From this by 5.32 follows that $n < i$ and $i < n + 1$ which is a contradiction. Hence the assumption $\vartheta_n(x)\ \mathbf{T_i'}\ \vartheta_{n+1}(x)$ is false.

5.34 $\quad x \in \mathbf{ch} \wedge n,m \leqslant \lambda_x \rightarrow (\vartheta_n(x)\ \mathbf{T_i}\ \vartheta_m(x) \equiv n + 1 = m)$

Proof. Suppose that the hypothesis of the theorem is true. Let us assume additionally that $\vartheta_n(x)\ \mathbf{T_i}\ \vartheta_m(x)$. Then, clearly, $\vartheta_n(x)\ \mathbf{T_c}\ \vartheta_m(x)$, and by 5.32 $n < m$. Now, suppose that $n + 1 \neq m$. Then $n + 1 < m$, whence by 5.30 $\vartheta_{n+1}(x) \in \mathbf{Esg}^{\vee}x$, therefore by 5.32 $\vartheta_n(x)\ \mathbf{T_c}\ \vartheta_{n+1}(x)$ and $\vartheta_{n+1}(x)\ \mathbf{T_c}\ \vartheta_m(x)$, contrary to the supposition $\vartheta_n(x)\ \mathbf{T_i}\ \vartheta_m(x)$. Thus the implication

$$\vartheta_n(x)\ \mathbf{T_i}\ \vartheta_m(x) \rightarrow n + 1 = m$$

is established. The converse implication follows immediately from theorem 5.33.

5.35 $\quad x \in \mathbf{ch} \wedge n < \lambda_x \rightarrow \vartheta_n(x)\ \mathbf{p}\ \vartheta_{n+1}(x)$

Proof. From the hypothesis it follows by 5.30 and 5.33 that $\vartheta_n(x) \in \mathbf{Esg}^{\vee}x$, $\vartheta_{n+1}(x) \in \mathbf{Esg}^{\vee}x$ and $\vartheta_n(x)\ \mathbf{T_i}\ \vartheta_{n+1}(x)$. Thus by 5.9 $\vartheta_n(x)\ \mathbf{p}\ \vartheta_{n+1}(x)$.

5.36 $\quad x \in \mathbf{ch} \wedge n < \lambda_x \rightarrow \vartheta_{n+1}(x)\ \mathbf{s}\ \vartheta_n(x)$ (by 5.30, 5.35, 5.23)

5.37 $\quad x \in \mathbf{ch} \wedge n < \lambda_x \wedge \vartheta_{n+1}(x) \in \mathsf{UUK} \rightarrow \vartheta_n(x) = \mathbf{p}`\vartheta_{n+1}(x)$ (by 5.35, 5.3)

5.38 $\quad x \in \mathbf{ch} \wedge n < \lambda_x \wedge \vartheta_n(x) \in \mathsf{UUK} \rightarrow \vartheta_{n+1}(x) = \mathbf{s}`\vartheta_n(x)$ (by 5.36, 5.14)

5.39 $\quad u \in \mathsf{UI} \rightarrow \vartheta_1(u) \in \mathbf{0}$ (by 3.23)

5.40 $\quad u \in \mathsf{UI} \rightarrow \vartheta_{\lambda_u}(u) \in \mathbf{0}$ (by 3.24)

5.41 $\quad y\ \mathbf{p}\ x \rightarrow y\ \mathbf{p}\ \vartheta_1(x)$

Proof. It is easy to prove that if $y\ \mathbf{p}\ x$, then $y\ \mathbf{T_i}\ \vartheta_1(x)$. Using 5.9 (where we substitute $y \cup x$ for x) we infer that $y\ \mathbf{p}\ \vartheta_1(x)$.

5.42 $$y \mathbf{s} x \rightarrow y \mathbf{s} \vartheta_{\lambda_x}(x)$$

Proof. From the hypothesis follows $\vartheta_{\lambda_x}(x)\,\mathbf{T}_\mathrm{i}\, y$, whence by 5.20 $y \mathbf{s} \vartheta_{\lambda_x}(x)$.

5.43 $$x \in \mathbf{ch} \wedge \vartheta_1(x) \notin \mathbf{0} \rightarrow \bigvee_y (y = \mathbf{p}`x)$$

Proof. The existence of a predecessor y is proved by a reasoning similar to that employed in the first part of the proof of 5.4. The uniqueness of y follows from 5.41 and 5.3.

5.44 $$x \in \mathbf{ch} \wedge \vartheta_{\lambda_x}(x) \notin \mathbf{0} \rightarrow \bigvee_y (y = \mathbf{s}`x)$$

Proof. The existence of a successor y is proved by a reasoning similar to that employed in the first part of the proof of 5.15. The uniqueness of y follows from 5.42 and 5.14.

Chapter 6

UTTERANCES AND PHRASES

In this chapter we are going to discuss more closely two special kinds of phonetic chains, namely utterances and phrases. The term 'utterance' has been used in previous chapters but merely in an informal way. We have used this term to denote an element of an idiolect, i.e. an element of the set $\mathsf{U}\mathbf{I}$. Presently the notion of utterance will be precisely defined. At the same time it will be slightly generalized. Henceforth, by *utterance* we shall mean a phonetic chain containing at least one proper elementary segment, and, both, beginning and ending with a pause. Of course, utterances, understood in this way, may contain a number of internal pauses. It is also obvious that if $u \in \mathsf{U}\mathbf{I}$, then u is an utterance in the above meaning, but at the same time there may exist utterances which are not elements of the set $\mathsf{U}\mathbf{I}$. The following two definitions introduce formally the notion of utterance:

$$6.1\ \mathbf{Ut} \underset{\mathrm{df}}{=} \{x,y\colon x\,\mathbf{Ch}\,y \wedge \bigcup\mathsf{U}\mathbf{K} \cap \mathbf{P}^{\vee}x \neq \Lambda \wedge \vartheta_1(x) \in \mathbf{0} \wedge \vartheta_{\lambda_x}(x) \in \mathbf{0}\}$$

$$6.2\ \mathbf{ut} \underset{\mathrm{df}}{=} \mathbf{Ut}\langle \mathsf{U}\mathbf{I}\rangle$$

The first of the above definitions introduces the *relation of being an utterance in*. According to it, x is an utterance in y, in symbols: $x\ \mathbf{Ut}\ y$, if and only if x is a phonetic chain in y, x contains at least one elementary proper segment, and the first and the last segment in x are pauses. The symbol **Ut** may be used in various contexts. If e.g. $y \in \mathsf{U}\mathbf{I}$, then $\mathbf{Ut}^{\vee}y$ is the set of all utterances which may be distinguished in y. $\mathbf{Ut}\langle\iota\rangle$ is the set of all utterances in the idiolect ι, and $\mathbf{Ut}\langle\mathsf{U}\mathbf{I}\rangle$ is the set of all utterances. The last set, in accordance with 6.2, we denote shortly by **ut**.

It is worth while to emphasize, that our notion of utterance is not synonymous with the analogous colloquial notion and even slightly diverges from the definitions which are usually presented by the linguists and which refer to non-phonetic criteria. However, our definition seems to be relatively close to that by Harris: 'An utterance is any stretch of talk, by one person, before and after which there is silence on the part of the person.' [1] The difference lies only

[1] Z. S. Harris [7], p. 14.

in that Harris locates the pauses before and after the utterance, while we consider them as parts of the utterance itself. This seems to us more convenient. That the utterance should be a 'stretch of talk, by one person', is expressed in our definition as the requirement that the utterance should be a chain.[1]

Now we shall present a few simple and obvious theorems referring to utterances.

6.3 $u \in \mathsf{UI} \rightarrow u\ \mathbf{Ut}\ u$ (by 4.12, 3.17, 5.39, 5.40, 6.1)

6.4 $\mathsf{UI} \subset \mathbf{ut}$ (by 6.3)

6.5 $\iota \subset \mathbf{Ut}\langle\iota\rangle$ (by 6.3)

6.6 $\mathbf{ut} \subset \mathbf{ch}$ (by 6.1)

6.7 $\mathbf{ut} \subset \mathbf{ln} \cap \mathbf{mo}'$ (by 6.6, 4.18)

In a similar way to the notion of utterance we now introduce the notion of *phrase*. Our understanding of this notion will be entirely in line with the following definition given by Bloch: 'Any fraction of an utterance between two immediately successive pauses [. . .] is a phrase.'[2]

6.8 $\mathbf{Phr} \underset{\mathrm{df}}{=} \{x,y\colon x\ \mathbf{Ch}\ y \wedge \mathbf{0} \cap \mathbf{P}^{\vee}x = \Lambda \wedge \mathbf{p}\text{'}x \in \mathbf{0} \wedge \mathbf{s}\text{'}x \in \mathbf{0}\}$

6.9 $\mathbf{phr} \underset{\mathrm{df}}{=} \mathbf{Phr}\langle\mathsf{UI}\rangle$

The first of these definitions introduces the *relation of being a phrase in*, the second introduces the set of all phrases.

6.10 $\mathbf{phr} \subset \mathbf{ch}$ (by 6.8)

6.11 $x \in \mathbf{phr} \wedge n \leqslant \lambda_x \rightarrow \vartheta_n(x) \in \mathsf{UUK}$ (by 6.8)

6.12 $x,y \in \mathbf{phr} \rightarrow x = y \vee \mathbf{P}^{\vee}x \cap \mathbf{P}^{\vee}y = \Lambda$

Proof. Let us suppose, for *reductio ad absurdum*, that $x,y \in$ **phr,** $x \neq y$ and $\mathbf{P}^{\vee}x \cap \mathbf{P}^{\vee}y \neq \Lambda$. It follows from these suppositions by 6.10 and 6.8 that $x,y \in \mathbf{ch}$ and $\mathbf{P}^{\vee}x \cap \mathbf{P}^{\vee}y \cap \mathbf{P}\langle\mathsf{UUK}\rangle \neq \Lambda$. Thus, by 4.35 $x \cup y \in \mathbf{ch}$, that is, $x \cup y\ \mathbf{Ch}\ u$, for some $u \in \mathsf{UI}$.

Since $x \neq y$, therefore by 4.10 $\mathbf{Esg}^{\vee}x \neq \mathbf{Esg}^{\vee}y$. Thus, there is a segment z which belongs to only one of the sets $\mathbf{Esg}^{\vee}x$ and $\mathbf{Esg}^{\vee}y$. Assume that e.g. $z \in \mathbf{Esg}^{\vee}x$ and $z \notin \mathbf{Esg}^{\vee}y$. It is clear that

$$\mathbf{Esg}^{\vee}x \cap \mathbf{Esg}^{\vee}y \subset \mathbf{Esg}^{\vee}u.$$

Therefore, by 4.11, either z completely precedes all elements of $\mathbf{Esg}^{\vee}y$ or z is completely preceded by all elements of $\mathbf{Esg}^{\vee}y$. Suppose

[1] In connection with this, compare chapter 1, the remarks about the notion of an idiolect.

[2] B. Bloch [4], p. 19.

that the first alternative holds. (In case the second holds the reasoning is analogous.) We may assume that z is the last among all those segments of x, which precede all segments of y. Using 4.27 we may easily prove that $z\ \mathbf{T}_i\ \vartheta_1(y)$. From this by 5.13 follows $z\ \mathbf{T}_i\ y$. Moreover, using 3.34 it is easily proved that $z \cup y \in \mathbf{ch}$. From this, by 5.3, follows that $z = \mathbf{p}`y$. But $z \in \mathbf{Esg}^{\vee}x$, hence $z \in \mathsf{UUK}$, and consequently $\mathbf{p}`y \notin \mathbf{0}$, contrary to our supposition $y \in \mathbf{phr}$. Every case which is omitted here leads in a similar way to a contradiction.

6.13 $$\mathsf{UU}\mathbf{K} \subset \mathbf{P}\langle\mathbf{phr}\rangle$$

Proof. Let $x \in \mathsf{UU}\mathbf{K}$. Then by A10 $x \in \mathbf{P}\langle\mathsf{U}\mathbf{I}\rangle$, that is, for some $u \in \mathsf{U}\mathbf{I}$, $x\ \mathbf{P}\ u$. Let us take into account the last segment y such that $y \in \mathbf{0} \cap \mathbf{Esg}^{\vee}u$ and $y\ \mathbf{T}_c\ x$, and the first segment z such that $z \in \mathbf{0} \cap \mathbf{Esg}^{\vee}u$ and $x\ \mathbf{T}_c\ z$. It is easily proved that

$$\mathbf{S}`(\mathbf{Esg}^{\vee}u \cap \mathbf{T}_c{}^{\vee}z \cap \breve{\mathbf{T}}_c{}^{\vee}y) \in \mathbf{phr}$$

and

$$x \in \mathbf{P}^{\vee}\mathbf{S}`(\mathbf{Esg}^{\vee}u \cap \mathbf{T}_c{}^{\vee}z \cap \breve{\mathbf{T}}_c{}^{\vee}y).$$

6.14 $$\mathbf{phr} \subset \mathbf{P}\langle\mathbf{ut}\rangle \qquad \text{(by 6.10, 4.8, 6.4)}$$

The last theorem confirms the accordance of our definition of 'phrase' with Bloch's definition, where it is explicitly stated that a phrase is always a part of an utterance.

In connection with the above considerations on the notions of an utterance and of a phrase the following question arise. Is it possible to define the notion of a word by means available in our system? This problem seems to be rather difficult. Nevertheless, it may be, in a certain sense, positively answered. It seems, namely, that all definitions of a word which are given hitherto by linguists and which employ no extraphonetic (e.g. semantical or morphological) notions may be reconstructed in our system. We shall return to this problem in the next chapter.

Chapter 7

PHONETIC EQUIVALENCE AND THE NOTION OF WORD

We shall say that two given segments are *phonetically equivalent* if either both are pauses or have exactly the same phonetic features. In other words, two segments are phonetically equivalent if they are phonetically undistinguishable, that is cannot be distinguished by means of phonetic criteria.

The notion of phonetic equivalence may be easily extended to any phonetic chains. We say that two phonetic chains are phonetically equivalent if they have the same length and their successive segments are respectively phonetically equivalent. This generalization follows the idea of Harris who writes: 'Equivalent utterances are then defined as being equivalent in all their segments; distinct utterances are non-equivalent in at least one of their segments.' [1] The fact that Harris speaks about the equivalence of utterances and not of phonetic chains is not essential here.

Since, according to our terminology, segments are phonetic chains, the notion of phonetic equivalence of segments is a particular case of the notion of equivalence of chains. Therefore, we shall present only one formal definition of the relation of phonetic equivalence, namely the definition of the equivalence of chains.

7.1 $$\mathbf{E} \underset{\mathrm{df}}{=} \{x,y\colon x,y \in \mathbf{ch} \wedge \lambda_x = \lambda_y \wedge \bigwedge_i (i \leqslant \lambda_x \rightarrow \rightarrow (\vartheta_i(x) \in \mathbf{0} \wedge \vartheta_i(y) \in \mathbf{0}) \vee \bigwedge_X (X \in \mathrm{U}\mathbf{K} \rightarrow \rightarrow (\vartheta_i(x) \in X \equiv \vartheta_i(y) \in X)))\}$$

According to the above definition x is phonetically equivalent to y, in symbols: $x\,\mathbf{E}\,y$, if and only if x and y are phonetic chains of the same length and for every i which is not greater than the length of these chains either $\vartheta_i(x)$ and $\vartheta_i(y)$ are pauses or $\vartheta_i(x)$ and $\vartheta_i(y)$ have exactly the same phonetic features.[2]

7.2 $$\mathbf{E} \in \mathrm{refl}(\mathbf{ch})$$ (by 7.1)

[1] Z. S. Harris [7], p. 34.

[2] As regards the notion of phonetic feature compare chapter 1.

7.3 $$C`\mathbf{E} = \mathbf{ch}$$ (by 7.1, 7.2)

7.4 $$\mathbf{E} \in \text{refl}$$ (by 7.2, 7.3)

7.5 $$\mathbf{E} \in \text{sym}$$ (by 7.1)

7.6 $$\mathbf{E} \in \text{trans}$$

Proof. Assume that $x\,\mathbf{E}\,y$ and $y\,\mathbf{E}\,z$. Then

(1) $$x,z \in \mathbf{ch} \wedge \lambda_x = \lambda_z$$

and, for $i \leqslant \lambda_x$, either

(a$_1$) $$\vartheta_i(x) \in \mathbf{0} \wedge \vartheta_i(y) \in \mathbf{0} \qquad \text{or}$$

(a$_2$) $$\bigwedge_X (X \in \mathsf{U}\mathbf{K} \longrightarrow (\vartheta_i(x) \in X \equiv \vartheta_i(y) \in X))$$

and either

(b$_1$) $$\vartheta_i(y) \in \mathbf{0} \wedge \vartheta_i(z) \in \mathbf{0} \qquad \text{or}$$

(b$_2$) $$\bigwedge_X (X \in \mathsf{U}\mathbf{K} \longrightarrow (\vartheta_i(y) \in X \equiv \vartheta_i(z) \in X)).$$

In the case when (a$_1$) and (b$_1$) hold, we have $\vartheta_i(x) \in \mathbf{0}$ and $\vartheta_i(z) \in \mathbf{0}$, which together with (1) gives $x\,\mathbf{E}\,z$. In the case when (a$_1$) and (b$_2$) hold, we have $\vartheta_i(y) \in \mathbf{0}$, whence by 3.12 $\vartheta_i(y) \notin \mathsf{UU}\mathbf{K}$. Then by virtue of (b$_2$) $\vartheta_i(z) \notin \mathsf{UU}\mathbf{K}$, that is $\vartheta_i(z) \in \mathbf{0}$. Thus in this case we also have $\vartheta_i(x) \in \mathbf{0}$ and $\vartheta_i(z) \in \mathbf{0}$, which together with (1) gives $x\,\mathbf{E}\,z$. In the case when (a$_2$) and (b$_1$) hold our reasoning is similar. Finally, in the case when (a$_2$) and (b$_2$) hold we have obviously

$$\bigwedge_X (X \in \mathsf{U}\mathbf{K} \longrightarrow (\vartheta_i(x) \in X \equiv \vartheta_i(z) \in X)).$$

Thus in every case we have $x\,\mathbf{E}\,z$.

7.7 $\mathbf{E} \in \text{eq}$ (by 7.4, 7.5, 7.6)

7.8 $x,y \in \mathbf{esg} \longrightarrow (x\,\mathbf{E}\,y \equiv x,y \in \mathbf{0} \vee \bigwedge_X (X \in \mathsf{U}\mathbf{K} \longrightarrow (x \in X \equiv y \in X)))$

Proof. If $x,y \in \mathbf{esg}$, then $x,y \in \mathbf{ch}$, and, by 4.6 $\lambda_x = \lambda_y = 1$, $\vartheta_1(x) = x$ and $\vartheta_1(y) = y$. According to these facts, the condition formulated in definition 7.1 may be simplified as in the present theorem.

7.9 $$x \in \mathbf{0} \longrightarrow \bigwedge_y (x\,\mathbf{E}\,y \equiv y \in \mathbf{0})$$

Proof. Assume that $x \in \mathbf{0}$. Then $\lambda_x = 1$. Suppose, additionally, that $x\,\mathbf{E}\,y$. Then clearly $\lambda_y = 1$, whence $y \in \mathbf{esg}$. Thus by 7.8 either $x,y \in \mathbf{0}$ or

(2) $$\bigwedge_X (X \in \mathsf{U}\mathbf{K} \longrightarrow (x \in X \equiv y \in X)).$$

Since $x \in \mathbf{0}$, therefore by 3.12 $x \notin \mathsf{UU}\mathbf{K}$. Thus, in case when (2) holds, we have $y \notin \mathsf{UU}\mathbf{K}$, and since $y \in \mathbf{esg}$, therefore $y \in \mathbf{0}$. In this way the implication

$$x \, \mathbf{E} \, y \rightarrow y \in \mathbf{0}$$

is established. The converse implication follows immediately from theorem 7.8.

The above theorem shows that any two pauses are phonetically equivalent and, moreover, that only a pause may be phonetically equivalent to a pause. Thus, for instance, two pauses with different durations are, in accordance with our theory, always phonetically equivalent. This does not mean that pauses with different durations cannot be differentiated by ear. Our theorem expresses merely the statement that the phonetic and phonological role of all real pauses is the same, no matter whether they last a minute or an hour.

Now, let us return to the problem of the definition of a word, mentioned at the end of the previous chapter. Frankly we agree with Jones[1] that it is impossible to give an exact and at the same time fully adequate definition of a word, especially if we limit ourselves to the means of phonetics and phonology. However, this opinion is not shared by all linguists and several definitions have been proposed. One of the last attempts to define a word by phonetic and phonological means is presented is Jassem's paper [12] where among others we read:

'The analysis presented below is based on two principal assumptions: (1) that the phonological analysis of a given language has been previously performed, and (2) that there are grounds for deciding what phonic chains (sequences of phonemes) exist in the language (that is, really occur in this language). . . . The assumption (2) means that it is possible to assert the real existence in the given language of sequences longer even than a phrase.

'In our opinion these assumptions are sufficient for the structural definition of a word. In the course of this work we shall make further reference to the fact that in accordance with structuralistic assumptions as well as with principles of the theory of information we avoid semantic criteria. We should like to point out here that in our method we do not assume any previous morphological analysis.' [2]

If the opinions expressed in the above excerpt are right, this means doubtlessly that Jassem's theory of word can be reconstructed in our system. Unfortunately, in certain points this theory is not clear to us, and, moreover, is rather too complicated for us to present here its logical reconstruction or to quote it or even to give

[1] Cf. D. Jones [13], § 7.

[2] W. Jassem [12], p. 36.

a short summary of it. We shall therefore confine ourselves to quoting and reconstructing some simpler conceptions. At first let us cite some original statements of certain linguists.

L. Bloomfield in [5] defines successively:

'The vocal features common to same or partly same utterances are *forms*; the corresponding stimulus-reaction features are *meanings*.

'Thus a form is a recurrent vocal feature which has meaning, and a meaning is a recurrent stimulus-reaction feature which corresponds to a form.

'A *minimum* X is an X which does not consist entirely of lesser X's.

'A form which may be an utterance is *free*.

'A minimum free form is a *word*.'

Harris summarizes Bloomfield's conception when discussing his own idea of the notion of word, as follows: 'Every word . . . occurs occasionally by itself as a complete utterance. No word is divisible into smaller sections each of which occurs by itself (except, in special circumstances) as a complete utterance. . . . Using this property, Bloomfield defined the word in general as a minimum utterance.' [1]

L. R. Palmer defines a word as 'the smallest speech unit (= constantly recurring sound-pattern) capable of functioning as a complete utterance'.[2]

Ch. F. Hockett gives the following definition: 'A word is thus any segment of a sentence bounded by successive points at which pausing is possible.' [3]

Apart from the external differences of all of the above definitions, the main intention seems to be approximately the same for all of them. This intention is probably most clear in the definitions by Harris and Palmer. We propose to make it precise by means available in our system. We shall begin with the definitions of two auxiliary notions, namely the notions of quasiphrasal partition and word-partition of a phrase.

We say that a set X is a *quasi-phrasal partition of* the phrase x with respect to the idiolect ι if and only if x is a phrase of the idiolect ι, the mereological sum of X is identical with x, all elements of X are chains contained in x, all elements of X are phonetically equivalent to certain whole phrases of the idiolect ι and finally no two different elements of the set X overlap. In other words, if x is a

[1] Z. S. Harris [7], p. 327.

[2] This definition is quoted from Jones [13], p. 3.—Let us add, that according to Jones the definition of word, given by Palmer is probably the most adequate from all possible definitions.

[3] Ch. F. Hockett [8], p. 167.

phrase of ι, we shall obtain a quasi-phrasal partition of x whenever we cut x in chains so that each of these chains is phonetically equivalent to a whole phrase of the idiolect ι.

As may be easily seen every phrase has at least one quasi-phrasal partition with respect to an appropriate idiolect. For, if x is a phrase in a certain idiolect, then already the set $[x]$ is such a partition. Of course we have here the trivial case of 'cutting' the phrase x into one chain only. Let us notice, however, that for many phrases no other quasi-phrasal partitions do exist. Thus, for example, if x is a phrase due to the uttering of the English *yes*!, then x certainly has only one quasi-phrasal partition, namely the trivial partition $[x]$ mentioned above. However, it is true that many phrases—especially the longer ones—have also non-trivial quasi-phrasal partitions, often even more than one or two.

In order to indicate that X is a quasi-phrasal partition of x with respect to ι we write $X\,\mathbf{Qpt}^{(\iota)}\,x$. The precise definition of the relation $\mathbf{Qpt}^{(\iota)}$ is as follows:

7.10 $$\mathbf{Qpt}^{(\iota)} \underset{\mathrm{df}}{=} \{X,x\colon x \in \mathbf{Phr}\langle\iota\rangle \wedge x = \mathbf{S}`X \wedge \wedge X \subset \mathbf{ch} \cap \mathbf{P}^{\vee}x \cap \mathbf{E}\langle\mathbf{Phr}\langle\iota\rangle\rangle \wedge \wedge \bigwedge_{y,z} (y,z \in X \wedge y \neq z \rightarrow \mathbf{P}^{\vee}y \cap \mathbf{P}^{\vee}z = \Lambda)\}$$

The following theorem is an immediate consequence of the above definition:

7.11 $$x \in \mathbf{Phr}\langle\iota\rangle \rightarrow [x]\,\mathbf{Qpt}^{(\iota)}\,x$$

Now, let us discuss our second auxiliary notion, i.e. the notion of a word-partition of a phrase. We say that a set X is a *word-partition of* a phrase x with respect to ι if and only if X is a quasi-phrasal partition of x with respect to ι and there does not exist a quasi-phrasal partition Y of x such that $Y \neq X$ and the elements of Y are parts of elements of X. Roughly speaking, a quasi-phrasal partition X of the phrase x is its word-partition if the further division of chains belonging to X cannot result in a new quasi-phrasal partition of the phrase x.

The relation of being a word-partition with respect to ι we denote by $\mathbf{Wpt}^{(\iota)}$. The exact definition is as follows:

7.12 $$\mathbf{Wpt}^{(\iota)} \underset{\mathrm{df}}{=} \{X,x\colon X\,\mathbf{Qpt}^{(\iota)}\,x \wedge \sim \bigvee_{Y} (Y\,\mathbf{Qpt}^{(\iota)}\,x \wedge \wedge Y \neq X \wedge Y \subset \mathbf{P}\langle X\rangle)\}$$

7.13 $$x \in \mathbf{Phr}\langle\iota\rangle \rightarrow \mathbf{Wpt}^{(\iota)\vee}x \neq \Lambda$$

Proof. Let $x \in \mathbf{Phr}\langle\iota\rangle$. Then, by 7.11, there exists an X_1 such that

X_1 $\mathbf{Qpt}^{(\iota)}$ x. If $\sim X_1$ $\mathbf{Wpt}^{(\iota)}$ x, then, by 7.12, there is an X_2 such that X_2 $\mathbf{Qpt}^{(\iota)}$ x, $X_2 \neq X_1$ and $X_2 \subset \mathbf{P}\langle X_1 \rangle$. If $\sim X_2$ $\mathbf{Wpt}^{(\iota)}$ x, then there exists an X_3 such that X_3 $\mathbf{Qpt}^{(\iota)}$ x, $X_3 \neq X_2$ and $X_3 \subset \mathbf{P}\langle X_2 \rangle$. Suppose that $X_3 = X_1$. Then, by virtue of the inclusion $X_2 \subset \mathbf{P}\langle X_1 \rangle$, we have $X_2 \subset \mathbf{P}\langle X_3 \rangle$. From this and the inclusion $X_3 \subset \mathbf{P}\langle X_2 \rangle$ and the fact that different elements of X_2 as well as different elements of X_3 do not overlap, we infer the equality $X_3 = X_2$. Since this equality is false, therefore the supposition that $X_3 = X_1$ is also false. Thus $X_3 \neq X_1$, and consequently, all the sets X_1, X_2, X_3 are distinct. If again $\sim X_3$ $\mathbf{Wpt}^{(\iota)}$ x, then there exists an X_4 such that X_4 $\mathbf{Qpt}^{(\iota)}$ x, $X_4 \neq X_3$ and $X_4 \subset \mathbf{P}\langle X_3 \rangle$. Suppose $X_4 = X_2$. Then, by virtue of the inclusion $X_3 \subset \mathbf{P}\langle X_2 \rangle$, we have $X_3 \subset \mathbf{P}\langle X_4 \rangle$ and consequently $X_3 = X_4$, which is false. Thus $X_4 \neq X_2$. Suppose now that $X_4 = X_1$. Since

$$X_3 \subset \mathbf{P}\langle X_2 \rangle \subset \mathbf{P}\langle \mathbf{P}\langle X_1 \rangle \rangle \subset \mathbf{P}\langle X_1 \rangle,$$

therefore $X_3 \subset \mathbf{P}\langle X_4 \rangle$, whence $X_3 = X_4$. But the last equality is false. Thus $X_4 \neq X_1$, and consequently all the sets X_1, X_2, X_3, X_4 are distinct.

Continuing the above reasoning either we shall find a set X_n such that X_n $\mathbf{Wpt}^{(\iota)}$ x or we shall get an infinite sequence $X_1, X_2, X_3, \ldots, X_i, \ldots$ of quasi-phrasal partitions of x such that $X_i \neq X_j$, for $i \neq j$. The second alternative is, however, impossible, since the number of all possible quasi-phrasal partitions of x is finite and less than or equal to the number of all possible ways of dividing x into non-overlapping phonetic chains. The last number is equal exactly to

$$\sum_{k=0}^{\lambda_x - 1} \binom{\lambda_x - 1}{k}.$$

The above theorem shows that there exists at least one word-partition for each phrase of a given idiolect. However, in our system we are unable to prove that there is only one partition of this kind, that is, that the set $\mathbf{Wpt}^{(\iota)\vee}x$ consists of only one element. This, however, seems to agree with intuition. For, although it is difficult to give a real example of a phrase which would have two different word-partitions, there are no reasons for considering it impossible.

Having the notion of word-partition at our disposal it is easy to formulate an exact definition of the notion of a *word*, which would be in accordance with the intentions of the definitions by Bloomfield, Palmer and Hockett, quoted above. For, if X $\mathbf{Wpt}^{(\iota)}$ x, then the elements of X are words in the phrase x. Therefore the set of words of a given idiolect ι may be defined as the sum of all sets $X, Y, Z, \ldots$

which are word partitions of some phrases of the idiolect ι. If we denote the set of words of the idiolect ι by $\mathbf{wd}^{(\iota)}$ we may formulate the definition:

7.14 $$\mathbf{wd}^{(\iota)} \underset{\mathrm{df}}{=} \bigcup \mathbf{Wpt}^{(\iota)} \langle \mathbf{Phr}\langle\iota\rangle\rangle$$

In accordance with this definition we have the following equivalence:

7.15 $$y \in \mathbf{wd}^{(\iota)} \equiv \bigvee_X \bigvee_x (X\, \mathbf{Wpt}^{(\iota)} x \wedge x \in \mathbf{Phr}\langle\iota\rangle \wedge y \in X)$$

The question may be raised whether 7.14 actually renders the intentions of the definitions by Bloomfield, Palmer and Hockett. In our opinion, this is the case. So far as Bloomfield's and Palmer's definitions are concerned, it seems even quite certain; (of course, it must be remembered that our terminology differs slightly from that of these authors). Only Hockett's definition may arouse greater doubts. It seems, however, that it should not be taken too literally, since in the literal understanding it may lead to absurd consequences such as, for instance, that in Polish every syllable is a word.

Obviously, we do not maintain that our definition of a word is adequate in relation to the colloquial understanding of the notion. Like Bloomfield's or Palmer's definitions it is too narrow. It seems, however, that the problem of obtaining a more adequate definition of a word is not absolutely hopeless and that our method may prove useful in further investigations in this field.

To conclude we have to indicate the following circumstance. Words, in the sense of our definition, are, in fact, concrete utterances of word-forms. For example, two utterances (even by one speaker) of the English *book* are two different words. Therefore, it would be necessary to formulate another notion of word, namely of a word in the abstract sense. This may be done by assuming, e.g., that words in the abstract sense are **E**-equivalence classes in the set of words in the sense of the definition 7.14. And so, e.g., the set of all concrete utterances of the English *book* would constitute one word in the abstract sense. It seems, however, that instead of **E**-equivalence classes it would be more appropriate to use here equivalence classes with respect to the phonological equivalence, that is, with respect to the relation of the phonemic structures' identity. The notion of the phonemic structure of a phonetic chain will be defined in chapter 13.

Chapter 8

PHONES AND PHONIC SYSTEMS

The **E**-equivalence classes in **esg** will be called *phones*. The class of all phones will be denoted by Π_0.

8.1 $$\Pi_0 \underset{\mathrm{df}}{=} \mathfrak{A}(\mathbf{E}, \mathbf{esg})$$

Immediately from this definition we infer the following corollaries:

8.2 $$X \in \Pi_0 \equiv \bigvee_x (x \in \mathbf{esg} \wedge \bigwedge_y (y \in X \equiv y \,\mathbf{E}\, x \wedge y \in \mathbf{esg}))$$

8.3 $$X \in \Pi_0 \rightarrow X \subset \mathbf{esg}$$

According to the above theorems, phones are sets of elementary segments. In particular, if $x \in \mathbf{esg}$, then the set of all elementary segments which are phonetically equivalent to x is a phone. Under our understanding of the notion of set, phones are simply common features of phonetically equivalent elementary segments. In other words and more accurately: a phone is something that is common to those and only those elementary segments which are phonetically equivalent to a given (arbitrarily chosen) elementary segment. Notice, that our distinction of elementary segments and of phones is analogous to Jones' distinction of concrete speech-sounds and of abstract speech-sounds.

Since $\mathbf{esg} \subset \mathbf{ch} = \mathbf{C}\text{‘}\mathbf{E}$, therefore using 7.7 we derive the following theorems:

8.4 $$\mathbf{E} \in \mathrm{eq}(\mathbf{esg})$$

8.5 $$x \in \mathbf{esg} \rightarrow \bigvee_X (X \in \Pi_0 \wedge x \in X)$$

8.6 $$X, Y \in \Pi_0 \rightarrow X = Y \vee X \cap Y = \Lambda$$

8.7 $$X \in \Pi_0 \rightarrow X \neq \Lambda$$

The next theorem gives an example of a phone.

8.8 $$\mathbf{0} \in \Pi_0$$

Proof. Since $\mathbf{0} \neq \Lambda$ and $\mathbf{0} \subset \mathbf{esg}$, therefore there is an x such that $x \in \mathbf{0} \cap \mathbf{esg}$. From this by 7.9 follows

$$\bigwedge_y (y \in \mathbf{0} \equiv y\,\mathbf{E}\,x \wedge y \in \mathbf{esg}),$$

and by 8.2 we have $\mathbf{0} \in \Pi_0$.

Of course, the phone $\mathbf{0}$ is not the most interesting among all phones. On the contrary it is only a subsidiary phone. Therefore, it may be called the *improper phone*. The other phones will be called *proper*. The set of proper phones will be symbolized by Π.

8.9 $$\Pi \underset{\mathrm{df}}{=} \Pi_0 - [\mathbf{0}]$$

Those phones which contain segments taken from a given idiolect ι, that is, those phones which are, so to say, represented in ι, will be called phones of the idiolect ι. The set of all phones of ι will be symbolized by $\Pi_0^{(\iota)}$, and the set of all proper phones of ι by $\Pi^{(\iota)}$.

8.10 $$\Pi_0^{(\iota)} \underset{\mathrm{df}}{=} \Pi_0 \cap \{X\colon X \cap \mathbf{Esg}\langle\iota\rangle \neq \Lambda\}$$

8.11 $$\Pi^{(\iota)} \underset{\mathrm{df}}{=} \Pi_0^{(\iota)} - [\mathbf{0}]$$

If $X \in \Pi_0$ and x is a segment belonging to X, then we say that X is a *phonic form* of the segment x. The relation of being a phonic form will be denoted by π.

8.12 $$\pi \underset{\mathrm{df}}{=} \{X, x\colon X \in \Pi_0 \wedge x \in X\}$$

8.13 $$x \in \mathbf{esg} \rightarrow \bigvee_X (X = \pi\text{‘}x)$$ (by 8.5, 8.6, 8.12)

If $x \in \mathbf{esg}$, then the symbol $\pi\text{‘}x$ denotes the unique phone which contains x. Using this symbol we state the following obvious theorems. Easy proofs of them are omitted.

8.14 $$x \in \mathbf{esg} \rightarrow \pi\text{‘}x \in \Pi_0$$

8.15 $$x \in \bigcup\bigcup\mathbf{K} \rightarrow \pi\text{‘}x \in \Pi$$

8.16 $$x \in \mathbf{0} \rightarrow \pi\text{‘}x = \mathbf{0}$$

8.17 $$x \in \mathbf{esg} \rightarrow x \in \pi\text{‘}x$$

8.18 $$x \in \mathbf{Esg}\langle\iota\rangle \rightarrow \pi\text{‘}x \in \Pi_0^{(\iota)}$$

8.19 $$x, y \in \mathbf{esg} \rightarrow (x\,\mathbf{E}\,y \equiv \pi\text{‘}x = \pi\text{‘}y)$$

We shall now define the notion of *phonic structure* of a phonetic chain. This notion will be of great importance for our subsequent considerations. Let us begin with intuitive explanations.

Let x be an arbitrary phonetic chain. With x we may associate a finite sequence of all elementary segments which are parts of x. Let

(1) $$z_1, z_2, \ldots, z_n,$$

where $n = \lambda_x$, be the sequence of the above type such that the order of its terms mirrors the time order of segments in the chain x. Let us now consider the sequence of phones

(2) $$X_1, X_2, \ldots, X_n,$$

such that $z_i \in X_i$, for every $i \leqslant n$. Thus (2) is simply the sequence of the phonic forms of successive segments belonging to (1). The sequence (2) constructed in this way will be called the phonic structure of the chain x. It will be symbolized by $\varphi(x)$. Clearly, $\varphi(x)$ is always a finite sequence of phones, and its form (in particular, its length) depends on the choice of the chain x. It is also clear, that the terms of $\varphi(x)$ may recur. Finally, notice that the so-called narrow (as opposed to the broad) phonetic transcription of a speech-chain consists in descripting the phonic structure of the chain.

Let us note that the sequence (1) is simply the function $\vartheta(x)$ and that it may be equivalently represented thus:

(3) $$\vartheta_1(x), \vartheta_2(x), \ldots, \vartheta_n(x).$$

On the other hand, (2) as the sequence of the phonic forms of the elements of (1) may now be represented as follows:

(4) $$\pi`\vartheta_1(x), \pi`\vartheta_2(x), \ldots, \pi`\vartheta_n(x).$$

It is now clear that the phonic structure of x, that is $\varphi(x)$, may be defined simply as the relative product of π and $\vartheta(x)$.

8.20 $$\varphi(x) \underset{\text{df}}{=} \pi/\vartheta(x)$$

The following three theorems show that $\varphi(x)$ is in fact a sequence of phones with λ_x terms. The simple proofs of these theorems are omitted.

8.21 $$x \in \mathbf{ch} \longrightarrow \mathrm{D}`\varphi(x) \subset \Pi_0$$

8.22 $$x \in \mathbf{ch} \longrightarrow \mathrm{\complement}`\varphi(x) = \{n : n \leqslant \lambda_x\}$$

8.23 $$x \in \mathbf{ch} \longrightarrow \varphi(x) \in \mathrm{fnc}$$

If $x \in \mathbf{ch}$ and $n \leqslant \lambda_x$, then the symbol $\varphi(x)`n$ denotes the n-th term of the phonic structure of the chain x. This symbol will be abbreviated according to the following definition:

8.24 $$\varphi_n(x) \underset{\text{df}}{=} \varphi(x)`n$$

8.25 $$x \in \mathbf{ch} \wedge n \leqslant \lambda_x \longrightarrow \varphi_n(x) \in \Pi_0$$

8.26 $$x \in \mathbf{ch} \wedge n \leqslant \lambda_x \longrightarrow \varphi_n(x) = \pi`\vartheta_n(x)$$

8.27 $$u \in \mathbf{UI} \longrightarrow \varphi_1(u) = \mathbf{0}$$ (by 5.39)

8.28 $$u \in \mathbf{UI} \longrightarrow \varphi_{\lambda_u}(u) = \mathbf{0}$$ (by 5.4)

8.29 $$x \in \mathbf{ch} \wedge n,m \leqslant \lambda_x \longrightarrow (\varphi_n(x) = \varphi_m(x) \equiv \vartheta_n(x)\, \mathbf{E}\, \vartheta_m(x))$$

8.30 $$x,y \in \mathbf{ch} \longrightarrow (\varphi(x) = \varphi(y) \equiv x\, \mathbf{E}\, y)$$

As has been mentioned above, the sequence $\varphi(x)$ strictly depends on the chain x. This dependence has a functional character and, strictly speaking, we should have defined here the function φ itself as the function which assigns respective phonic structures $\varphi(x)$, $\varphi(y)$, . . . to various phonetic chains x, y, . . . In this case φ is a certain relation between sequences of phones and phonetic chains, therefore we may consider the image $\varphi\langle X\rangle$ where X is e.g. a set of chains. The notation $\varphi\langle X\rangle$ will be used below in the definition of the notion of phonic system.

What is a phonic system? Similarly to other notions introduced in this chapter the notion of phonic system, so far, has not been used in phonology. Various phonologists speak only and as a rule rather vaguely about the so-called phonological systems. Perhaps the clearest writer on this subject is Ch. F. Hockett. He defines the phonological system as 'a stock of phonemes (or phonologic units) and the arrangements in which they occur relative to each other'.[1] The notion of the phonological system will be discussed at the end of this work, however, we adduce this quotation from Hockett here in order to elucidate our intuitive notion of phonic system. For we want the notion of phonic system to be a kind of 'subphonemic' analogue of the notion of phonological system. Slightly modifying Hockett's words we may say that a phonic system in our sense is 'a stock of phones and the arrangements in which they occur relative to each other'. This statement certainly does not provide a direct basis for answering the question what a phonic system is in the formal language of our axiomatic system. Therefore, we shall try to analyse the notion of phonic system more closely. First of all let us point out that like the notion of phonological system, the notion of phonic system requires a relativization to a definite idiolect. Therefore we shall not speak merely about a phonic system, but about a phonic system of the idiolect ι. When may we say that we know the phonic system of an idiolect ι? In accordance with the above explanation we may say so when we know

(*a*) the set of all proper phones of the idiolect ι i.e. the set $\Pi^{(\iota)}$, and
(*b*) the set of all sequences of proper phones realized in the idiolect ι.

The latter point may be rendered precise in various ways. The most appropriate seems to be the assumption that this point concerns the set of sequences of phones which are phonic structures of certain phrases of the idiolect ι, that is the set $\varphi\langle\mathbf{Phr}\langle\iota\rangle\rangle$.

After these explanations, it will be clear that the *phonic system of*

[1] Ch. F. Hockett [9], p. 14. A similar definition may be also found in a later book by the same author [8], p. 137.

the idiolect ι is simply the ordered pair the first element of which is the set $\Pi^{(\iota)}$, and the second element—the set $\varphi\langle\mathbf{Phr}\langle\iota\rangle\rangle$. The phonic system of the idiolect ι will be denoted by $\mathfrak{S}_\pi^{(\iota)}$. Here is the formal definition:

8.31 $$\mathfrak{S}_\pi^{(\iota)} \underset{\text{df}}{=} \langle\Pi^{(\iota)}, \varphi\langle\mathbf{Phr}\langle\iota\rangle\rangle\rangle$$

In a quite analogous way the notion of the phonological system of the idiolect ι will be defined later. It is possible to treat mutatis mutandis the above intuitive explanations as preparatory also for the definition of phonological system.

It would be worthwhile to indicate that the phonic systems of two different idiolects need, by no means, be different. Therefore it may occur that $\iota_1 \neq \iota_2$ but $\mathfrak{S}_\pi^{(\iota_1)} = \mathfrak{S}_\pi^{(\iota_2)}$. This will happen, as a rule, when the idiolects ι_1 and ι_2 represent the same language or dialect, but the possibility is not excluded that this may happen in other circumstances, too.

Chapter 9

UNIT-LENGTH SEGMENTS

The notion of unit-length segment is one of the fundamental notions of the structuralistic theory of phoneme. As a rule, the unit-length segments are obtained by linking together into one whole several elementary segments following one another. Which segments are to be linked together is settled by certain general principles and depends upon the properties of the language considered. It is clear that in our system the role of language is assumed by the idiolect. Therefore the notion of the unit-length segment is of a relative character. It makes no sense to speak about unit-length segments simply, but only about the unit-length segments of a given idiolect. In this respect there exists an essential difference between the notion of the unit-length segment and that of elementary segment: the first is relative while the second is absolute.

Before we formulate a precise definition of the class of all unit-length segments of an idiolect ι, we shall quote some explanations on this subject by the linguists themselves. Let us start with the most authoritative linguist in this field, that is with Z. S. Harris. Here are his words:

'This procedure sees to it that the length of the segmental elements should be that of phonemes. It provides that the segments should be neither longer nor shorter than is necessary to differentiate phonemically distinct utterances, so that minimally different utterances will differ in only one of their segments. [. . .]

'We join into one segment any succession (even if discontinuous) of segments which always occur together in a particular environment. [. . .]

'More generally, if in a given portion of many utterances (a given environment) segment *A* never occurs without segment *B*, we consider $A + B$ to constitute together one segment. For this procedure it is not required that *B* should also never occur without *A*: *B* may occur independently of *A*, as [h] does in *hill*. It is also not required that *A* be always attended by *B* in any environment: after [s], [t] occurs without [h], but our joining of [t] and [h] was limited to the position between silence and vowel. [. . .]

'All our segments now have this in common: there are as many segments in each utterance throughout the language as will enable us to distinguish each utterance from each other utterance which is not a repetition of it, and no more. [. . .]

'It will be seen that the conditions of 5.3 [i.e. of the preceding fragment] are precisely true of phonemes, so that we may say that each of these unit-length segments now has the length of one phoneme.'[1]

Similar statements may be found in Jassem who instead of the term 'unit-length segment' uses the term 'sound' (Polish 'głoska'). Among others, he writes: 'If any *two segments always occur together* in a particular position, then these two segments constitute *one sound*.'[2]

In a somewhat different manner H. Pilch describes the procedure of obtaining unit-length segments.[3] According to him the phonologist should compare in a systematic way different utterances and distinguish in them the maximal phonetically equivalent parts and the non-equivalent remainders. Parts obtained in this way should again be compared one with another and with whole utterances and should be further divided according to the same principle. This procedure is to be repeated to the moment (and Pilch does not doubt that such a moment must come) when it becomes unproductive, that means, to the moment when any two resulting parts are either phonetically equivalent or do not have any equivalent fragments whatever. These indivisible parts of utterances Pilch calls phonemic segments. It is fairly clear that these segments are what Harris meant by unit-length segments. At any rate this seems to be Pilch's intention.

Jassem and Pilch are themselves fully aware of the relative character of the notion of unit-length segment (in their terminology, sound and phonemic segment, respectively). Here are their own statements on this subject: 'Compounds of the same or almost the same segments may constitute in one language compounds of sounds and in another individual sounds.'[4] 'Da die phonematische Segmentierung sich auf den Bau einer bestimmten Sprache und nicht auf die physikalische Struktur von "Lauten" gründet, kann es durchaus vorkommen, daß wir akustisch, artikulatorisch und auditiv gleiche oder ähnliche Geräusche in verschiedenen Sprachen verschieden segmentieren.'[5]

We shall now try to reconstruct the notion of unit-length segment

[1] Z. S. Harris [7], pp. 42, 43 and 44.
[2] W. Jassem [10], p. 20.
[3] Cf. H. Pilch [20], pp. 88–91.
[4] W. Jassem [11], pp. 26–27.
[5] H. Pilch [20], p. 91.

in our axiomatic system. Generally speaking our definition will follow the line of Harris' procedures, that is, the procedures of linking certain elementary segments. For this purpose Pilch's procedures, that is, the procedures of dividing utterances, would be quite satisfactory. We shall, however, adopt a different approach.

Although perhaps this is not apparent from the explanations of Harris, Jassem or Pilch, the notion of unit-length segment is, in fact, very complicated and it is not easy to define it precisely. In order to make our task easier, we are assuming that there never arises a need to link more than three elementary segments into one unit-length segment and therefore in our definition of the class of unit-length segments we do not need to consider the general case of summing *n* segments. Although our assumption is not in accordance with the general formulation of Harris' principle of linking elementary segments, we are inclined to accept it for various reasons. First of all, an exact an adequate phrasing of the general principle for *n* segments is a very difficult task. (Of course Harris' phrasing cannot be taken too seriously.) Secondly, none of concrete examples given by Harris or Jassem contradicts our assumption. Thirdly, it is highly improbable that such an example will be found. Fourthly, even if such an example turned up the number of elementary segments appearing in it would be small (e.g. 4) and it would not be difficult to adjust our theory to this concrete number without generalizing to *n* segments.

We shall begin with some auxiliary definitions.

We say that the elementary segments x, y, z (in this order) *are inseparable in* the idiolect ι, in symbols: $\mathbf{Isp}^{(\iota)}(x,y,z)$, if and only if x, y, z are proper elementary segments of the idiolect ι, x is the predecessor of y, y is the predecessor of z, and (here we are speaking inexactly, even incorrectly) in the environment in which the whole chain $x \cup y \cup z$ occurs, there occurs neither the segment y alone nor the chain $x \cup y$ alone nor the chain $y \cup z$ alone.

The above vague and incorrect formulation will facilitate the understanding of the following exact definition:

9.1 $$\mathbf{Isp}^{(\iota)} \underset{\mathrm{df}}{=} \{x,y,z\colon x,y,z \in \bigcup\mathbf{UK} \cap \mathbf{P}\langle\iota\rangle \wedge x = \mathbf{p}\text{‘}y \wedge y = \mathbf{p}\text{‘}z \wedge$$
$$\wedge \bigwedge_{v}(v \in \mathbf{Ch}\langle\iota\rangle \wedge \lambda_v = 3 \rightarrow \sim(\varphi_1(v) = \pi\text{‘}\mathbf{p}\text{‘}x \wedge \varphi_2(v) = \pi\text{‘}y \wedge$$
$$\wedge \varphi_3(v) = \pi\text{‘}\mathbf{s}\text{‘}z)) \wedge \bigwedge_{v}(v \in \mathbf{Ch}\langle\iota\rangle \wedge \lambda_v = 4 \rightarrow$$
$$\rightarrow \sim(\varphi_1(v) = \pi\text{‘}\mathbf{p}\text{‘}x \wedge \varphi_2(v) = \pi\text{‘}x \wedge \varphi_3(v) = \pi\text{‘}y \wedge$$
$$\wedge \varphi_4(v) = \pi\text{‘}\mathbf{s}\text{‘}z) \wedge \sim(\varphi_1(v) = \pi\text{‘}\mathbf{p}\text{‘}x \wedge \varphi_2(v) = \pi\text{‘}y \wedge$$
$$\wedge \varphi_3(v) = \pi\text{‘}z \wedge \varphi_4(v) = \pi\text{‘}\mathbf{s}\text{‘}z))\}$$

If $X = [x,y,z]$, where x, y, z are inseparable elementary segments in ι, then we say that X is a *three-segmental complex in* ι. The class of all three-segmental complexes in ι will be symbolized by $\mathbf{sgcm}_3^{(\iota)}$.

9.2 $$\mathbf{sgcm}_3^{(\iota)} \underset{\mathrm{df}}{=} \{X\colon \bigvee_{x,y,z} (X = [x,y,z] \wedge \mathbf{Isp}^{(\iota)}(x,y,z))\}$$

We shall say that a segment x *is left-inseparable from* another segment y in ι, in symbols: $x\ \mathbf{Isp}_1^{(\iota)}\ y$, if and only if x and y are proper elementary segments in ι, x is the predecessor of y, neither x nor y is an element of a three-segmental complex in ι and (our wording here is incorrect) y never occurs alone in any environment in which the whole chain $x \cup y$ occurs. The exact definition of this relation is as follows:

9.3 $$\mathbf{Isp}_1^{(\iota)} \underset{\mathrm{df}}{=} \{x,y\colon x,y \in \cup\cup\mathbf{K} \cap \mathbf{P}\langle\iota\rangle \wedge x = \mathbf{p}`y \wedge$$
$$\wedge \sim \bigvee_X (X \in \mathbf{sgcm}_3^{(\iota)} \wedge (x \in X \vee y \in X)) \wedge \bigwedge_v (v \in \mathbf{Ch}\langle\iota\rangle \wedge$$
$$\wedge \lambda_v = 3 \rightarrow \sim (\varphi_1(v) = \pi`\mathbf{p}`x \wedge \varphi_2(v) = \pi`y \wedge$$
$$\wedge \varphi_3(v) = \pi`\mathbf{s}`y))\}$$

Quite analogous to this one is the definition of the *relation of being right-inseparable*, symbolized by $\mathbf{Isp}_r^{(\iota)}$.

9.4 $$\mathbf{Isp}_r^{(\iota)} \underset{\mathrm{df}}{=} \{x,y\colon x,y \in \cup\cup\mathbf{K} \cap \mathbf{P}\langle\iota\rangle \wedge x = \mathbf{s}`y \wedge$$
$$\wedge \sim \bigvee_X (X \in \mathbf{sgcm}_3^{(\iota)} \wedge (x \in X \vee y \in X)) \wedge \bigwedge_v (v \in \mathbf{Ch}\langle\iota\rangle \wedge$$
$$\wedge \lambda_v = 3 \rightarrow \sim(\varphi_1(v) = \pi`\mathbf{p}`y \wedge \varphi_2(v) = \pi`y \wedge$$
$$\wedge \varphi_3(v) = \pi`\mathbf{s}`x))\}$$

If $X = [x,y]$, where x is left- or right-inseparable from y in ι, then we say that X is a *two-segmental complex in* ι. The class of all two-segmental complexes in ι will be denoted by $\mathbf{sgcm}_2^{(\iota)}$.

9.5 $$\mathbf{sgcm}_2^{(\iota)} \underset{\mathrm{df}}{=} \{X\colon \bigvee_{x,y}(X = [x,y] \wedge (x\ \mathbf{Isp}_1^{(\iota)}\ y \vee x\ \mathbf{Isp}_r^{(\iota)}\ y))\}$$

Now we shall state some theorems which follow from the given definitions.

9.6 $$\mathbf{Isp}^{(\iota)}(x,y,z) \wedge v = x \cup y \cup z \rightarrow v \in \mathbf{Ch}\langle\iota\rangle \wedge \lambda_v = 3$$

Proof. If $\mathbf{Isp}^{(\iota)}(x,y,z)$, then $x,y,z \in \cup\cup\mathbf{K} \cap \mathbf{P}\langle\iota\rangle$, $x = \mathbf{p}`y$ and $y = \mathbf{p}`z$. Thus, for some $u \in \iota$, $z \in \cup\cup\mathbf{K} \cap \mathbf{P}^{\vee}u$. From this by 5.11 follows $y \in \mathbf{Esg}^{\vee}u$ and $x \in \mathbf{Esg}^{\vee}u$. Moreover, by 5.1, $x \cup y \in \mathbf{ch}$ and $y \cup z \in \mathbf{ch}$. From this by 4.35 it follows that $x \cup y \cup z \in \mathbf{ch}$. Since $x,y,z \in \mathbf{Esg}^{\vee}u$, therefore $x \cup y \cup z \in \mathbf{P}^{\vee}u$ and by 4.29 $x \cup y \cup z \in \mathbf{Ch}^{\vee}u$.

Thus $x \mathbin{\dot\cup} y \mathbin{\dot\cup} z \in \mathbf{Ch}\langle\iota\rangle$. Clearly, all the segments x, y, z are distinct and on account of A11 and 3.15 there is no other segment in the chain $x \mathbin{\dot\cup} y \mathbin{\dot\cup} z$. Thus the length of $x \mathbin{\dot\cup} y \mathbin{\dot\cup} z$ is 3.

9.7 $\mathbf{Isp}^{(\iota)}(x,y,z) \rightarrow \vartheta_1(x \mathbin{\dot\cup} y \mathbin{\dot\cup} z) = x \wedge \vartheta_2(x \mathbin{\dot\cup} y \mathbin{\dot\cup} z) = y \wedge$
$\wedge \vartheta_3(x \mathbin{\dot\cup} y \mathbin{\dot\cup} z) = z \wedge \mathbf{p}\text{‘}(x \mathbin{\dot\cup} y \mathbin{\dot\cup} z) = \mathbf{p}\text{‘}x \wedge \mathbf{s}\text{‘}(x \mathbin{\dot\cup} y \mathbin{\dot\cup} z) = \mathbf{s}\text{‘}z$

Proof. If $\mathbf{Isp}^{(\iota)}(x,y,z)$, then $x \mathbin{\dot\cup} y \mathbin{\dot\cup} z$ is a chain of length 3, $\mathbf{Esg}^{\vee}(x \mathbin{\dot\cup} y \mathbin{\dot\cup} z) = [x,y,z]$ and, moreover, $x\, \mathbf{T}_{\mathrm{i}}\, y$ and $y\, \mathbf{T}_{\mathrm{i}}\, z$. By 5.29 there exist numbers $n, m, k \in [1, 2, 3]$ such that $x = \vartheta_n(x \mathbin{\dot\cup} y \mathbin{\dot\cup} z)$, $y = \vartheta_m(x \mathbin{\dot\cup} y \mathbin{\dot\cup} z)$ and $z = \vartheta_k(x \mathbin{\dot\cup} y \mathbin{\dot\cup} z)$. Therefore $\vartheta_n(x \mathbin{\dot\cup} y \mathbin{\dot\cup} z)\, \mathbf{T}_{\mathrm{i}}\, \vartheta_m(x \mathbin{\dot\cup} y \mathbin{\dot\cup} z)$ and $\vartheta_m(x \mathbin{\dot\cup} y \mathbin{\dot\cup} z)\, \mathbf{T}_{\mathrm{i}}\, \vartheta_k(x \mathbin{\dot\cup} y \mathbin{\dot\cup} z)$. From this by 5.34 we infer that $n + 1 = m$ and $m + 1 = k$, whence $n = 1, m = 2$ and $k = 3$.

Since $x \notin \mathbf{0}$, therefore by 5.43 there does exist $\mathbf{p}\text{‘}(x \mathbin{\dot\cup} y \mathbin{\dot\cup} z)$, and by 5.41 $\mathbf{p}\text{‘}(x \mathbin{\dot\cup} y \mathbin{\dot\cup} z)$ is the predecessor of x. From this by 5.4 follows $\mathbf{p}\text{‘}(x \mathbin{\dot\cup} y \mathbin{\dot\cup} z) = \mathbf{p}\text{‘}x$. In a similar way, using 5.44, 5.42 and 5.15, it is proved also that $\mathbf{s}\text{‘}(x \mathbin{\dot\cup} y \mathbin{\dot\cup} z) = \mathbf{s}\text{‘}z$.

The easy proofs of the next six theorems are omitted.

9.8 $(x\, \mathbf{Isp}^{(\iota)}_{\mathrm{l}}\, y \vee x\, \mathbf{Isp}^{(\iota)}_{\mathrm{r}}\, y) \wedge v = x \mathbin{\dot\cup} y \rightarrow v \in \mathbf{Ch}\langle\iota\rangle \wedge \lambda_v = 2$

9.9 $x\, \mathbf{Isp}^{(\iota)}_{\mathrm{l}}\, y \rightarrow \vartheta_1(x \mathbin{\dot\cup} y) = x \wedge \vartheta_2(x \mathbin{\dot\cup} y) = y \wedge$
$\wedge \mathbf{p}\text{‘}(x \mathbin{\dot\cup} y) = \mathbf{p}\text{‘}x \wedge \mathbf{s}\text{‘}(x \mathbin{\dot\cup} y) = \mathbf{s}\text{‘}y$

9.10 $x\, \mathbf{Isp}^{(\iota)}_{\mathrm{r}}\, y \rightarrow \vartheta_1(x \mathbin{\dot\cup} y) = y \wedge \vartheta_2(x \mathbin{\dot\cup} y) = x \wedge$
$\wedge \mathbf{p}\text{‘}(x \mathbin{\dot\cup} y) = \mathbf{p}\text{‘}y \wedge \mathbf{s}\text{‘}(x \mathbin{\dot\cup} y) = \mathbf{s}\text{‘}x$

9.11 $X \in \mathbf{sgcm}^{(\iota)}_3 \rightarrow X \subset \mathsf{UUK} \cap \mathbf{P}\langle\iota\rangle$

9.12 $X \in \mathbf{sgcm}^{(\iota)}_2 \rightarrow X \subset \mathsf{UUK} \cap \mathbf{P}\langle\iota\rangle$

9.13 $X \in \mathbf{sgcm}^{(\iota)}_3 \wedge Y \in \mathbf{sgcm}^{(\iota)}_2 \rightarrow X \cap Y = \Lambda$

If $[x,y,z]$ is a three-segmental complex in ι, then the sum $x \mathbin{\dot\cup} y \mathbin{\dot\cup} z$ is called a *ternary compound segment in* ι.

If $[x,y]$ is a two-segmental complex in ι, then the sum $x \mathbin{\dot\cup} y$ is called a *binary compound segment in* ι.

The binary and also the ternary compound segments in ι will be called *compound segments in* ι.

The respective sets $\mathbf{csg}^{(\iota)}_3$, $\mathbf{csg}^{(\iota)}_2$ and $\mathbf{csg}^{(\iota)}$ are exactly defined as follows:

9.14 $$\mathbf{csg}^{(\iota)}_3 \underset{\mathrm{df}}{=} \mathbf{S}\langle\mathbf{sgcm}^{(\iota)}_3\rangle$$

9.15 $$\mathbf{csg}^{(\iota)}_2 \underset{\mathrm{df}}{=} \mathbf{S}\langle\mathbf{sgcm}^{(\iota)}_2\rangle$$

9.16 $$\mathbf{csg}^{(\iota)} \underset{\mathrm{df}}{=} \mathbf{csg}^{(\iota)}_3 \cup \mathbf{csg}^{(\iota)}_2$$

The set $\mathbf{usg}^{(\iota)}$ of all *proper unit-length segments in* ι and the set

$\mathbf{usg}_0^{(\iota)}$ of all *unit-length segments in* ι may now be defined as follows:

9.17 $\mathbf{usg}^{(\iota)} \underset{\text{df}}{=} \mathbf{csg}^{(\iota)} \cup ((\mathsf{U}\mathsf{U}\mathbf{K} \cap \mathbf{P}\langle\iota\rangle) - \mathsf{U}(\mathbf{sgcm}_3^{(\iota)} \cup \mathbf{sgcm}_2^{(\iota)}))$

9.18 $\mathbf{usg}_0^{(\iota)} \underset{\text{df}}{=} \mathbf{usg}^{(\iota)} \cup (\mathbf{0} \cap \mathbf{P}\langle\iota\rangle)$

As it is seen from 9.17, we recognize as proper unit-length segments in ι all compound segments in ι and all those elementary proper segments in ι which belong to no segmental complex and, consequently, are not parts of some compound segments.

We turn now to some elementary theorems.

9.19 $x \in \mathbf{usg}^{(\iota)} \rightarrow \mathbf{Esg}^{\vee}x \subset \mathsf{U}\mathsf{U}\mathbf{K}$ (by 9.11, 9.12, A11)

9.20 $x \in \mathbf{csg}^{(\iota)} \rightarrow \mathbf{Esg}^{\vee}x \in \mathbf{sgcm}_3^{(\iota)} \cup \mathbf{sgcm}_2^{(\iota)}$

Proof. If $x \in \mathbf{csg}^{(\iota)}$, then $x = \mathbf{S}`X$, where $X \in \mathbf{sgcm}_3^{(\iota)} \cup \mathbf{sgcm}_2^{(\iota)}$. Clearly, $X \subset \mathbf{Esg}^{\vee}x$. To complete the proof it is sufficient to show that $\mathbf{Esg}^{\vee}x \subset X$. Now, if $y \in \mathbf{Esg}^{\vee}x$, then $y\ \mathbf{P}\ x$ and, by 9.19, $y \in \mathsf{U}\mathsf{U}\mathbf{K}$. Therefore, for some $z \in X$, $\mathbf{P}^{\vee}y \cap \mathbf{P}^{\vee}z \neq \Lambda$. Moreover, by 9.11 and 9.12 $z \in \mathsf{U}\mathsf{U}\mathbf{K}$, so that by 3.15 $y = z$ and consequently $y \in X$. Thus the inclusion $\mathbf{Esg}^{\vee}x \subset X$ is established.

9.21 $\mathbf{usg}_0^{(\iota)} \subset \mathbf{Ch}\langle\iota\rangle$ (by 9.6, 9.8, 4.16)

9.22 $\mathbf{Esg}\langle\iota\rangle \subset \mathbf{P}\langle\mathbf{usg}_0^{(\iota)}\rangle$

Proof. If $x \in \mathbf{Esg}\langle\iota\rangle$, then $x \in \mathbf{P}\langle\iota\rangle$ and $x \in \mathbf{esg}$. If, now, $x \in \mathbf{0}$, then by 9.18 $x \in \mathbf{usg}_0^{(\iota)}$, so that $x \in \mathbf{P}\langle\mathbf{usg}_0^{(\iota)}\rangle$. Suppose $x \in \mathsf{U}\mathsf{U}\mathbf{K}$. Then either $x \in \mathbf{P}\langle\mathbf{csg}^{(\iota)}\rangle$ (in the case when $x \in \mathsf{U}(\mathbf{sgcm}_3^{(\iota)} \cup \mathbf{sgcm}_2^{(\iota)})$) or $x \in \mathbf{usg}^{(\iota)}$ (in the case when $x \notin \mathsf{U}(\mathbf{sgcm}_3^{(\iota)} \cup \mathbf{sgcm}_2^{(\iota)})$). Thus we always have $x \in \mathbf{P}\langle\mathbf{usg}_0^{(\iota)}\rangle$.

9.23 $u \in \iota \wedge x \in \mathbf{usg}^{(\iota)} \wedge \mathbf{P}^{\vee}u \cap \mathbf{P}^{\vee}x \neq \Lambda \rightarrow x\ \mathbf{P}\ u$

Proof. If $x \in \mathbf{usg}^{(\iota)}$, then by 9.21 $x \in \mathbf{ch}$ and consequently $x = \mathbf{S}`\mathbf{Esg}^{\vee}x$. If additionally $\mathbf{P}^{\vee}u \cap \mathbf{P}^{\vee}x \neq \Lambda$, where $u \in \iota$, then there exist a point v, a segment $y \in \mathbf{Esg}^{\vee}x$ and a segment $z \in \mathbf{Esg}^{\vee}u$ such that $v \in \mathbf{P}^{\vee}y \cap \mathbf{P}^{\vee}z$. By 9.19 $y \in \mathsf{U}\mathsf{U}\mathbf{K}$. Hence by A11 $z \in \mathsf{U}\mathsf{U}\mathbf{K}$ and by 3.15 $y = z$. Thus $y\ \mathbf{P}\ u$.

According to definition 9.17 there are possible the three following cases:

(*a*) $x \in \mathsf{U}\mathsf{U}\mathbf{K}$. Then $[x] = \mathbf{Esg}^{\vee}x = [y] = [z]$, whence $x\ \mathbf{P}\ u$.

(*b*) $x \in \mathbf{csg}_2^{(\iota)}$. Then $\mathbf{Esg}^{\vee}x \in \mathbf{sgcm}_2^{(\iota)}$ and there is a w such that $w \neq y$ and $[y,w] = \mathbf{Esg}^{\vee}x$. From this it follows that either $w = \mathbf{p}`y$ or $w = \mathbf{s}`y$. In both the cases we have by 5.11 and 5.25 $w\ \mathbf{P}\ u$, whence finally $x\ \mathbf{P}\ u$.

(*c*) $x \in \mathbf{csg}_3^{(\iota)}$. In this case our reasoning is similar to that in (*b*), but with the proviso that we have to distinguish three cases corresponding to the following three possibilities: $y = \vartheta_1(x)$, $y = \vartheta_2(x)$, $y = \vartheta_3(x)$.

9.24 $$u \in \iota \wedge x\,\mathbf{P}\,u \rightarrow \mathbf{P}^{\vee}x \cap \mathbf{P}\langle \mathbf{P}^{\vee}u \cap \mathbf{usg}_0^{(\iota)} \rangle \neq \Lambda$$

Proof. From the hypothesis by A4 follows $\mathbf{P}^{\vee}x \cap \mathbf{P}\langle \mathbf{Esg}^{\vee}u \rangle \neq \Lambda$. From this by 9.22 follows $\mathbf{P}^{\vee}x \cap \mathbf{P}\langle \mathbf{usg}_0^{(\iota)} \rangle \neq \Lambda$. Thus, there is a $y \in \mathbf{usg}_0^{(\iota)}$ such that $\mathbf{P}^{\vee}x \cap \mathbf{P}^{\vee}y \neq \Lambda$. Clearly, $\mathbf{P}^{\vee}u \cap \mathbf{P}^{\vee}y \neq \Lambda$. If, now, $y \in \mathbf{usg}^{(\iota)}$, then by 9.23 $y\,\mathbf{P}\,u$, whence

(1) $$\mathbf{P}^{\vee}x \cap \mathbf{P}\langle \mathbf{P}^{\vee}u \cap \mathbf{usg}_0^{(\iota)} \rangle \neq \Lambda.$$

Suppose $y \in \mathbf{0}$. By I.3.7 there is a z such that $z \in \mathbf{pn} \cap \mathbf{P}^{\vee}x \cap \mathbf{P}^{\vee}u \cap \mathbf{P}^{\vee}y$. From this by 3.16 we infer that there is a v such that $z\,\mathbf{P}\,v$ and $v \in \mathbf{Esg}^{\vee}u$. Since $z\,\mathbf{P}\,y$, where $y \in \mathbf{0}$, therefore by A11 $v \in \mathbf{0}$. Thus $v \in \mathbf{P}^{\vee}u \cap \mathbf{usg}_0^{(\iota)}$ and obviously $\mathbf{P}^{\vee}x \cap \mathbf{P}^{\vee}v \neq \Lambda$. From this again follows (1).

9.25 $$u \in \iota \rightarrow \mathbf{P}^{\vee}u \cap \mathbf{P}\langle \mathbf{usg}^{(\iota)} \rangle \neq \Lambda$$

Proof. If $u \in \iota$, then by A5 $\mathbf{P}^{\vee}u \cap \mathbf{P}\langle \mathsf{UUK} \rangle \neq \Lambda$. From this by 9.22 and A11 follows the thesis of our theorem.

9.26 $u_1, u_2 \in \mathsf{UI} \wedge \mathbf{P}^{\vee}u_1 \cap \mathbf{P}^{\vee}u_2 \cap \mathbf{P}\langle \mathbf{usg}^{(\iota)} \rangle \neq \Lambda \rightarrow u_1 \mathbin{\dot\cup} u_2 \in \mathbf{P}\langle \mathsf{UI} \rangle$ (by A9, 9.19)

9.27 $\mathbf{usg}_0^{(\iota)} \subset \mathbf{mo}' \cap \mathbf{P}\langle \mathsf{UI} \rangle$ (by 9.21, 4.18, 4.8)

9.28 $\mathbf{P}\langle \mathbf{usg}^{(\iota)} \rangle \cap \mathbf{P}\langle \mathbf{0} \rangle = \Lambda$ (by 9.21, 9.19, A11)

It is easily seen that theorems 9.24–9.28 correspond in a sense to axioms A4, A5, A9, A10 and A11. The difference between them is that instead of UUK and $\mathsf{UUK} \cup \mathbf{0}$ we have in these theorems $\mathbf{usg}^{(\iota)}$ and $\mathbf{usg}_0^{(\iota)}$, respectively. Moreover, on account of the relative nature of unit-length segments we have in 9.24 and 9.25 $u \in \iota$ instead of $u \in \mathsf{UI}$.

Note that we are not able to deduce similar counterparts of A7 and A8. Nevertheless, these counterparts will be necessary for our purposes. In fact, we must introduce a new notion of segmenting function corresponding to the notion of unit-length segment. In order to establish the above mentioned counterparts we have, however, to strengthen the foundations of our system. We make this by adjoining to it the following new axiom:

A15. $X, Y \in \mathbf{sgcm}_3^{(\iota)} \vee X, Y \in \mathbf{sgcm}_2^{(\iota)} \rightarrow X = Y \vee X \cap Y = \Lambda$

This axiom states that any two three-segmental complexes and also any two two-segmental complexes are either identical or disjoint. On account of 9.13, it follows from A15 that any two complexes are either identical or disjoint. From this we have as a further corollary, that any two different unit-length proper segments are external to each other, that is, they do not overlap.

Let us note that Harris should have adopted in chapter 5 of his book an assumption similar to our A15. For, without such an assumption Harris is unable to prove (though he intends it to be provable) that his unit-length segments do not overlap.

It should be noted that axiom A15 is by no means obvious, and, what is more, it may turn out to be empirically false. This is not very likely. Were this, however, the case, our theory of unit-length segments would have to be modified.

We now give some theorems based on A15.

9.29 $$X, Y \in \mathbf{sgcm}_3^{(\iota)} \cup \mathbf{sgcm}_2^{(\iota)} \rightarrow X = Y \vee X \cap Y = \Lambda$$

Proof. This theorem follows from A15 and 9.13. It furnishes a strengthening of the axiom A15 by weakening its predecessor.

9.30 $$x,y \in \mathbf{usg}^{(\iota)} \rightarrow x = y \vee \mathbf{P}^{\vee}x \cap \mathbf{P}^{\vee}y = \Lambda$$

Proof. Assume that $x,y \in \mathbf{usg}^{(\iota)}$ and $\mathbf{P}^{\vee}x \cap \mathbf{P}^{\vee}y \neq \Lambda$. By 9.21 $x,y \in \mathbf{ch}$, and by 9.19 $\mathbf{P}^{\vee}x \cap \mathbf{P}^{\vee}y \cap \mathbf{P}\langle \bigcup\bigcup\mathbf{K}\rangle \neq \Lambda$. From this, using 4.33, we infer that

(2) $$\mathbf{Esg}^{\vee}x \cap \mathbf{Esg}^{\vee}y \cap \bigcup\bigcup\mathbf{K} \neq \Lambda.$$

According to definition 9.17 we must distinguish several cases.

(*a*) $x,y \in \bigcup\bigcup\mathbf{K}$. In this case we infer from (2) by 4.6 that $x = y$.

(*b*) $x \in \bigcup\bigcup\mathbf{K} \wedge y \in \mathbf{csg}^{(\iota)}$. Then by (2) $x \in \mathbf{Esg}^{\vee}y$, whence by 9.20 $x \in \bigcup(\mathbf{sgcm}_3^{(\iota)} \cup \mathbf{sgcm}_2^{(\iota)})$. From this by 9.17 it follows that $x \notin \mathbf{usg}^{(\iota)}$, contrary to the assumption. In a similar way we show that the case when $x \in \mathbf{csg}^{(\iota)} \wedge y \in \bigcup\bigcup\mathbf{K}$ is also impossible.

(*c*) $x,y \in \mathbf{csg}^{(\iota)}$. By virtue of 9.20 we have:

$$\mathbf{Esg}^{\vee}x \in \mathbf{sgcm}_3^{(\iota)} \cup \mathbf{sgcm}_2^{(\iota)},$$
$$\mathbf{Esg}^{\vee}y \in \mathbf{sgcm}_3^{(\iota)} \cup \mathbf{sgcm}_2^{(\iota)}.$$

From this and (2) by 9.29 follows the equality: $\mathbf{Esg}^{\vee}x = \mathbf{Esg}^{\vee}\mathbf{y}$. Thus, by 9.21 and 4.10 $x = y$.

9.31 $$u \in \iota \rightarrow \mathbf{T}_e \in \mathrm{con}(\mathbf{P}^{\vee}u \cap \mathbf{usg}_0^{(\iota)})$$

Proof. Assume that $u \in \iota$, $x,y \in \mathbf{P}^{\vee}u \cap \mathbf{usg}_0^{(\iota)}$ and $x \neq y$.

(*a*) If $x,y \in \mathbf{0}$, then by A7 either $x\, \mathbf{T}_c\, y$ or $y\, \mathbf{T}_c\, x$.

(*b*) If $x \in \mathbf{0}$ and $y \in \mathbf{usg}^{(\iota)}$, then by 9.19 $x \notin \mathbf{P}^{\vee}y$. Since $y \in \mathbf{ch}$, we infer from this that either x completely precedes all elementary segments in y (that is, $\mathbf{Esg}^{\vee}y \subset \mathbf{T}_c{}^{\wedge}x$) or x is completely preceded by all elementary segments in y (that is, $\mathbf{Esg}^{\vee}y \subset \mathbf{T}_c{}^{\vee}x$). Thus we have either $x\, \mathbf{T}_c\, y$ or $y\, \mathbf{T}_c\, x$.

(*c*) Suppose $x,y \in \mathbf{usg}^{(\iota)}$. Since $x \neq y$, therefore by 9.30

$$\mathbf{P}^{\vee}x \cap \mathbf{P}^{\vee}y = \Lambda.$$

Hence $\vartheta_1(x) \neq \vartheta_1(y)$. By virtue of A7 we have either $\vartheta_1(x)\, \mathbf{T}_c\, \vartheta_1(y)$ or $\vartheta_1(y)\, \mathbf{T}_c\, \vartheta_1(x)$. If $x \in \bigcup\bigcup\mathbf{K}$ or $y \in \bigcup\bigcup\mathbf{K}$, then obviously either

$x\ \mathbf{T_c}\ y$ or $y\ \mathbf{T_c}\ x$. Therefore we may assume that $x,y \in \mathbf{csg}^{(\iota)}$ and e.g. that $\vartheta_1(x)\ \mathbf{T_c}\ \vartheta_1(y)$. Let z be an arbitrary elementary segment in x distinct from $\vartheta_1(x)$. Then $\vartheta_1(x)\ \mathbf{T_c}\ z$ and, moreover, $\sim\vartheta_1(y)\ \mathbf{T_c}\ z$, since in the opposite case in view of 4.11 $\vartheta_1(y) \in \mathbf{P}^{\vee}x$ would hold, which is impossible. Hence $z\ \mathbf{T_c}\ \vartheta_1(y)$. Thus, we have proved that $\mathbf{Esg}^{\vee}x \subset \mathbf{T_c}^{\vee}\vartheta_1(y)$. It follows from this that $x\ \mathbf{T_c}\ \vartheta_1(y)$ and, consequently, $x\ \mathbf{T_c}\ y$. In a similar way we may prove that if $\vartheta_1(y)\ \mathbf{T_c}\ \vartheta_1(x)$, then $y\ \mathbf{T_c}\ x$.

9.32 $$u \in \iota \longrightarrow 3 \leqslant \overline{\overline{\mathbf{P}^{\vee}u \cap \mathbf{usg}_0^{(\iota)}}} < \aleph_0$$

Proof. The number of unit-length segments in u is equal to or less than the number of elementary segments in u. But in accordance with 3.21 the last number is finite. Further, it follows from 3.25 and 3.17 that there are at least three different unit-length segments in u.

9.33 $$u \in \iota \wedge X \neq \Lambda \wedge X \subset \mathbf{P}^{\vee}u \cap \mathbf{usg}_0^{(\iota)} \longrightarrow \bigvee_x (x \in X \wedge \bigwedge_y (y \in X \longrightarrow x\ \mathbf{T_e}\ y)) \wedge \bigvee_v (v \in X \wedge \bigwedge_z (z \in X \longrightarrow z\ \mathbf{T_e}\ v))$$

Proof. It follows from the general properties of $\mathbf{T_e}$ and from theorem 9.31 that $\mathbf{T_e}$ is an ordering in the set $\mathbf{P}^{\vee}u \cap \mathbf{usg}_0^{(\iota)}$. Moreover, it follows from 9.32 that this is a well-ordering of a finite type.

It is easily seen that theorems 9.31 and 9.33 are the counterparts of the axioms A7 and A8 which we were looking for. Hence we may formulate the following general corollary: all the theorems concerning elementary segments, formulated in chapter 3 and proved by using only the axioms A1–A11 will remain theorems of our system, if we reformulate them in such a way as to refer to unit-length segments; the method of such a reformulation is indicated in our remarks after theorem 9.28. We formulate below (without proofs) some theorems of this kind.

9.34 $\mathbf{usg}^{(\iota)} \neq \Lambda$

9.35 $u \in \iota \longrightarrow u = \mathbf{S}`(\mathbf{P}^{\vee}u \cap \mathbf{usg}_0^{(\iota)})$

9.36 $u \in \iota \wedge x,y \in \mathbf{P}^{\vee}u \cap \mathbf{usg}_0^{(\iota)} \longrightarrow x = y \vee \mathbf{P}^{\vee}x \cap \mathbf{P}^{\vee}y = \Lambda$

9.37 $u \in \iota \wedge x \in \mathbf{pn} \cap \mathbf{P}^{\vee}u \longrightarrow \dot{\bigvee_y}\,(x\ \mathbf{P}\ y \wedge y \in \mathbf{P}^{\vee}u \cap \mathbf{usg}_0^{(\iota)})$

9.38 $u \in \iota \longrightarrow \mathbf{P}^{\vee}u \cap \mathbf{usg}^{(\iota)} \neq \Lambda$

9.39 $3 \leqslant \overline{\overline{\mathbf{usg}_0^{(\iota)}}} < \aleph_0$

9.40 $0 < \overline{\overline{\mathbf{usg}^{(\iota)}}} < \aleph_0$

Chapter 10

COMPOUND FEATURES

As we have emphasized in chapter 1 we understand phonetic features as certain sets of elementary segments. Hence, it is quite obvious that these features do not pertain to compound segments. Consequently, if we wish to speak about features of unit-length segments, we must use another, more general, notion of a phonetic feature. To this end we introduce the notion of a compound feature. Obviously, the compound features are also understood as sets, namely, sets of unit-length segments. The notion of a compound feature is precisely defined below in 10.3. The first two definitions introduce only certain convenient abbreviations.

10.1 $\mathbf{csg}_3 \underset{\mathrm{df}}{=} \bigcup_{\iota} \mathbf{csg}_3^{(\iota)}$

10.2 $\mathbf{csg}_2 \underset{\mathrm{df}}{=} \bigcup_{\iota} \mathbf{csg}_2^{(\iota)}$

10.3 $\mathbf{cf}(\mathscr{X}) \underset{\mathrm{df}}{=} \{X\colon \bigvee_{Y,Z,V} (Y, Z, V \in \mathscr{X} \wedge (X = \{z\colon z \in \mathbf{csg}_2 \wedge$

$\wedge \vartheta_1(z) \in Y \wedge \vartheta_2(z) \in Z\} \vee X = \{z\colon z \in \mathbf{csg}_3 \wedge$

$\wedge \vartheta_1(z) \in Y \wedge \vartheta_2(z) \in Z \wedge \vartheta_3(z) \in V\}))\}$

The elements of the family $\mathbf{cf}(\mathscr{X})$ will be called *compound features of the kind* $\mathscr{X}$. According to definition 10.3 X is a compound feature of the kind $\mathscr{X}$, in symbols: $X \in \mathbf{cf}(\mathscr{X})$, if and only if either (*a*) there exist two phonetic features Y, Z such that Y and Z are features of the kind $\mathscr{X}$, X is the set of all binary compound segments the first elementary segment of which has the property Y and the second the property Z, or (*b*) there exist three phonetic features Y, Z, V such that Y, Z and V are features of the kind $\mathscr{X}$ and X is the set of all ternary compound segments the successive elementary segments of which have the properties Y, Z, V, respectively.

We shall illustrate now the notion of a compound feature of a given kind by a concrete example. Let, e.g. x be the first unit-length segment of a phrase due to the uttering of the English sentence *Damn you*! Then x is composed of two elementary segments the first of which is voiceless and the second is voiced.[1] One might say, that the unit-length segment x is voiceless-voiced. If now $\mathscr{X}$ is that kind of phonetic features which contains the features of being voiceless and of being voiced, and X is the set of all binary compound segments in which the first elementary segment is voiceless and the second is voiced, then in accordance with 10.3 the set X may be recognized as a compound feature of the kind $\mathscr{X}$. This feature might be called the feature of being a voiceless-voiced unit-length segment. It is easily seen that X is not the only compound feature of the kind $\mathscr{X}$. There may exist additionally voiced-voiceless, voiced-voiced and voiceless-voiceless unit-length segments, and, moreover, eight sorts of ternary compound segments.

10.4 $\mathscr{X} \in \mathbf{K} \wedge X_1, X_2 \in \mathbf{cf}(\mathscr{X}) \rightarrow X_1 = X_2 \vee X_1 \cap X_2 = \Lambda$

Proof. Suppose that $x \in X_1 \cap X_2$ and

$$X_1 = \{z\colon z \in \mathbf{csg}_2 \wedge \vartheta_1(z) \in Y_1 \wedge \vartheta_2(z) \in Z_1\},$$
$$X_2 = \{z\colon z \in \mathbf{csg}_2 \wedge \vartheta_1(z) \in Y_2 \wedge \vartheta_2(z) \in Z_2\},$$

where $Y_1, Z_1, Y_2, Z_2 \in \mathscr{X}$. Then $\vartheta_1(x) \in Y_1 \cap Y_2$ and $\vartheta_2(x) \in Z_1 \cap Z_2$. From this by A14 we infer that $Y_1 = Y_2$ and $Z_1 = Z_2$, whence $X_1 = X_2$.

In the case when X_1 and X_2 are sets of ternary compound segments the reasoning is similar.

10.5 $$x \in \mathbf{csg}^{(\iota)} \wedge \mathscr{X} \in \mathbf{K} \rightarrow \dot{\bigvee_X}(X \in \mathbf{cf}(\mathscr{X}) \wedge x \in X)$$

Proof. Suppose that $x \in \mathbf{csg}_2^{(\iota)}$ and $\mathscr{X} \in \mathbf{K}$. By 9.19 $\vartheta_1(x) \in \mathsf{UUK}$ and $\vartheta_2(x) \in \mathsf{UUK}$. From this by 3.3 we infer that there is exactly one Y and exactly one Z such that $Y, Z \in \mathscr{X}$, $\vartheta_1(x) \in Y$ and $\vartheta_2(x) \in Z$.

Let now

$$X = \{z\colon z \in \mathbf{csg}_2 \wedge \vartheta_1(z) \in Y \wedge \vartheta_2(z) \in Z\}.$$

Then obviously $x \in X$ and, in accordance with 10.3, $X \in \mathbf{cf}(\mathscr{X})$. The uniqueness of the feature X follows from 10.4. In the case when $x \in \mathbf{csg}_3^{(\iota)}$ our reasoning is similar.

10.6 $$\mathscr{X} \in \mathbf{K} \rightarrow \mathbf{csg}^{(\iota)} \subset \mathsf{U}\mathbf{cf}(\mathscr{X})$$ (by 10.5)

10.7 $$\mathscr{X} \in \mathbf{K} \rightarrow \bigcup_{\iota} \mathbf{csg}^{(\iota)} \subset \mathsf{U}\mathbf{cf}(\mathscr{X})$$ (by 10.6)

10.8 $$\mathscr{X} \in \mathbf{K} \rightarrow \bigcup_{\iota} \mathbf{usg}^{(\iota)} \subset \mathsf{U}(\mathscr{X} \cup \mathbf{cf}(\mathscr{X}))$$

[1] This example is taken from Jassem [10], § 46.—The sound [d] appearing in the phrase under consideration is initially voiceless, and thus, in accordance with the understanding of the notion of a segment which is accepted in linguistics, it consists of two (elementary) segments.

Proof. Using 9.17, A13 and 10.7 it is easily proved that if $\mathscr{X} \in \mathbf{K}$, then

$$\bigcup_{\iota} \mathbf{usg}^{(\iota)} \subset \bigcup\bigcup \mathbf{K} \cup \bigcup_{\iota} \mathbf{csg}^{(\iota)} \subset \bigcup \mathscr{X} \cup \bigcup \mathbf{cf}(\mathscr{X}) = \bigcup(\mathscr{X} \cup \mathbf{cf}(\mathscr{X})).$$

Having in mind compound features, we shall introduce a new notion of a kind of phonetic features. Roughly speaking the kinds of features in the new sense result from kinds in the previous sense (cf. chapter 1) by adding corresponding compound features to them. To be more accurate, by a *kind in the generalized sense of phonetic features* we mean any sum $\mathscr{Y} \cup \mathbf{cf}(\mathscr{Y})$, where $\mathscr{Y} \in \mathbf{K}$, i.e. $\mathscr{Y}$ is a kind of features in the previous sense. The family of all kinds in the generalized sense will be denoted by $\mathbf{K}^*$.

10.9 $$\mathbf{K}^* \underset{\text{df}}{=} \{\mathscr{X} : \bigvee_{\mathscr{Y}}(\mathscr{Y} \in \mathbf{K} \wedge \mathscr{X} = \mathscr{Y} \cup \mathbf{cf}(\mathscr{Y}))\}$$

Elements of $\bigcup \mathbf{K}^*$ may be called *phonetic features in the generalized sense*. Clearly, all phonetic features in the previous sense (i.e. elements of $\bigcup \mathbf{K}$) are also phonetic features in the generalized sense.

10.10 $$\bigcup \mathbf{K} \subset \bigcup \mathbf{K}^*$$

10.11 $$\bigcup\bigcup \mathbf{K} \subset \bigcup\bigcup \mathbf{K}^*$$

10.12 $$\bigcup\bigcup \mathbf{K}^* \cup \mathbf{0} \subset \mathbf{mo}' \cap \mathbf{P}\langle \bigcup \mathbf{I} \rangle$$

10.13 $$\mathbf{P}\langle \bigcup\bigcup \mathbf{K}^* \rangle \cap \mathbf{P}\langle \mathbf{0} \rangle = \Lambda$$

Theorems 10.12 and 10.13 are given here on account of their similarity to the axioms A10 and A11, respectively.

10.14 $$\mathscr{X} \in \mathbf{K}^* \rightarrow \bigcup_{\iota} \mathbf{usg}^{(\iota)} \subset \bigcup \mathscr{X}$$

Proof. If $\mathscr{X} \in \mathbf{K}^*$, then by 10.4 $\mathscr{X} = \mathscr{Y} \cup \mathbf{cf}(\mathscr{Y})$, where $\mathscr{Y} \in \mathbf{K}$. By 10.8

$$\bigcup_{\iota} \mathbf{usg}^{(\iota)} \subset \bigcup(\mathscr{Y} \cup \mathbf{cf}(\mathscr{Y})),$$

that is

$$\bigcup_{\iota} \mathbf{usg}^{(\iota)} \subset \bigcup \mathscr{X}.$$

10.15 $$\bigcup\bigcup \mathbf{K} \cup \bigcup_{\iota} \mathbf{usg}^{(\iota)} = \bigcup\bigcup \mathbf{K}^*$$

Proof. The inclusion

$$\bigcup\bigcup \mathbf{K} \cup \bigcup_{\iota} \mathbf{usg}^{(\iota)} \subset \bigcup\bigcup \mathbf{K}^*$$

follows from 10.11 and 10.14. The converse inclusion follows from 10.4 and 10.3.

Notice that the inclusion $\bigcup\bigcup \mathbf{K}^* \subset \bigcup_{\iota} \mathbf{usg}^{(\iota)}$ is not true. For, if x is a binary compound segment, then we have, for instance, $\vartheta_1(x) \in \bigcup\bigcup\mathbf{K}$ and $\vartheta_1(x) \notin \bigcup_\iota \mathbf{usg}^{(\iota)}$.

10.16 $$\mathscr{X} \in \mathbf{K}^* \rightarrow \bigcup\bigcup\mathbf{K}^* \subset \bigcup\mathscr{X}$$

Proof. If $\mathscr{X} \in \mathbf{K}^*$, then $\mathscr{X} = \mathscr{Y} \cup \mathbf{cf}(\mathscr{Y})$, where $\mathscr{Y} \in \mathbf{K}$. Hence by A13 $\bigcup\bigcup\mathbf{K} \subset \bigcup\mathscr{Y} \subset \bigcup\mathscr{X}$. From this by 10.14 follows

$$\bigcup\bigcup\mathbf{K} \cup \bigcup_\iota \mathbf{usg}^{(\iota)} \subset \bigcup\mathscr{X},$$

whence by 10.15 we derive the thesis of our theorem.

10.17 $$\mathscr{X} \in \mathbf{K}^* \wedge X_1, X_2 \in \mathscr{X} \rightarrow X_1 = X_2 \vee X_1 \cap X_2 = \Lambda$$

Proof. Suppose $\mathscr{X} \in \mathbf{K}^*$. Then $\mathscr{X} = \mathscr{Y} \cup \mathbf{cf}(\mathscr{Y})$, where $\mathscr{Y} \in \mathbf{K}$. If now $X_1, X_2 \in \mathscr{X}$, then either (*a*) $X_1, X_2 \in \mathscr{Y}$, or (*b*) $X_1 \in \mathscr{Y}$, $X_2 \in \mathbf{cf}(\mathscr{Y})$, or (*c*) $X_1 \in \mathbf{cf}(\mathscr{Y})$, $X_2 \in \mathscr{Y}$, or (*d*) $X_1, X_2 \in \mathbf{cf}(\mathscr{Y})$. In the case when (*a*) holds, the thesis of our theorem is derived by A14. In the case (*d*) we use 10.4; and in the two remaining cases we employ the fact that $\mathbf{csg}^{(\iota)} \cap \bigcup\bigcup\mathbf{K} = \Lambda$.

Theorems 10.16 and 10.17 correspond, in a sense, to the axioms A13 and A14, respectively.

10.18 $$x, y \in \mathbf{usg}^{(\iota)} \rightarrow (x\,\mathbf{E}\,y \equiv \bigwedge_X (X \in \bigcup\mathbf{K}^* \rightarrow \rightarrow (x \in X \equiv y \in X)))$$

Proof. Assume that $x, y \in \mathbf{csg}_2^{(\iota)}$. Then $\lambda_x = \lambda_y = 2$ and

$$\mathbf{Esg}^{\vee}x \cup \mathbf{Esg}^{\vee}y \subset \bigcup\bigcup\mathbf{K}.$$

If now $x\,\mathbf{E}\,y$, then, by 7.1, for every $i \in [1, 2]$, we have

(1) $$\bigwedge_Y (Y \in \bigcup\mathbf{K} \rightarrow (\vartheta_i(x) \in Y \equiv \vartheta_i(y) \in Y))$$

Let now $X \in \bigcup\mathbf{K}^*$ and $x \in X$. Then $X \in \mathscr{Y} \cup \mathbf{cf}(\mathscr{Y})$, for some $\mathscr{Y} \in \mathbf{K}$. Since $x \in X$ and $\lambda_x = 2$, therefore $X \notin \mathscr{Y}$. Hence $X \in \mathbf{cf}(\mathscr{Y})$. It follows from this, that

(2) $$X = \{z: z \in \mathbf{csg}_2 \wedge \vartheta_1(z) \in Y_1 \wedge \vartheta_2(z) \in Y_2\},$$

where $Y_1, Y_2 \in \mathscr{Y}$. Clearly, $\vartheta_1(x) \in Y_1$ and $\vartheta_2(x) \in Y_2$. From this and (1) we infer that also $\vartheta_1(y) \in Y_1$ and $\vartheta_2(y) \in Y_2$, whence by (2) $y \in X$. In a similar way it is proved that if $X \in \bigcup\mathbf{K}^*$ and $y \in X$ then $x \in X$. Thus, our assumption entails the implication:

(3) $$x\,\mathbf{E}\,y \rightarrow \bigwedge_X (X \in \bigcup\mathbf{K}^* \rightarrow (x \in X \equiv y \in X)).$$

To prove the converse implication, we assume that $\sim x\,\mathbf{E}\,y$. Then by 7.1 there is a $Y \in \bigcup\mathbf{K}$ and an $i \in [1, 2]$ such that $\vartheta_i(x) \in Y$ and $\vartheta_i(y) \notin Y$. Let $\mathscr{Y}$ be the kind of phonetic features which contains Y. Hence $\mathscr{Y} \in \mathbf{K}$ and $Y \in \mathscr{Y}$. We may assume that e.g. $i = 1$ (for, if

$i = 2$, the reasoning is analogous). Thus $\vartheta_1(x) \in Y$ and $\vartheta_1(y) \notin Y$. Let

$$X = \{z\colon z \in \mathbf{csg}_2 \wedge \vartheta_1(z) \in Y \wedge \vartheta_2(z) \in Z\},$$

where Z is the unique feature of kind $\mathscr{Y}$ which pertains to the segment $\vartheta_2(x)$. (The existence of such a feature is guaranteed by 3.3). Then $X \in \mathbf{cf}(\mathscr{Y})$ and, consequently, $X \in \mathsf{U}\mathbf{K}^*$. Moreover, $x \in X$, but $y \notin X$, since $\vartheta_1(y) \notin Y$. Hence

$$\sim \bigwedge_X (X \in \mathsf{U}\mathbf{K}^* \rightarrow (x \in X \equiv y \in X)).$$

Thus, the converse of implication (3) is established.

In the case when $x,y \in \mathbf{csg}_3^{(i)}$ the proof is quite analogous. In the case when $x,y \in \mathsf{UU}\mathbf{K}$ the proof is simple. All other cases may be disregarded, for, if $X \in \mathsf{U}\mathbf{K}^*$, then all elements of X must be of the same length.

Chapter 11

SOUNDS AND PHONETIC SYSTEMS

E-equivalence classes in the set $\mathbf{usg}_0^{(\iota)}$ will be called *sounds* of the idiolect ι. The class of all sounds of ι will be symbolized by $\Sigma_0^{(\iota)}$.

11.1 $$\Sigma_0^{(\iota)} \underset{\text{df}}{=} \mathfrak{A}(\mathbf{E}, \mathbf{usg}_0^{(\iota)})$$

The following two theorems follow at once from the above definition.

11.2 $$X \in \Sigma_0^{(\iota)} \equiv \bigvee_x (x \in \mathbf{usg}_0^{(\iota)} \wedge \bigwedge_y (y \in X \equiv y\, \mathbf{E}\, x \wedge y \in \mathbf{usg}_0^{(\iota)}))$$

11.3 $$X \in \Sigma_0^{(\iota)} \rightarrow X \subset \mathbf{usg}_0^{(\iota)}$$

According to the above theorems, sounds are sets of unit-length segments. In particular, if $x \in \mathbf{usg}_0^{(\iota)}$, then the set of all unit-length segments of ι which are phonetically equivalent to x is a sound of ι. Thus, sounds of the idiolect ι are simply common features of phonetically equivalent unit-length segments of this idiolect.

Doubtlessly, our definition of sound is in accord with the intention of the following explication given by Pilch: 'Eine Klasse hörbar gleicher Segmente nennen wir einen Laut.'[1] We are speaking here only of the intention, since Pilch's definition, if literally understood, certainly is not adequate and does not express the author's proper intention. For, if x, y, z are three different, but phonetically equivalent unit-length segments in an idiolect ι, then in accordance with Pilch's definition—though certainly not with his intention—the set $[x, y]$ is a sound. Needless to say this set is not a sound in the sense of our own definition.

The distinction between unit-length segments and sounds is to a great extent analogous to that between elementary segments and phones. Nevertheless, the analogy is not complete, for, the terms appearing in the last distinction are, in a sense, absolute, whereas those in the first one are relativized to the idiolect.

11.4 $$\mathbf{E} \in \mathrm{eq}(\mathbf{usg}_0^{(\iota)})$$

[1] H. Pilch [20], p. 91. By 'Segmente' the author means here his 'phonematische Segmente', that is our unit-length segments.

11.5 $$x \in \mathbf{usg}_0^{(\iota)} \rightarrow \bigvee_X (X \in \Sigma_0^{(\iota)} \wedge x \in X)$$

11.6 $$X, Y \in \Sigma_0^{(\iota)} \rightarrow X = Y \vee X \cap Y = \Lambda$$

11.7 $$X \in \Sigma_0^{(\iota)} \rightarrow X \neq \Lambda$$

11.8 $$\mathbf{0} \cap \mathbf{P}\langle\iota\rangle \in \Sigma_0^{(\iota)}$$

The last theorem gives an example of a particular sound of the idiolect ι. Namely, the set of all pauses in a given idiolect constitutes a sound. This sound may be called the *improper sound.* The other sounds will be called *proper*. The set of all proper sounds of ι will be symbolized by $\Sigma^{(\iota)}$.

11.9 $$\Sigma^{(\iota)} \underset{\mathrm{df}}{=} \Sigma_0^{(\iota)} - [\mathbf{0} \cap \mathbf{P}\langle\iota\rangle]$$

If X is a sound of ι and $x \in X$, then we say that X is the *phonetic form* of the segment x with respect to ι. The relation of being the phonetic form with respect to ι will be denoted by σ_ι.

11.10 $$\sigma_\iota \underset{\mathrm{df}}{=} \{X{,}x\colon X \in \Sigma_0^{(\iota)} \wedge x \in X\}$$

11.11 $$x \in \mathbf{usg}_0^{(\iota)} \rightarrow \bigvee_X (X = \sigma_\iota{}^{\backprime}x)$$

11.12 $$x \in \mathbf{usg}_0^{(\iota)} \rightarrow \sigma_\iota{}^{\backprime}x \in \Sigma_0^{(\iota)}$$

11.13 $$x \in \mathbf{usg}^{(\iota)} \rightarrow \sigma_\iota{}^{\backprime}x \in \Sigma^{(\iota)}$$

11.14 $$x \in \mathbf{0} \cap \mathbf{P}\langle\iota\rangle \rightarrow \sigma_\iota{}^{\backprime}x = \mathbf{0} \cap \mathbf{P}\langle\iota\rangle$$

11.15 $$x \in \mathbf{usg}_0^{(\iota)} \rightarrow x \in \sigma_\iota{}^{\backprime}x$$

11.16 $$x{,}y \in \mathbf{usg}_0^{(\iota)} \rightarrow (x\,\mathbf{E}\,y \equiv \sigma_\iota{}^{\backprime}x = \sigma_\iota{}^{\backprime}y)$$

The notion of the phonic form of an elementary segment defined in chapter 8 has been used there in defining the notion of the phonic structure of a phonetic chain. Now, the notion of the phonetic form will be employed to an analogous end. Namely, we shall define the notion of the phonetic structure of a phonetic chain. But before this we must introduce some auxiliary notions. For, it is clear, that we may not use here the function $\vartheta(x)$, which was employed in chapter 8, because this function gives a numbering of elementary segments and not of unit-length segments in a chain. Moreover, we must also replace the notion of the length of a chain by a new one.

The following definition introduces the *relation of being a unit-length segment in x with respect to ι.*

11.17 $$\mathbf{Usg}_\iota \underset{\mathrm{df}}{=} \{x{,}y\colon x\,\mathbf{P}\,y \wedge x \in \mathbf{usg}_0^{(\iota)}\}$$

11.18 $$\mathbf{Usg}_\iota{}^{\vee}x = \mathbf{P}^{\vee}x \cap \mathbf{usg}_0^{(\iota)}$$

11.19 $x \in \mathbf{usg}_0^{(\iota)} \rightarrow \mathbf{Usg}_\iota{}^{\vee}x = [x]$

A new notion of the length of phonetic chain is introduced in 11.20. The *length in the new sense* of a given chain is measured by the number of unit-length segments contained in the chain. On account of the relative nature of the notion of unit-length segment, the new notion of length must be relativized to the idiolect.

11.20 $\lambda_x^\iota \underset{\mathrm{df}}{=} \overline{\overline{\mathbf{Usg}_\iota{}^{\vee}x}}$

11.21 $x \in \mathbf{Ch}\langle\iota\rangle \rightarrow 0 \leqslant \lambda_x^\iota < \aleph_0$

It is quite obvious that λ_x^ι is a finite number. It is to be emphasized, however, that unlike in 5.25 0 may not be substituted by 1 in the above theorem. For, if e.g. $x \in \mathbf{sgcm}_3^{(\iota)}$, then obviously $x \in \mathbf{Ch}\langle\iota\rangle$ and $\lambda_x^\iota = 0$. It is also clear from this example that $x \in \mathbf{Ch}\langle\iota\rangle$ does not necessarily entail the equality $x = \mathbf{S}`\mathbf{Usg}_\iota{}^{\vee}x$. The chains for which the last equality is true will be called *complete chains* in ι. The set of all chains of this kind will be denoted by $\mathbf{cch}^{(\iota)}$.

11.22 $\mathbf{cch}^{(\iota)} \underset{\mathrm{df}}{=} \mathbf{Ch}\langle\iota\rangle \cap \{x : x = \mathbf{S}`\mathbf{Usg}_\iota{}^{\vee}x\}$

11.23 $\mathbf{Ut}\langle\iota\rangle \subset \mathbf{cch}^{(\iota)}$

Proof. Suppose $x \in \mathbf{Ut}\langle\iota\rangle$. Then $x \in \mathbf{Ch}\langle\iota\rangle$, $\vartheta_1(x) \in \mathbf{0}$ and $\vartheta_{\lambda_x}(x) \in \mathbf{0}$. First, we want to show that

(1) $\mathbf{Esg}^{\vee}x \subset \mathbf{P}\langle\mathbf{Usg}_\iota{}^{\vee}x\rangle.$

To this end we assume that $y \in \mathbf{Esg}^{\vee}x$. If, now, $y \in \mathbf{0}$, then clearly $y \in \mathbf{Usg}_\iota{}^{\vee}x$ and consequently $y \in \mathbf{P}\langle\mathbf{Usg}_\iota{}^{\vee}x\rangle$. Therefore, we may assume that $y \in \mathsf{UUK}$. Then, by 9.22 we infer that $y \in \mathbf{P}\langle\mathbf{usg}^{(\iota)}\rangle$. Hence, there is a $z \in \mathbf{usg}^{(\iota)}$ such that $y \in \mathbf{P}^{\vee}z$. We may also assume that $z \in \mathbf{csg}^{(\iota)}$. (For, in the case when $z \in \mathsf{UUK}$, we have by 3.15 $y = z$ and consequently $y \in \mathbf{P}\langle\mathbf{Usg}_\iota{}^{\vee}x\rangle$.) Then by 9.16 either $z \in \mathbf{csg}_2^{(\iota)}$ or $z \in \mathbf{csg}_3^{(\iota)}$. Suppose that the first alternative holds. Then z is composed of two elementary segments. Obviously, y is one of these segments. Hence

(2) $\mathbf{P}^{\vee}x \cap \mathbf{P}^{\vee}z \neq \Lambda.$

Since $x \in \mathbf{Ut}\langle\iota\rangle$, therefore for some $u \in \iota$, $x \in \mathbf{P}^{\vee}u$. From this and (2) follows that $\mathbf{P}^{\vee}u \cap \mathbf{P}^{\vee}z \neq \Lambda$. Hence by 9.23 $z \in \mathbf{P}^{\vee}u$. We need to prove that $z \in \mathbf{P}^{\vee}x$. First of all, let us notice that one of those elementary segments which are parts of z, namely y, is a part of x. The second of those elementary segments is either the predecessor or the successor of y, and, moreover, it is not a pause. It follows from this that this segment lies in the utterance u either between $\vartheta_1(x)$ and y or between y and $\vartheta_{\lambda_x}(x)$; and consequently it is also a part of x, since $x\,\mathbf{Ch}\,u$. Hence we conclude that the whole unit-length segment z is a part of x. Consequently $y \in \mathbf{P}\langle \mathbf{Usg}_\iota{}^\vee x\rangle$. In the case when $z \in \mathbf{csg}_3^{(\iota)}$, our reasoning is similar, though somewhat longer on account of a greater number of possible cases. Thus, we may recognize (1) as proved.

From (1) follows that $\mathbf{S}‘\mathbf{Esg}^\vee x \in \mathbf{P}^\vee\mathbf{S}‘\mathbf{P}\langle \mathbf{Usg}_\iota{}^\vee x\rangle$. Because $x = \mathbf{S}‘\mathbf{Esg}^\vee x$ and $\mathbf{S}‘\mathbf{P}\langle \mathbf{Usg}_\iota{}^\vee x\rangle = \mathbf{S}‘\mathbf{Usg}_\iota{}^\vee x$, we have $x \in \mathbf{P}^\vee\mathbf{S}‘\mathbf{Usg}_\iota{}^\vee x$, and since it is obvious that $\mathbf{S}‘\mathbf{Usg}_\iota{}^\vee x \in \mathbf{P}^\vee x$, therefore by I.3.17 we infer that $x = \mathbf{S}‘\mathbf{Usg}_\iota{}^\vee x$. From this by 11.22 follows that $x \in \mathbf{cch}^{(\iota)}$ and thus the proof is completed.

11.24 $$\mathbf{Phr}\langle \iota\rangle \subset \mathbf{cch}^{(\iota)}$$

The proof of this theorem is similar to that of the preceding theorem.

11.25 $$x \in \mathbf{cch}^{(\iota)} \rightarrow 1 \leqslant \lambda_x^\iota < \aleph_0$$

Proof. It is easily seen from the definition 11.22 that the hypothesis of the theorem implies that $\mathbf{Usg}_\iota{}^\vee x \neq \Lambda$. Hence in this case the thesis of 11.21 may be in fact strengthened.

11.26 $x \in \mathbf{cch}^{(\iota)} \rightarrow \mathbf{T}_e \in \text{word}\,(\mathbf{Usg}_\iota{}^\vee x)$ (by 9.31, 9.33)

It follows from the two last theorems that, if $x \in \mathbf{cch}^{(\iota)}$, then there is an ordinal correlator (isomorphism) of $\mathbf{T}_e$ with its field limited to $\mathbf{Usg}_\iota{}^\vee x$ and $\leqslant$ with its field limited to the set of natural numbers $[1, 2, \ldots, \lambda_x^\iota]$. It may also be shown that there is but one ordinal correlator of this kind. This unique ordinal correlator will be symbolized by $\vartheta^\iota(x)$. The parameter ι appears here for the sake of marking that the ordinal correlator depends on the idiolect ι. Moreover, the index ι serves to differentiate the symbols $\vartheta^\iota(x)$ and $\vartheta(x)$.

The formal definition of $\vartheta^\iota(x)$ will not be given here in symbolic form. We shall limit ourselves to stating it in words. Nevertheless, the corollaries from the definition will be put down in symbols.

11.27 $\vartheta^\iota(x)$ is the unique ordinal correlator of $\mathbf{T}_e$ with its field limited to $\mathbf{Usg}_\iota{}^\vee x$ and $\leqslant$ with its field limited to the set $[1, 2, \ldots, \lambda_x^\iota]$.

11.28 $$x \in \mathbf{cch}^{(\iota)} \rightarrow \vartheta^\iota(x) \in \text{crs} \wedge \mathbf{D}‘\vartheta^\iota(x) = \mathbf{Usg}_\iota{}^\vee x \wedge \mathbf{Cl}‘\vartheta^\iota(x) = \\ = \{n\colon n \leqslant \lambda_x^\iota\} \wedge \bigwedge_{y,z} \bigwedge_{n,m} (y\,\vartheta^\iota(x)\,n \wedge z\,\vartheta^\iota(x)\,m \rightarrow \\ \rightarrow (y\,\mathbf{T}_e\,z \equiv n \leqslant m))$$

11.29 $$\vartheta_n^\iota(x) \underset{\text{df}}{=} \vartheta^\iota(x)‘n$$

11.30 $$x \in \mathbf{cch}^{(\iota)} \wedge y \in \mathbf{Usg}_\iota{}^\vee x \rightarrow \bigvee_n (n \leqslant \lambda_x^\iota \wedge y = \vartheta_n^\iota(x))$$

11.31 $x \in \mathbf{cch}^{(\iota)} \wedge n \leqslant \lambda^{\iota}_{x} \rightarrow \vartheta^{\iota}_{n}(x) \in \mathbf{Usg}_{\iota}{}^{\vee}x$

11.32 $x \in \mathbf{cch}^{(\iota)} \wedge n,m \leqslant \lambda^{\iota}_{x} \rightarrow (\vartheta^{\iota}_{n}(x)\ \mathbf{T}_{\mathrm{e}}\ \vartheta^{\iota}_{m}(x) \equiv n \leqslant m)$

11.33 $x \in \mathbf{cch}^{(\iota)} \wedge n,m \leqslant \lambda^{\iota}_{x} \rightarrow (\vartheta^{\iota}_{n}(x)\ \mathbf{T}_{\mathrm{c}}\ \vartheta^{\iota}_{m}(x) \equiv n < m)$

11.34 $x \in \mathbf{cch}^{(\iota)} \wedge n \leqslant \lambda^{\iota}_{x} \rightarrow \vartheta^{\iota}_{n}(x)\ \mathbf{T}_{\mathrm{i}}\ \vartheta^{\iota}_{n+1}(x)$

11.35 $x \in \mathbf{cch}^{(\iota)} \wedge n,m \leqslant \lambda^{\iota}_{x} \rightarrow (\vartheta^{\iota}_{n}(x)\ \mathbf{T}_{\mathrm{i}}\ \vartheta^{\iota}_{m}(x) \equiv n + 1 = m)$

11.36 $u \in \mathbf{Ut}\langle\iota\rangle \rightarrow \vartheta^{\iota}_{1}(u) \in \mathbf{0}$

11.37 $u \in \mathbf{Ut}\langle\iota\rangle \wedge n = \lambda^{\iota}_{u} \rightarrow \vartheta^{\iota}_{n}(u) \in \mathbf{0}$

Using the functions σ_{ι} and $\vartheta^{\iota}(x)$ we shall define the notion of the phonetic structure of a complete phonetic chain. Now, if x is a complete phonetic chain in ι, then by the *phonetic structure* of this chain with respect to ι we mean the following sequence of sounds:

$$\sigma_{\iota}{}^{\text{‘}}\vartheta^{\iota}_{1}(x),\quad \sigma_{\iota}{}^{\text{‘}}\vartheta^{\iota}_{2}(x),\ \ldots,\quad \sigma_{\iota}{}^{\text{‘}}\vartheta^{\iota}_{n}(x),$$

where $n = \lambda^{\iota}_{x}$. The sequence will be denoted by $\varphi^{\iota}(x)$. Its formal definition is quite analogous to definition 8.20, which introduced the notion of phonic structure.

11.38 $\varphi^{\iota}(x) \underset{\mathrm{df}}{=} \sigma_{\iota}/\vartheta^{\iota}(x)$

11.39 $x \in \mathbf{cch}^{(\iota)} \rightarrow \mathrm{D}^{\text{‘}}\varphi^{\iota}(x) \subset \Sigma^{(\iota)}_{0}$

11.40 $x \in \mathbf{cch}^{(\iota)} \rightarrow \mathrm{Ɑ}^{\text{‘}}\varphi^{\iota}(x) = \{n\colon n \leqslant \lambda^{\iota}_{x}\}$

11.41 $x \in \mathbf{cch}^{(\iota)} \rightarrow \varphi^{\iota}(x) \in \mathrm{fnc}$

11.42 $\varphi^{\iota}_{n}(x) \underset{\mathrm{df}}{=} \varphi^{\iota}(x)^{\text{‘}}n$

11.43 $x \in \mathbf{cch}^{(\iota)} \wedge n \leqslant \lambda^{\iota}_{x} \rightarrow \varphi^{\iota}_{n}(x) \in \Sigma^{(\iota)}_{0}$

11.44 $x \in \mathbf{cch}^{(\iota)} \wedge n \leqslant \lambda^{\iota}_{x} \rightarrow (\varphi^{\iota}_{n}(x) = \sigma_{\iota}{}^{\text{‘}}\vartheta^{\iota}_{n}(x))$

11.45 $u \in \mathbf{Ut}\langle\iota\rangle \rightarrow \varphi^{\iota}_{1}(u) = \mathbf{0} \cap \mathbf{P}\langle\iota\rangle$

11.46 $u \in \mathbf{Ut}\langle\iota\rangle \wedge n = \lambda^{\iota}_{u} \rightarrow \varphi^{\iota}_{n}(u) = \mathbf{0} \cap \mathbf{P}\langle\iota\rangle$

11.47 $x \in \mathbf{cch}^{(\iota)} \wedge n,m \leqslant \lambda^{\iota}_{x} \rightarrow (\varphi^{\iota}_{n}(x) = \varphi^{\iota}_{m}(x) \equiv \vartheta^{\iota}_{n}(x)\ \mathbf{E}\ \vartheta^{\iota}_{m}(x))$

11.48 $x,y \in \mathbf{cch}^{(\iota)} \rightarrow (\varphi^{\iota}(x) = \varphi^{\iota}(y) \equiv x\ \mathbf{E}\ y)$

We conclude this chapter with the definition of the *phonetic system of* ι. The phonetic system of ι will be symbolized by $\mathfrak{S}^{(\iota)}_{\sigma}$. Its formal definition is as follows:

11.49 $$\mathfrak{S}^{(\iota)}_{\sigma} \underset{\mathrm{df}}{=} \langle \Sigma^{(\iota)}, \varphi^{\iota}\langle \mathbf{Phr}\langle\iota\rangle\rangle\rangle$$

Chapter 12

DISTRIBUTION OF SOUNDS

The notion of the distribution of sounds, of morphemes and of other linguistic entities is one of the main components of the conceptual apparatus of contemporary descriptive linguistics. We shall be concerned here exclusively with the notion of distribution of sounds. It is this notion which is necessary when defining the notion of a phoneme.

Our definition of the distribution of sounds will be fitted to the intentions contained in the following explanation given by Harris: 'The distribution of an element is the total of all environments in which it occurs, i.e. the sum of all the (different) positions (or occurrences) of an element relative to the occurrence of other elements.' [1]

In the first place we shall introduce some auxiliary notions and symbols.

12.1 $$\mathbf{bch}^{(\iota)} \underset{\text{df}}{=} \mathbf{cch}^{(\iota)} \cap \{x: \bigwedge_i (1 < i \leqslant \lambda^{\iota}_x \rightarrow \varphi^{\iota}_i(x) \in \Sigma^{(\iota)})\}$$

12.2 $$\mathbf{ech}^{(\iota)} \underset{\text{df}}{=} \mathbf{cch}^{(\iota)} \cap \{x: \bigwedge_i (1 \leqslant i < \lambda^{\iota}_x \rightarrow \varphi^{\iota}_i(x) \in \Sigma^{(\iota)})\}$$

The elements of the set $\mathbf{bch}^{(\iota)}$ may be called *beginning chains* in ι. In accordance with the first definition, x is a beginning chain in ι, in symbols: $x \in \mathbf{bch}^{(\iota)}$, if and only if x is a complete chain in ι and at most the first unit-length segment in x is a pause. The elements of the set $\mathbf{ech}^{(\iota)}$ may be called *ending chains* in ι. In accordance with the second of the above definitions, x is an ending chain in ι, in symbols: $x \in \mathbf{ech}^{(\iota)}$, if and only if x is a complete chain in ι and at most the last unit-length segment in x is a pause. The terms 'beginning chain' and 'ending chain' are used here only because the set $\mathbf{bch}^{(\iota)}$ contains (among others) all the complete chains which are beginnings of utterances, and the set $\mathbf{ech}^{(\iota)}$ contains (among others) all the complete chains,which are ending parts of utterances.

All sequences with two terms, the first term of which is a beginning chain in ι and the second term is an ending chain in ι will be

[1] Z. S. Harris [7], pp. 15–16.

called *environmental pairs*[1] in ι. On account of the fact that sequences with two terms are functions the converse domain of which is the set [1, 2], the set $\mathbf{ep}^{(\iota)}$ of all environmental pairs in ι may be formally defined as follows:

12.3 $$\mathbf{ep}^{(\iota)} \underset{\mathrm{df}}{=} \{\varrho\colon \varrho \in \mathrm{fnc} \wedge \mathrm{C\!I}`\varrho = [1, 2] \wedge \varrho`1 \in \mathbf{bch}^{(\iota)} \wedge \wedge \varrho`2 \in \mathbf{ech}^{(\iota)}\}$$

If ϱ is an environmental pair in ι, x is a proper unit-length segment in ι, $\varrho`1$ immediately precedes $x$, $x$ immediately precedes $\varrho`2$ and the sum $\varrho`1 \mathbin{\dot\cup} x \mathbin{\dot\cup} \varrho`2$ is a (complete) chain in ι, then we say that ϱ is an *environment of* x in ι (in symbols: $\varrho\ \mathbf{En}_\iota\ x$).

12.4 $$\mathbf{En}_\iota \underset{\mathrm{df}}{=} \{\varrho,x\colon \varrho \in \mathbf{ep}^{(\iota)} \wedge x \in \mathbf{usg}^{(\iota)} \wedge \varrho`1\ \mathbf{T}_\mathrm{i}\ x \wedge \wedge x\ \mathbf{T}_\mathrm{i}\ \varrho`2 \wedge \varrho`1 \mathbin{\dot\cup} x \mathbin{\dot\cup} \varrho`2 \in \mathbf{cch}^{(\iota)}\}$$

12.5 $$\mathbf{D}`\mathbf{En}_\iota \subset \mathbf{ep}^{(\iota)}$$

12.6 $$\mathrm{C\!I}`\mathbf{En}_\iota = \mathbf{usg}^{(\iota)}$$

Proof. It is easily seen from definition 12.4 that $\mathrm{C\!I}`\mathbf{En}_\iota \subset \mathbf{usg}^{(\iota)}$. To prove the converse inclusion, let us suppose that $x \in \mathbf{usg}^{(\iota)}$. Then by 9.21 for some $u \in \iota$, $x\ \mathbf{P}\ u$, and by 9.28 x is not a pause. Consequently x is different from the first as well as from the last unit-length segment in u (by 11.36 and 11.37). Hence, if $X = \mathbf{Usg}_\iota{}^\vee u \cap \mathbf{T}_\mathrm{c}{}^\vee x$ and $Y = \mathbf{Usg}_\iota{}^\vee u \cap \mathbf{T}_\mathrm{c}{}^\wedge x$, then $X \neq \Lambda$, $Y \neq \Lambda$ and the sequence ϱ with two terms such that $\varrho`1 = \mathbf{S}`X$ and $\varrho`2 = \mathbf{S}`Y$ is an environment of x in ι.

12.7 $$x \in \mathbf{usg}^{(\iota)} \longrightarrow \mathbf{En}_\iota{}^\vee x \neq \Lambda$$

12.8 $$X \in \Sigma^{(\iota)} \longrightarrow \mathbf{En}_\iota\langle X\rangle \neq \Lambda$$

12.9 $$\varrho\ \mathbf{En}_\iota\ x \wedge \varrho\ \mathbf{En}_\iota\ y \longrightarrow x = y \vee x,y \in \mathbf{Phr}\langle\iota\rangle$$

Proof. Suppose that $\varrho\ \mathbf{En}_\iota\ x$ and $\varrho\ \mathbf{En}_\iota\ y$. Moreover, assume that $x,y \notin \mathbf{Phr}\langle\iota\rangle$. We shall prove that $x = y$. For the sake of clarity we shall write simply ϱ_1 and ϱ_2 instead of $\varrho`1$ and $\varrho`2$ respectively.

From our suppositions it follows, that x, $y \in \mathbf{usg}^{(\iota)}$, $\varrho_1 \mathbin{\dot\cup} x \mathbin{\dot\cup} \varrho_2 \in \mathbf{cch}^{(\iota)}$ and $\varrho_1 \mathbin{\dot\cup} y \mathbin{\dot\cup} \varrho_2 \in \mathbf{cch}^{(\iota)}$. From this we infer that for some $u_1,u_2 \in \iota$, we have $\varrho_1 \mathbin{\dot\cup} x \mathbin{\dot\cup} \varrho_2 \in \mathbf{Ch}^\vee u_1$ and $\varrho_1 \mathbin{\dot\cup} y \mathbin{\dot\cup} \varrho_2 \in \mathbf{Ch}^\vee u_2$. Because by 9.19 and 9.21 $\mathbf{0} \cap \mathbf{Esg}^\vee x = \Lambda$ and $x \in \mathbf{ch}$, so by 5.5 and 5.16 there does exist the predecessor $\mathbf{p}`x$ as well as the successor $\mathbf{s}`x$. But $x \notin \mathbf{Phr}^\vee u_1$, hence by 6.8 either $\mathbf{p}`x \in \mathsf{UU}\mathbf{K}$ or $\mathbf{s}`x \in \mathsf{UU}\mathbf{K}$. We may assume, e.g. that the second alternative holds. Then, it is easy to prove that $\mathbf{s}`x = \vartheta_1(\varrho_2)$. Obviously, there exists also the

[1] This notion is somewhat similar to Bloch's notion of a disjunction. Cf. B. Bloch [4], p. 13.

predecessor $\mathbf{p}`\mathbf{s}`x$, and, since $x\ \mathbf{T}_{\mathrm{i}}\ \varrho_2$ and $y\ \mathbf{T}_{\mathrm{i}}\ \varrho_2$, therefore $\mathbf{p}`\mathbf{s}`x = \vartheta_{\lambda_x}(x) = \vartheta_{\lambda_y}(y)$. Thus $\mathbf{P}^{\vee}x \cap \mathbf{P}^{\vee}y \neq \Lambda$, whence by 9.30 $x = y$.

12.10 $\quad x \neq y \wedge x, y \notin \mathbf{Phr}\langle\iota\rangle \rightarrow \mathbf{En}_{\iota}{}^{\vee}x \cap \mathbf{En}_{\iota}{}^{\vee}y = \Lambda$

12.11 $\quad X, Y \in \Sigma^{(\iota)} \wedge X \neq Y \wedge \varrho \in \mathbf{En}_{\iota}\langle X\rangle \cap \mathbf{En}_{\iota}\langle Y\rangle \rightarrow$

$$\rightarrow \varrho`1 \in \mathbf{0} \wedge \varrho`2 \in \mathbf{0}$$

Proof. From the hypothesis follows by 11.6 that $X \cap Y = \Lambda$. Therefore, if $\varrho\ \mathbf{En}_{\iota}\ x$ and $\varrho\ \mathbf{En}_{\iota}\ y$, where $x \in X$ and $y \in Y$, then $x \neq y$. It follows from this (by 12.10) that $x, y \in \mathbf{Phr}\langle\iota\rangle$. But then the thesis of our theorem is obvious.

The last theorem explicitly shows that the set $\mathbf{En}_{\iota}\langle X\rangle$, where $X \in \Sigma^{(\iota)}$, is not yet what a linguist would call the distribution of the sound X. For, it is essential for the linguistic understanding of the notion of distribution that different sounds may have also non-pausal contexts in common.

Now, we shall define an auxiliary function $\mathbf{F}_{\iota}$. This function might be called the *transforming function* with respect to ι. It will assign to every environmental pair ϱ in ι an appropriate sequence of phonetic structures of the chains $\varrho`1$ and $\varrho`2$, namely, the sequence with two terms the first term of which is $\varphi^{\iota}(\varrho`1)$ and the second is $\varphi^{\iota}_{\mathrm{I}}(\varrho`2)$.

12.12 $\quad \mathbf{F}_{\iota} \underset{\mathrm{df}}{=} \{\xi,\varrho\colon \xi \in \mathrm{fnc} \wedge \mathrm{C\!\!\!I}`\xi = [1, 2] \wedge \rho \in \mathbf{ep}^{(\iota)} \wedge \xi`1 = \varphi^{\iota}(\varrho`1) \wedge$

$$\wedge\ \xi`2 = \varphi^{\iota}(\varrho`2)\}$$

Using the function $\mathbf{F}_{\iota}$ we shall formulate now the main definition of the present chapter.

12.13
$$\mathbf{D}_{\iota} \underset{\mathrm{df}}{=} \mathbf{F}_{\iota}/\mathbf{En}_{\iota}$$

According to the above definition ξ takes the relation $\mathbf{D}_{\iota}$ to x if and only if there is an environmental pair ϱ such that $\xi = \mathbf{F}_{\iota}`\varrho$ and $\varrho \in \mathbf{En}_{\iota}{}^{\vee}x$. Should we call $\mathbf{F}_{\iota}`\varrho$ the phonetic structure of the environmental pair ϱ, the above definition could be expressed also in the following way: ξ takes the relation $\mathbf{D}_{\iota}$ to x if and only if ξ is the phonetic structure of an environment of x. If $X \in \Sigma^{(\iota)}$, then $\mathbf{D}_{\iota}\langle X\rangle$ is the set of all phonetic structures of all environments of elements of the sound X. Just this set, in our opinion, may be called the *distribution of the sound* X in the idiolect ι. This explication seems to be quite adequate to Harris' usage of the notion of the distribution of a sound.

12.14
$$x \in \mathbf{usg}^{(\iota)} \rightarrow \mathbf{D}_{\iota}{}^{\vee}x \neq \Lambda$$

12.15
$$X \in \Sigma^{(\iota)} \rightarrow \mathbf{D}_{\iota}\langle X\rangle \neq \Lambda$$

Using the notion of distribution (or, strictly speaking, the relation $\mathbf{D}_{\iota}$) we shall define two important relations between sounds, namely, the relation of being a free variant and the relation of complementarity.

If the distributions of two sounds in a given idiolect ι are the same, then we say that one of these sounds is a *free variant* of the other in the idiolect ι. The relation of being a free variant in the idiolect ι will be symbolized by $\mathbf{Fv}_\iota$.

12.16 $$\mathbf{Fv}_\iota \underset{\mathrm{df}}{=} \{X, Y\colon X, Y \in \Sigma^{(\iota)} \wedge \mathbf{D}_\iota\langle X\rangle = \mathbf{D}_\iota\langle Y\rangle\}$$

It is quite obvious that the relation $\mathbf{Fv}_\iota$, defined above, is reflexive in $\Sigma^{(\iota)}$ and, moreover, symmetric and transitive. Thus we have the theorem:

12.17 $$\mathbf{Fv}_\iota \in \mathrm{eq}(\Sigma^{(\iota)})$$

Two sounds X and Y, the distributions of which are disjoint, that is, such that $\mathbf{D}_\iota\langle X\rangle \cap \mathbf{D}_\iota\langle Y\rangle = \Lambda$, are said to be *complementary* to each other. Thus, we may formulate the following definition.

12.18 $$\mathbf{Cm}^1_\iota \underset{\mathrm{df}}{=} \{X, Y\colon X, Y \in \Sigma^{(\iota)} \wedge \mathbf{D}_\iota\langle X\rangle \cap \mathbf{D}_\iota\langle Y\rangle = \Lambda\}$$

This definition, however, cannot be considered as a full explication of the notion of complementarity as it is used by the linguists. For, when—in accordance with our definition—$X\,\mathbf{Cm}^1_\iota\,Y$, the linguist will always say that X is complementary (or in complementary distribution) to Y. But according to the linguistic intuition the holding of the relation $\mathbf{Cm}^1_\iota$ between X and Y is not a necessary condition for X to be complementary to Y. Here is an expressive quotation from Bloch's work: '[. . .] the segments [u·] and [ü·] in pre-English are in some phrases immediately preceded and immediately followed by the same sequences,[1] and hence appear to have some of their environments in common—for instance in *[mu·s] 'mouse' and *[mü·si] 'mice'; but if we state the environments of [u·] and [ü·] in such a way as to include the following vowel, the two segments turn out to be in complementary distribution: [ü·] occurs only in environments that contain the segment [i] or [j] in the following sequence, [u·] occurs only in environments that do not contain such a segment.' [2]

Wishing to grasp the proper linguistic meaning of the relation of complementarity we must treat as complementary also any two sounds X and Y which although having some common contexts have at the same time the following property: there exists a constant

[1] Strictly speaking, we should speak here of sequences (that is chains, in our terminology) which have the same phonetic structure. Similarly, it is incorrect to refer to [u·] and [ü·] as segments but as sounds. However, Bloch does not differentiate between individuals and abstracts.

[2] B. Bloch [4], p. 23.

factor such that every common context of these sounds may be enlarged so that X will occur in a context including this constant factor and Y in a context without this factor. This explanation is obviously not precise. And, what is more, the task of transforming it into a formal definition seems very difficult.[1] Therefore we shall take as our basis another, slightly different explanation which also seems to fit with a sufficient adequacy Bloch's examples. We shall namely treat as complementary also any two sounds X and Y which have some common contexts, but all these contexts may be enlarged so that certain differences will occur.

It is obvious that no environment ϱ in which the first element begins with a pause and the second ends with a pause can be enlarged (since then the pause would cease to be a beginning or an end). If we call such environments *maximal*, the latter explanation may be more exactly formulated in the following way: Every two sounds X and Y the distributions of which are neither disjoint nor equal but such that the product $\mathbf{D}_\iota\langle X\rangle \cap \mathbf{D}_\iota\langle Y\rangle$ does not contain phonetic structures of any maximal environments, are also complementary.

Let us point out that it may well be that the above explanation defines a somewhat wider relation than does the former one. For, in a certain idiolect some sounds may turn out to be complementary not because of phonetic conditions which have been spoken about in the first explanation, but because of a kind of lexical poverty of the given idiolect. However, such situation is hardly probable and we shall not take it into consideration.

The first of the definitions given below introduces the auxiliary notion of a *maximal environmental pair* in ι. For the sake of graphic simplicity the index λ occurring in this definition stands for $\lambda^\iota_{\varrho'2}$. The second definition introduces the *relation of complementarity in the second sense*.

12.19 $$\mathbf{mep}^{(\iota)} \underset{\mathrm{df}}{=} \mathbf{ep}^{(\iota)} \cap \{\varrho : \vartheta^\iota_1(\varrho`1) \in \mathbf{0} \wedge \vartheta^\iota_\lambda(\varrho`2) \in \mathbf{0}\}$$

12.20 $$\mathbf{Cm}^2_\iota \underset{\mathrm{df}}{=} \{X, Y\colon X, Y \in \Sigma^{(\iota)} \wedge \mathbf{D}_\iota\langle X\rangle \cap \mathbf{D}_\iota\langle Y\rangle \neq \Lambda \wedge$$
$$\wedge\, \mathbf{D}_\iota\langle X\rangle \neq \mathbf{D}_\iota\langle Y\rangle \wedge \mathbf{D}_\iota\langle X\rangle \cap \mathbf{D}_\iota\langle Y\rangle \cap \mathbf{F}_\iota\langle \mathbf{mep}^{(\iota)}\rangle = \Lambda\}$$

The *relation of complementarity in the general sense* may now be defined simply as the sum of the above two 'partial' complementarity relations. It will be denoted by $\mathbf{Cm}_\iota$.

[1] Of course, it is easily possible to adjust our definitions (22) and (23) given in [3] to the present system, but they do not seem to be satisfactory. In fact, they are too complicated and moreover certain properties, essential from the intuitive point of view, of the relation of complementarity, cannot be derived from them.

12.21 $$\mathbf{Cm}_\iota \underset{\mathrm{df}}{=} \mathbf{Cm}^1_\iota \cup \mathbf{Cm}^2_\iota$$

According to the above definition, X is complementary to Y in ι, in symbols: $X\,\mathbf{Cm}_\iota\,Y$, if and only if X and Y are sounds in ι which are complementary to each other in the first or in the second sense.

Now we shall state some simple theorems which follow from the given definitions.

12.22 $$X\,\mathbf{Cm}^1_\iota\,Y \rightarrow \sim X\,\mathbf{Fv}_\iota\,Y$$

Proof. If $X\,\mathbf{Cm}^1_\iota\,Y$, then $X, Y \in \Sigma^{(\iota)}$ and, in accordance with 12.15, $\mathbf{D}_\iota\langle X\rangle \neq \Lambda$ and $\mathbf{D}_\iota\langle Y\rangle \neq \Lambda$. Suppose $X\,\mathbf{Fv}_\iota\,Y$. Then, by 12.16, $\mathbf{D}_\iota\langle X\rangle \cap \mathbf{D}_\iota\langle Y\rangle = \mathbf{D}_\iota\langle X\rangle \neq \Lambda$, which on account of 12.18 contradicts the hypothesis of the theorem, and proves our supposition false.

12.23 $$X\,\mathbf{Cm}^2_\iota\,Y \rightarrow \sim X\,\mathbf{Fv}_\iota\,Y$$

This theorem follows immediately from 12.16 and 12.20. From 12.22 and 12.23 follow the next two corollaries.

12.24 $$X\,\mathbf{Cm}_\iota\,Y \rightarrow \sim X\,\mathbf{Fv}_\iota\,Y$$

12.25 $$X\,\mathbf{Fv}_\iota\,Y \rightarrow \sim X\,\mathbf{Cm}_\iota\,Y$$

From 12.18 and 12.20 we infer at once that the relations $\mathbf{Cm}^1_\iota$ and $\mathbf{Cm}^2_\iota$ exclude each other.

12.26 $$X\,\mathbf{Cm}^1_\iota\,Y \rightarrow \sim X\,\mathbf{Cm}^2_\iota\,Y$$

12.27 $$X\,\mathbf{Cm}^2_\iota\,Y \rightarrow \sim X\,\mathbf{Cm}^1_\iota\,Y$$

12.28 $$X\,\mathbf{Cm}_\iota\,Y \rightarrow X \neq Y$$

This theorem states that the relation $\mathbf{Cm}_\iota$ is irreflexive and follows from the corresponding definitions and theorem 12.15.

12.29 $$\mathbf{Cm}_\iota \in \mathrm{sym}$$

Proof. It is easily seen from definitions 12.18 and 12.20 that both relations $\mathbf{Cm}^1_\iota$ and $\mathbf{Cm}^2_\iota$ are symmetric. Therefore the relation $\mathbf{Cm}_\iota$ as the sum of two symmetric relations must also be symmetric.

12.30 $$X\,\mathbf{Cm}_\iota\,Y \wedge Y\,\mathbf{Fv}_\iota\,Z \rightarrow X\,\mathbf{Cm}_\iota\,Z$$

Proof. If $Y\,\mathbf{Fv}_\iota\,Z$ and $X\,\mathbf{Cm}^1_\iota\,Y$, then by virtue of 12.16 and 12.18 $X\,\mathbf{Cm}^1_\iota\,Z$. If $Y\,\mathbf{Fv}_\iota\,Z$ and $X\,\mathbf{Cm}^2_\iota\,Y$, then by 12.16 and 12.20 $X\,\mathbf{Cm}^2_\iota\,Z$. Thus, in accordance with 12.21, our theorem is established.

12.31 $$x \in \mathbf{usg}^{(\iota)} \rightarrow \dot{\bigvee_{\rho}}(\varrho \in \mathbf{mep}^{(\iota)} \cap \mathbf{En}_\iota{}^{\vee}x)$$

Proof. Let $x \in \mathbf{usg}^{(\iota)}$. It is easy to show (with the help of 6.12) that there exists exactly one v such that $v \in \mathbf{Phr}\langle\iota\rangle$ and $x\,\mathbf{P}\,v$. Let now

$$y = \mathbf{S}`([\mathbf{p}`v] \cup (\mathbf{Usg}_\iota{}^{\vee}v \cap \mathbf{T}_c{}^{\vee}x))$$

and

$$z = \mathbf{S}`([\mathbf{s}`v] \cup (\mathbf{Usg}_\iota{}^\vee v \cap \mathbf{T}_c{}^\wedge x)).$$

Then the sequence ϱ with two terms such that $\varrho`1 = y$ and $\varrho`2 = z$, is the unique maximal environmental pair which is an environment of $\boldsymbol{x}$.

Chapter 13

PHONEMES AND THE FUNDAMENTAL HYPOTHESES OF PHONOLOGY

We shall now try to define the main notion of theoretical phonology, namely the notion of phoneme. We shall start by quoting definitions of 'phoneme' by different linguists by way of introduction to the theoretical problems connected with that notion.

According to Jones 'a phoneme is a family of sounds in a given language which are related in character and are used in such a way that no one member ever occurs in a word in the same phonetic context as any other member'.[1]

Harris defines phoneme as follows:

'We take any segment and note the sum of environments in which it occurs [. . .]. We then cast about for some other segment which never occurs in any of the environments in which the first segment occurs [. . .]. We say that such a segment is complementary to the first one. We then look for a segment which is complementary to the first two (i.e. which never occurs in any environment in which either of the first two occurs) [. . .]. We continue the search until we can no longer find a segment which is complementary to all the previous segments. At this point we close the list of these mutually complementary segments and begin afresh with a new segment for which we will seek other complementaries, forming a second set of mutually complementary segments.

'We take any number of segments, each of which is complementary to every other one we have taken, and say that they comprise a single class which we call a phoneme.' [2]

Jassem's definition:

'A phoneme is

(1) either a single sound contrasting with any other sound but not excluding any other and not indifferent to any other,

(2) or a group of sounds excluding each other, having at least one relevant feature in common,

(3) or a group of sounds indifferent to each other.' [3]

[1] D. Jones [13], p. 10, § 31.

[2] Z. S. Harris [7], p. 61.

[3] W. Jassem [10], pp. 44–5.—We should explain that in accordance with

H. Pilch writes:

'Wir haben eben gesehen, daß manche Lautelemente in komplementärer Verteilung stehen und manche Lautelemente miteinander phonetisch verwandt sind. Lautelemente, die durch diese beiden Eigenschaften gleichzeitig, gekennzeichnet sind, heißen phonematisch gleich. [. . .] Phonetisch verwandte Elemente in freiem Wechsel sind phonematisch gleich. [. . .] Wir können nun die Segmente weiter ordnen in der Weise, daß wir phonematisch einander gleiche Segmente zu einer Klasse zusammenfassen [. . .]. Eine solche Klasse phonematisch gleicher Segmente heißt ein Phonem.' [1]

Considering the above definitions we could conclude that the definition of the notion of phoneme in the idiolect ι should be as follows:

(1) The set of phonemes of idiolect $\iota \underset{\mathrm{df}}{=} \{\mathscr{X} : \mathscr{X} \subset \Sigma^{(\iota)} \wedge \ldots\}$

It is quite clear that the condition $\mathscr{X} \subset \Sigma^{(\iota)}$ is needed here: all the above definitions agree that phonemes are sets of sounds. Although Harris and Pilch speak about sets of segments, it is evident that by segment the authors mean not a concrete physical thing but an abstract entity, that is, what we here call a sound.

Of course, in order to obtain a concrete definition of the form (1) the dots in definiens should be replaced by a conjunction of appropriate conditions which warrant that $\mathscr{X}$ has all the properties determining that something is a phoneme.

However, the formula (1) is not an appropriate schema for the definition of phoneme (in ι): no definition constructed according to the schema (1) would be adequate. The reason for this is as follows. The acceptance of a definition formulated according to (1) would mean that for each idiolect there is only one way of grouping sounds into phonemes. However, as has been known for more than thirty years this assumption is false. (This fact was pointed out for the first time in 1934 by a Chinese linguist Yuen Ren Chao in his work under the significant title: *The Non-Uniqueness of Phonemic Solutions of Phonetic Systems.*)

Regarding this matter Harris writes in the introduction to his book: 'The methods described here do not eliminate non-uniqueness in linguistic descriptions. It is possible for different linguists, working on the same material, to set up different phonemic and morphemic

---

Jassem's terminology, two sounds are contrasting with each other if they have some (but not all) environments in common, on the other hand, they are indifferent if they have all environments in common, that is, if they are free variants.

[1] H. Pilch [20], pp. 56, 59 and 92.

elements, to break phonemes into simultaneous components or not to do so, to equate two sequences of morphemes as being mutually substitutable or not to do so.' [1]

Here is another, even more expressive quotation of Harris' book dealing with the same problem:

'At a time when phonemic operations were less frequently and less explicitly carried out, there was discussion as to what had to be done in order to arrive at "the phonemes" and how one could discover "the phonemes" of a language. Today we can say that any grouping of complementary segments may be called phonemic. As phonemic problems in various languages came to be worked out, and possibilities of alternative analysis were revealed, it became clear that the ultimate elements of the phonology of a language upon which all linguists analysing that language could be expected to agree, were the distinct (contrasting) segments (positional variants, or allophones) rather than the phonemes. The phonemes resulted from a classification of complementary segmental elements; and this could be carried out in various ways. For a particular language, one phonemic arrangement may be more convenient, in terms of particular criteria, than other arrangements. The linguistic requisite is not that a particular arrangement be presented, but that the criteria which determine the arrangement be explicit.' [2]

The reason for the fact that there exist more than one way of grouping sounds into phonemes seems to lie in that the relation $\mathbf{Cm}_\iota$ is not transitive; this is, at least partly, evident from the definitions quoted at the beginning of this chapter. Let us assume, for instance, that $\Sigma^{(\iota)} = [X_1, X_2, X_3, X_4]$ and

$$X_1 \,\mathbf{Cm}_\iota\, X_2, \qquad X_2 \,\mathbf{Cm}_\iota\, X_4,$$
$$X_1 \,\mathbf{Cm}_\iota\, X_3, \qquad X_3 \,\mathbf{Cm}_\iota\, X_4,$$
$$X_1 \,\mathbf{Cm}_\iota\, X_4, \qquad \sim X_2 \,\mathbf{Cm}_\iota\, X_3,$$

and let us try to group X_1, X_2, X_3, X_4 into phonemes according to Harris' rules. It is obvious that two ways of such grouping are possible: in one the sets $[X_3]$, $[X_1, X_2, X_4]$ are phonemes, in the other $[X_2]$, $[X_1, X_3, X_4]$. Each time we obtain two phonemes, but different ones in each case. Obviously, all this is true under the condition that different phonemes are required to be always disjoint. For, if we do not make this requirement, there exists in our case only one way of grouping sounds into phonemes, namely: $[X_1, X_2, X_4]$, $[X_1, X_3, X_4]$. It seems, however, that the requirement of disjointness is one of the guiding ideas for all theoretical phonologists. Although sometimes

[1] Z. S. Harris [7], p. 2.

[2] Z. S. Harris [7], p. 72, footnote 28.

they admit some exceptions in this respect,[1] this happens very seldom and only in certain exceptional circumstances, and, moreover, with explicit qualification as an exception from the generally accepted principle. 'It is to be taken as axiomatic—writes Jones—that one sound cannot belong to two phonemes of a language. There are possibly some rare exceptions to this.'[2] Pilch writes in a similar spirit, perhaps even more radically, since he includes no reference to possible exceptions; at the very beginning of his monograph he states: 'Bei unseren Darlegungen stellen wir uns auf den Standpunkt, daß aus hörbarer Gleichheit immer auch phonematische Gleichheit folge.' [3] A similar idea seems to be expressed in one of the parts of the introductory definition by Bloch: 'A phoneme is a class of sounds in the utterances of a given dialect, such that (*a*) all members of the class contain a feature absent from all other sounds, (*b*) the differences among them are in complementary distribution or free variation, and (*c*) the class belongs to a set of classes that are mutually contrasting and conjointly exhaustive.' [4] Point (*c*) of the above definition could perhaps be taken as saying—although rather awkwardly—that the class of phonemes should be a classification of sounds.

In the light of the above considerations it seems necessary to look for a schema of the definition of phoneme, different from (1).

In our opinion a definition of phoneme, which takes into account the fact of many possibilities of 'phonemic solutions' (that is, a definition in accordance with Harris' argument quoted above) should answer not the question what sets of sounds are phonemes (as is done by the schema (1)) but the question what ways of sound-grouping are phonemic or what sets are the sets of phonemes of a specific idiolect. If sets which can be regarded as sets of phonemes of an idiolect ι are called the phonemic bases of this idiolect, the required schema of the definition can be formulated as follows:

(2) The set of the phonemic bases of the idiolect $\iota \underset{\text{df}}{=} \{\mathsf{B}: \ldots\}$

Of course, in order to obtain a concrete definition of the notion of a phonemic basis constructed according to the schema (2) the dots should be replaced by the conjunction of appropriate conditions which ensure that B is a phonemic grouping of sounds, or in other words, B is a system of phonemes of the idiolect ι. We shall now try to formulate conditions of this kind. They will be as follows:

(i) $\mathsf{B} \in \mathrm{clsf}(\Sigma^{(\iota)})$

[1] Cf. Z. S. Harris [7], p. 65.
[2] D. Jones [13], p. 11.
[3] H. Pilch [20], p. xiii.
[4] B. Bloch [4], p. 5.

(ii) $\bigwedge_{\mathscr{X}} (\mathscr{X} \in \mathfrak{A}(\mathbf{Fv}_\iota, \Sigma^{(\iota)}) \rightarrow \bigvee_{\mathscr{Y}}(\mathscr{Y} \in \mathsf{B} \wedge \mathscr{X} \subset \mathscr{Y}))$

(iii) $\bigwedge_{\mathscr{X}} \bigwedge_{X,Y} (\mathscr{X} \in \mathsf{B} \wedge X, Y \in \mathscr{X} \rightarrow X\,\mathbf{Fv}_\iota\,Y \vee X\,\mathbf{Cm}_\iota\,Y)$

(iv) $\bigwedge_{\mathscr{X},\mathscr{Y}} (\mathscr{X},\mathscr{Y} \in \mathsf{B} \wedge \mathscr{X} \neq \mathscr{Y} \rightarrow \bigvee_{\mathscr{Z}} \bigvee_{X,Y} (\mathscr{Z} \in \mathbf{K}^* \wedge X, Y \in \mathscr{Z} \wedge$
$\wedge X \neq Y \wedge \bigcup\mathscr{X} \subset X \wedge \bigcup\mathscr{Y} \subset Y))$

(v) $\bigwedge_{\mathsf{B}_1}$ (if B_1 fulfils the above conditions (i)—(iv), then $\overline{\overline{\mathsf{B}}} \leqslant \overline{\overline{\mathsf{B}}}_1$)

If the family of all phonemic bases of the idiolect ι is denoted by $\mathbf{PB}^{(\iota)}$ and if only the numbers (i)—(v) are used instead of the corresponding long formulas, we may formulate the following definition falling under the schema (2):

13.1 $$\mathbf{PB}^{(\iota)} \underset{\text{df}}{=} \{\mathsf{B}: \text{(i)} \wedge \text{(ii)} \wedge \text{(iii)} \wedge \text{(iv)} \wedge \text{(v)}\}$$

This is the main definition of the present work.

According to this definition B is a *phonemic basis* of the idiolect ι if and only if B fulfils all the requirements (i)—(v). If B is a phonemic basis of the idiolect ι, then the elements of B may be called *phonemes* of the idiolect ι in the basis B (or, with respect to the basis B).

Let us examine more closely the meaning of the conditions used in our definition.

The condition (i) says that B is a classification of the set of all proper sounds of the idiolect ι. It means that:

(a) Each phoneme in the basis B is a set of sounds of the idiolect ι. (Of course, some phonemes can be unit sets. Cf. point (1) in the above definition by Jassem).

(b) Each sound of the idiolect ι belongs to a phoneme in the basis B.

(c) Each two different phonemes in the basis B are disjoint, that is, no sound of the idiolect ι belongs to two different phonemes in the same phonemic basis.

The condition (ii) states that each $\mathbf{Fv}_\iota$-equivalence class in the set $\Sigma^{(\iota)}$ is contained in one phoneme in the basis B. In other words, each two sounds which are free variants of each other must be contained in the same phoneme.

At first sight the condition (ii) might seem to be rather alien in relation to the linguistic explanations of the notion of phoneme quoted at the beginning of this chapter. However, this is not so. As a matter of fact this condition does not differ much from the third point of Jassem's definition and from one of the principles in Pilch's definition; moreover, it is one of the essential components of Harris' theory, that is, the theory in which we are mainly interested and which is the principal object of the reconstruction undertaken in this work. The point is that for Harris 'the identification' of free variants is one of the first operations performed on the way from the living speech to the list of phonemes and, therefore, in discussing, as it were, the last act of his procedures—that is the grouping of segments into phonemes—Harris does not mention free variants. But the 'segments' which he groups into phonemes are, among others, the result of the identification of free variants. Following Harris strictly in this respect seemed pointless. A parallel treatment of the identification of free variants and of the identification of complementary sounds (referred to in the condition (iii)), seemed to us more reasonable.[1] In this respect our definition is quite close to those by Jassem and Pilch, and partly to Bloch's. One of the advantages of our approach is that the logical type of phonemes is lowered: they are objects of the type $((*))$ instead of $(((*)))$. It makes the whole theory clearer.

We have already pointed out the similarity between our condition (ii) and the third point of Jassem's definition. Let us point out now the difference between them. The difference lies in the following: According to Jassem the $\mathbf{Fv}_\iota$-equivalence classes appear to be phonemes, whereas according to our condition every such class is included in a certain phoneme. Hence our approach is more liberal. Let us illustrate it by an example. Let us assume that $X_1 \mathbf{Fv}_\iota X_2$ and $X_1 \mathbf{Fv}_\iota X_3$ and there are no other sounds in ι which would be free variants of X_1. Hence, in accordance with 12.17 $X_2 \mathbf{Fv}_\iota X_3$, and of course, $[X_1, X_2, X_3] \in \mathfrak{A}(\mathbf{Fv}_\iota, \Sigma^{(\iota)})$. Let us assume now that $X_1 \mathbf{Cm}_\iota X_4$. (Then by 12.29 and 12.30 we have $X_2 \mathbf{Cm}_\iota X_4$ and $X_3 \mathbf{Cm}_\iota X_4$). In this case, in accordance with Jassem's definition the class $[X_1, X_2, X_3]$ is a phoneme to which no sound may be added. Our condition (ii), on the other hand, does not exclude the possibility of regarding the whole class $[X_1, X_2, X_3, X_4]$ as one phoneme. In this respect our definition seems to be closer to the spirit of Harris' theory.

The condition (iii) of our definition says that if two sounds belong to the same phoneme, then they are free variants or, one is complementary to the other. Thus, if X and Y are sounds of ι and if neither X is a free variant of Y nor X is complementary to Y, then these sounds cannot be considered as belonging to the same phoneme. The above condition is rather a prohibition than a requirement. In this respect it differs from (ii) which was a typical requirement. The postulate (ii) unconditionally requires the grouping of free variants

[1] Even Harris himself, when adjusting his theory to a concrete example of its application in the phonemic analysis of Swahili, mentions equally to other principles the following one: 'If two segments vary freely with one another in every position in which they occur, they are grouped in one phoneme.' Cf. Z. S. Harris [7], p. 110.

into one phoneme, while the postulate (iii) only forbids the grouping in one phoneme of these sounds which are neither complementary to each other nor are free variants. As may be seen from the above, (iii) does not forbid grouping complementary sounds into one phoneme and in this, rather weak sense, it permits such grouping. Let us emphasize that it *only permits* and does not require. The difference in the treatment of free variants and complementary sounds is, therefore, evident. One might even suppose that this difference is too great and too radical from the point of view of the intentions of linguists who would rather be inclined to require the 'identification' of complementary sounds. But this is not so for two reasons. First of all, no linguist requires or can require the grouping of all complementary sounds, since in view of the fact that the relation $\mathbf{Cm}_t$ is not transitive (and in view of the actual situation in specific languages) phonemes would not be disjoint; therefore Harris as well as other phonologists only recommends grouping complementary sounds whenever it is possible. Secondly, the condition (v) of our definition provides a strengthening of (iii). The condition (v) is a certain principle of economy requiring the maximal reduction of the number of phonemes and thereby it requires the grouping into one phoneme of all complementary sounds for which this is possible from the point of view of other conditions. (This will be given further attention when discussing the condition (v)). This approach to the problem of complementary sounds seems to be fairly subtle and in accordance with the intentions of linguists.

The content of (iv) is as follows: If $\mathscr{X}$ and $\mathscr{Y}$ are any two different phonemes in the basis B, then there exist two different phonetic features X and Y (in the generalized sense) which are homogeneous (i.e. belong to the same kind in the generalized sense)—the feature X being the property [1] of all sounds belonging to the phoneme $\mathscr{X}$, and the feature Y of all sounds belonging to the phoneme $\mathscr{Y}$; of course, owing to the fact that X and Y are homogeneous and different, the feature X is not possessed by any sound belonging to $\mathscr{Y}$, and the feature Y by any sound belonging to $\mathscr{X}$, i.e. $\bigcup\mathscr{Y} \cap X = \Lambda$ and $\bigcup\mathscr{X} \cap Y = \Lambda$ (cf. 10.17).

The condition (iv) contains the two following important ideas:

(*a*) All sounds belonging to the same phoneme in a specific basis B have at least one phonetic feature in common.[2]

[1] We say that a feature X is a property of the sound Z if $Z \subset X$, that means, if every unit-length segment belonging to Z has the feature X.

[2] The exact proof in our system of this corollary requires the additional assumption that the basis B contains at least two different elements. This assumption certainly is true for all natural languages (and all sufficiently representative idiolects).

(*b*) Every two different phonemes in a specific basis B are differentiated by means of appropriate oppositional features.

Of course, (*b*) is simply a free translation of the condition (iv) in colloquial language, whereas (*a*) is a particular conclusion from (iv) and thereby from (*b*).

Let us consider now some similarities and differences between our condition (iv) and some conditions included in the definitions of various linguists which were quoted at the beginning of this chapter. Thus, Jones requires the sounds grouped in one phoneme to be 'related in character'. This requirement is doubtlessly concerned with the phonetic similarity of respective sounds, which is more or less what is expressed in the above corollary (*a*). This is presumably also Pilch's point, who requires that phonemically equivalent sounds should be phonetically related (phonetisch verwandt). In the definitions of the two authors we do not find, therefore, any trace of the idea expressed in (*b*). Such a trace, however, may be discovered in Jassem's definition. It may be seen in his usage of the notion of relevant feature, which denotes—according to respective explanations made by the author—all and only those features common to all elements of a phoneme, which are oppositional with respect to other phonemes. Of course, we may speak here only about a trace, since the requirement concerning the necessity of having common relevant features refers only to the grouping of complementary sounds. Nevertheless, this trace is quite evident, especially in view of the fact that Jassem himself—in one of his later articles—has developed it into, more or less, our point (*b*); he writes there: 'Phonemes are groups of sounds with definite relevant features which have all contexts in common, or which have no contexts in common and also sounds which are not contained in such groups but which have definite relevant features.' [1] However, our condition (iv) seems to be closest to the point (*a*) of Bloch's definition quoted above. They seem to concern exactly the same idea.

Thus in the definitions of Bloch, Jones, Jassem and Pilch we may find at least something meant by our condition (iv), whereas nothing of that sort is to be found in Harris' definition. However, the view that the idea expressed in (iv) is alien to Harris' theory, would be erroneous, since this idea seems to be clearly contained in Harris' theory.

'We may try—he writes—to group segments into phonemes in such a way that all the segments of each phoneme represent sounds having some feature in common which is not represented by any segment of any other phoneme: to use articulatory examples, all

[1] W. Jassem [11], p. 25.

segments included in /p/ would represent the feature of lip closure plus complete voicelessness (or fortisness) which would not be represented by any other segment. We would then be able to speak of the phoneme as representing this common feature, rather than as being a class of segments. Relations between phonemes would then represent relations between sound features.' [1]

Although the quoted passage is not quite clear, it seems to express the principle stated in our condition (iv). But this principle plays a secondary role in Harris' theory and is not necessarily obligatory. According to Harris, it does not determine what a phoneme is,[2] and therefore the author does not include it in his general definition of a phoneme. However, the acceptance of (iv) as an imperative principle and the inclusion of it in the general definition of a phoneme, seems to be in accordance with the intentions of the classical definition by Trubetzkoy and with the intentions of the majority of modern phonologists, many of whom (e.g. R. Jakobson and his school) regard essence of phoneme to be oppositional features. Such approach does not contradict the Harris theory: the difference lies only in attributing greater significance to the principle which is observed, never violated but somewhat neglected by Harris.

As has been mentioned above, condition (v) may be called the condition of economy. It may, of course, be presented in exact, symbolic form. To this end it is enough to substitute the statement 'B_1 fulfils the above conditions (i)–(iv)' by the conjunction of conditions (i′)–(iv′) which are obtained from (i)–(iv) respectively by substituting the variable B_1 for B. It is unnecessary to put down here the formula obtained in this way.

The content of (v) is reasonably clear. This condition says that if B is to be a phonemic basis of the idiolect ι, there cannot exist any classification B_1 of the set of sounds of the idiolect which would fulfil the conditions (i)–(iv) and would have less elements than B. Thus, if any two families B and B_1 fulfil the conditions (i)–(iv) and one of them contains more elements than the other, then the more numerous one is not a phonemic basis. Of course, it does not necessarily mean that the other family should be a phonemic basis. In any case, in order to obtain a phonemic basis of a specific idiolect we have to try to group sounds in such a way as to obtain the smallest number of sets of sounds. Thus we have to attempt to group together as many complementary sounds as possible.

The idea expressed in our condition (v) cannot be found in any of the definitions quoted at the beginning of this chapter. However, it

[1] Z. S. Harris [7], p. 64.
[2] Z. S. Harris [7], p. 72, footnote 28.

can be found if the entire theories of the linguists' mentioned are considered. In particular, it is one of the components of Harris' theory: 'A general desideratum is to have as few phonemes as possible.' [1] Harris did not, however, include this desideratum into his definition of the notion of a phoneme, since, again, he was convinced that it is only a subsidiary criterion not determining what a phoneme is. Such underestimation seems to disagree with the spirit of classical phonology. For, the discovery of the most economic means of reducing speech to writing has been, for a long time, one of the principal practical aims of phonology. It has, also, been known that the phonetic transcription in which each sound is associated with one specific symbol is not sufficiently economic, since it is possible to reduce considerably the number of symbols without blurring (from the point of view of native speakers) the transcription. Such a reduction may be obtained by 'identification' of certain sounds, that is, by appropriate 'phonemic grouping'. Of course, not just any reduction is meant but a reduction to the smallest possible number of units. This aim is precisely one of the main factors determining what the phonemes are. All other rules formulated by phonologists should be considered as secondary rather than vice versa, since all of them are subsidiary in relation to the principle of economy. The latter, expressing the essential aim of phonological investigations should be considered to be superior, in a sense. The omission of this principle in the definition of a phoneme would impoverish the very notion being defined.

As can be seen from the above explanations, the principles (i)–(v) are not a set of rules which enables us to obtain, automatically, the phonemic basis of a given idiolect. They are only some general principles which absolutely have to be observed. However, the decision whether they are really observed is not always simple. As a result the statement that a concrete classification of sounds is a phonemic basis must, as a rule, remain a hypothesis requiring (especially in view of (v)) verification.

Every precise definition of a notion is, in the first place, an alteration of this notion. Nevertheless the definition 13.1 seems to be a sufficiently adequate logical reconstruction of Harris' phonological theory. And even if it is not always true to the letter of Harris' theory, it preserves to my mind the spirit of this theory. It seems that one cannot require more from this kind of definition. For, if it were possible to construct a formal definition in complete accordance with Harris' text, this definition would not be necessary at all. After all, this would mean that Harris' book contains formulations which are sufficiently clear, unequivocal, precise, and so easy to

[1] Z. S. Harris [7], p. 63.

formalize. It is obvious, however, that a formalization of something easy to formalize is superfluous.

Certainly our definition will not satisfy all phonologists, particularly those who do not accept Harris' theory. However, it is possible that there will be some who will be ready to accept the definition 13.1 after some modifications. These modifications may be of various kinds. They may consist, e.g., in adding some new conditions or in omitting some of our postulates (i)–(v) or, ultimately, in some changes within particular conditions. We shall consider now one of the possibilities of the latter kind. Now, there seem to be reasons for formulating the condition (iv) in the following way:

$$\text{(iv}'\text{)}\quad \bigwedge_{\mathscr{X},\mathscr{Y}} (\mathscr{X},\mathscr{Y} \in \mathsf{B} \wedge \mathscr{X} \neq \mathscr{Y} \rightarrow \bigvee_{\mathscr{Z}} \bigvee_{X,Y} (\mathscr{Z} \in \mathbf{K}^* \wedge (X, Y \in \mathscr{Z} \vee$$
$$\vee (X = Y' \wedge (X \in \mathscr{Z} \vee Y \in \mathscr{Z}))) \wedge X \neq Y \wedge \bigcup \mathscr{X} \subset X \wedge$$
$$\wedge \bigcup \mathscr{Y} \subset Y))$$

(iv) and (iv′) differ in that instead of the condition $X, Y \in \mathscr{Z}$ in (iv), in (iv′) there is a more complicated condition $X, Y \in \mathscr{Z} \vee \vee (X = Y' \wedge (X \in \mathscr{Z} \vee Y \in \mathscr{Z}))$. Thus, it is not required here that X and Y be necessarily positive phonetic features of the kind $\mathscr{Z}$ and so it is not excluded that Y is a phonetic feature, and X is only the absence of the feature Y, that is, X is, so to speak, merely a negative feature. Of course, this relation between X and Y is formally expressed by the statement that X is the complement of the set Y, that is $X = Y'$.

The reasons for accepting (iv′) rather than (iv) are clear from the following considerations quoted from Jassem:

It happens sometimes (but very seldom) that a relevant feature should be defined negatively. The sounds in ***along*** and in *sof**a*** are examples of this in English. The first is a half-closed neutral, the second—a half-open neutral. It may seem that only the neutral articulation is their common feature (these two sounds are mutually excluded). If this were so, it would be impossible to state the opposition between the second vowel in *canvas* (which is identical with the vowel in ***along***) and the second vowel in *converse* (adjective). The vowel in *converse* is also neutral, but it is middle. Thus, here we have a more complicated case. On the one hand we have mutually excluded vowels which are both neutral but one is half-open and the second half-closed; on the other hand one of them is in opposition to a third vowel and this opposition cannot be described merely by the feature of neutral articulation. In this case we are obliged to establish a negative common feature, namely, a non-middle articulation, for our mutually excluded sounds. And thus we shall be able to describe the opposition between the vowels of *canvas* and of *converse* as consisting in the difference between middle and non-middle articulation.[1]

In spite of the above argument, we have used the condition (iv) and not (iv′) in the definition 13.1, since we are afraid that the condition (iv′) can be, generally speaking, too liberal. In our opinion, this problem requires more detailed linguistic examination.

The following are a few simple formal corollaries from the definition 13.1.

13.2 $$\mathsf{B} \in \mathbf{PB}^{(\iota)} \rightarrow 0 < \overline{\overline{\mathsf{B}}} < \aleph_0$$

13.3 $$\mathsf{B} \in \mathbf{PB}^{(\iota)} \wedge \mathscr{X} \in \mathsf{B} \rightarrow \mathscr{X} \neq \Lambda$$

Proof. Let us suppose that the hypothesis of the theorem is fulfilled and that at the same time $\mathscr{X} = \Lambda$. Then $\Lambda \in \mathsf{B}$. Let us consider the set $\mathsf{B}_1 = \mathsf{B} - [\Lambda]$. It is obvious that B_1 fulfils the conditions (i)–(iv) of the definition 13.1. And since in accordance with 13.2 B is a finite set, therefore $\overline{\overline{\mathsf{B}}}_1 < \overline{\overline{\mathsf{B}}}$. Hence it results in accordance with the condition (v) of the definition 13.1, that $\mathsf{B} \notin \mathbf{PB}^{(\iota)}$, contrary to our supposition.

13.4 $$\mathsf{B} \in \mathbf{PB}^{(\iota)} \wedge X \in \Sigma^{(\iota)} \rightarrow \dot{\bigvee_{\mathscr{X}}} (\mathscr{X} \in \mathsf{B} \wedge X \in \mathscr{X})$$

13.5 $$\mathsf{B}_1 \in \mathbf{PB}^{(\iota)} \wedge \mathsf{B}_2 \in \mathbf{PB}^{(\iota)} \rightarrow \overline{\overline{\mathsf{B}}}_1 = \overline{\overline{\mathsf{B}}}_2$$

Proof. If $\overline{\overline{\mathsf{B}}}_1 \neq \overline{\overline{\mathsf{B}}}_2$, then by 13.2, we would have either $\overline{\overline{\mathsf{B}}}_1 < \overline{\overline{\mathsf{B}}}_2$ or $\overline{\overline{\mathsf{B}}}_2 < \overline{\overline{\mathsf{B}}}_1$. In this case, however, in accordance with 13.1(v) we have either $\mathsf{B}_1 \notin \mathbf{PB}^{(\iota)}$ or $\mathsf{B}_2 \notin \mathbf{PB}^{(\iota)}$, which contradicts the hypothesis of the theorem.

13.6 $$\bigwedge_{X,Y} (X\, \mathbf{Fv}_\iota\, Y \rightarrow X = Y) \rightarrow \mathbf{PB}^{(\iota)} \neq \Lambda$$

Proof. Let B_1 be the family of all sets of the form $[X]$, where $X \in \Sigma^{(\iota)}$. In view of the assumption that $X\, \mathbf{Fv}_\iota\, Y$ always implies the equation $X = Y$, the family B_1 must fulfil the conditions (i)–(iv) of the definition 13.1. Of course,

$$\overline{\overline{\mathsf{B}}}_1 = \overline{\overline{\Sigma^{(\iota)}}} \leqslant \overline{\overline{\mathbf{usg}^{(\iota)}}} < \aleph_0$$

and, moreover, every family B which fulfils the conditions (i)–(iv) of the definition 13.1 does not contain more elements than B_1. Therefore all such families contain a finite number of elements. Hence among these families, there exists a family B_0 such that for every family B which fulfils the conditions (i)–(iv) we have $\overline{\overline{\mathsf{B}}}_0 \leqslant \overline{\overline{\mathsf{B}}}$. Therefore, B_0 fulfils also the condition (v) of the definition 13.1, that is, $\mathsf{B}_0 \in \mathbf{PB}^{(\iota)}$ and in consequence $\mathbf{PB}^{(\iota)} \neq \Lambda$.

[1] W. Jassem [10], pp. 43–44.

Let us consider now the following proposition

$$(\mathrm{H}_1) \qquad \bigwedge_{\iota}(\mathbf{PB}^{(\iota)} \neq \Lambda).$$

This proposition states that every idiolect has at least one phonemic basis. However, it is not a theorem of our system, that is to say, it cannot be derived from our axioms and definitions. This does not mean that the proposition (H_1) is false: in fact, it can be true although we are not able to prove it exclusively by means of the assumptions of our system. At any rate, if our definition 13.1 is correct from the linguistic point of view, that is, if it is adequate as an explication of the notion of the phoneme, known from the intuitive, informal phonology, the proposition (H_1) should be true (at least when in the set **I** we include only 'maximal' idiolects, that is, the idiolects which comprise the totality of the speech of all members of a speech community). The proposition (H_1) may be treated, therefore, as a test of adequacy of our definition and as a test of practical usefulness of the defined notion. Of course, (H_1) may be proved to be true or false only by means of empirical examination of particular languages.

The proposition (H_1) may be called the *first fundamental hypothesis of phonology*.

Let us consider now the reasons why it is impossible to prove the proposition (H_1) in our system and for which it is even uncertain whether it is true. These reasons lie in the conditions (ii) and (iv) of our definition. Although these conditions do not contradict each other, in certain idiolects they may happen to be incompatible. The first one requires that each two sounds being mutual free variants, must be grouped into one phoneme. The second requires the existence of certain features common to all elements of each phoneme and oppositional features for each two different phonemes. Whether both these conditions can be simultaneously fulfilled depends on certain specific properties of idiolect. As a rule this is possible, since the existence of different free variants is connected with the processes of language development, and hence, if $X \ \mathbf{Fv}_\iota \ Y$, X is only slightly different from Y, i.e. X and Y have almost all features in common. However, we cannot exclude *a priori* the possibility of the existence of such idiolects in which the conditions (ii) and (iv) are incompatible. If such idiolects exist, the proposition (H_1) is false and our definition 13.1 requires modification. What kind of modification would be required, is evident from the above considerations: namely, the condition (ii) of 13.1 should be omitted.[1] The definition modified in

[1] (ii) might be as well left and (iv) omitted, but this way of improving definition does not seem to be appropriate.

this way would treat the relations $\mathbf{Fv}_\iota$ and $\mathbf{Cm}_\iota$ identically, that is, in the same way as the definition 13.1 in its present form treats the relation $\mathbf{Cm}_\iota$: the 'identification' of free variants would not be imperative but only permissible (namely, only when other conditions, particularly (iv), make it possible). Moreover, having altered the definition 13.1 in this way, we would be able to prove the truth of the proposition (H_1). This proof would be similar to that of the theorem 13.6. It is also possible that our definition modified in this way would appeal more to some phonologists.

We shall define next two important notions of phonology, the notion of relevant (or phonemic) feature and the notion of distinctive feature. To begin with, let us point out that for the majority of phonologists the terms 'relevant' and 'distinctive' have the same meaning. Here they are given different meanings. It is not our own innovation. The differentiation between these two notions appears, for instance, in Jassem[1] and Pilch, and the latter uses the actual terms 'relevant' and 'distinctive' for this purpose. The respective definition by Pilch is as follows:

'Die einzelnen Schallmerkmale, die die Verwandschaft einer Klasse phonematisch gleicher Lautelemente ausmachen, nennen wir *phonematische* oder relevante Merkmale. [. . .] Von den relevanten scheiden wir die *distinktiven Merkmale*. Distinktiv sind nicht *sämtliche* Merkmale, die die Verwandschaft phonematisch gleicher Elemente ausmachen, sondern nur jenes *Mindestmaß* relevanter Merkmale, das für sich allein eine gegebene Klasse phonematisch gleicher Elemente gegenüber sämtlichen übrigen Lautelementen der gleichen Sprache abgrenzt.' [2]

These definitions require, of course, appropriate precisations and also certain modifications. First of all, let us say that it is not exactly sensible to speak simply about relevant or distinctive features. One should speak rather about relevant or distinctive features of something. But of what, sounds or phonemes? That should already be decided on in definitions. It appears to us that it would be most reasonable to speak about relevant features of sounds and distinctive features of phonemes. Considering the above modifications the explanation of both notions may be formulated as follows:

A *relevant feature* of the sound X in the idiolect ι and in respect to the phonemic basis B is every phonetic (in the generalized sense)

[1] W. Jassem [10], pp. 41–43. As a matter of fact Jassem uses a different terminology: instead of 'relevant' and 'distinctive' he writes 'fundamental' and 'relevant', respectively.

[2] H. Pilch [20], p. 57.

feature which pertains to the sound X (i.e. to every element of X) and to every sound Y which, together with the sound X belongs to the same phoneme in the basis B.

A *distinctive feature* of the phoneme $\mathscr{X}$ in the idiolect ι and with respect to the phonemic basis B is every relevant feature X of sounds belonging to $\mathscr{X}$, such that there exists a phoneme $\mathscr{Y}$ in the basis B and a relevant feature Y of sounds belonging to $\mathscr{Y}$, such that X is of the same kind as Y (that is, X and Y are homogeneous) and $X \neq Y$.

All features of the sound X which are not its relevant features may be called *irrelevant* or *non-phonemic features* of this sound (in the idiolect ι and in respect to the basis B).

On the other hand all relevant features of sounds belonging to the phoneme $\mathscr{X}$ which are not its distinctive features may be called *redundant features* of this phoneme (in the idiolect ι and in respect to the basis B).

The relativization of relevant and distinctive features to a definite phonemic basis B, which appears in the above definitions, is quite natural. For, the same sound X can have quite different relevant features if it is considered from the point of view of some other phonemic basis B_1. The quality and quantity of relevant features of a sound are dependent on what sounds it will be grouped with in one phoneme. Similarly, the quantity and quality of the distinctive features of particular phonemes depends on the phonemic basis.

Before we express the above definitions in symbolic form, let us introduce a certain auxiliary notion, namely, the relation of being a phonemic form of a sound (in respect to the idiolect ι and its given phonemic basis B). This relation we denote by $\Omega(\iota,\mathsf{B})$ and define as follows:

$\mathscr{X}$ is the *phonemic form* of the sound X of the idiolect ι and in respect to the phonemic basis B, in symbols: $\mathscr{X}\ \Omega(\iota,\mathsf{B})\ X$, if and only if $\mathscr{X} \in \mathsf{B}$ and $X \in \mathscr{X}$.

In order to speak about the phonemic form of the improper sound, i.e. the sound $\mathbf{0} \cap \mathbf{P}\langle\iota\rangle$, we shall enlarge the relation under discussion and assume that the set $[\mathbf{0} \cap \mathbf{P}\langle\iota\rangle]$ is the phonemic form of the improper sound. (This set may be called an *improper phoneme* of the idiolect ι.) Ultimately the definition of the relation $\Omega(\iota,\mathsf{B})$ may be formulated as follows:

13.7 $$\Omega(\iota,\mathsf{B}) \underset{\mathrm{df}}{=} \{\mathscr{X}, X: (\mathsf{B} \in \mathbf{PB}^{(\iota)} \wedge \mathscr{X} \in \mathsf{B} \wedge X \in \mathscr{X}) \vee \vee (X = \mathbf{0} \cap \mathbf{P}\langle\iota\rangle \wedge \mathscr{X} = [X])\}$$

The six theorems which follow are simple corollaries from the above definition and definition 13.1.

13.8 $\mathsf{B} \in \mathbf{PB}^{(\iota)} \wedge X \in \Sigma_0^{(\iota)} \rightarrow \bigvee_{\mathscr{X}} (\mathscr{X} = \Omega(\iota,\mathsf{B})`X)$

13.9 $\mathsf{B} \in \mathbf{PB}^{(\iota)} \wedge X \in \Sigma^{(\iota)} \rightarrow \Omega(\iota,\mathsf{B})`X \in \mathsf{B}$

13.10 $\mathsf{B} \in \mathbf{PB}^{(\iota)} \rightarrow \Omega(\iota,\mathsf{B})`(\mathbf{0} \cap \mathbf{P}\langle\iota\rangle) = [\mathbf{0} \cap \mathbf{P}\langle\iota\rangle]$

13.11 $\mathsf{B} \in \mathbf{PB}^{(\iota)} \wedge X \in \Sigma_0^{(\iota)} \rightarrow \Omega(\iota,\mathsf{B})`X \in \mathsf{B} \vee \Omega(\iota,\mathsf{B})`X = [X]$

13.12 $\mathsf{B} \in \mathbf{PB}^{(\iota)} \wedge X \in \Sigma_0^{(\iota)} \rightarrow X \in \Omega(\iota,\mathsf{B})`X$

13.13 $\mathsf{B} \in \mathbf{PB}^{(\iota)} \wedge X, Y \in \Sigma_0^{(\iota)} \rightarrow (\Omega(\iota,\mathsf{B})`X = \Omega(\iota,\mathsf{B})`Y \equiv$
$\equiv \bigvee_{\mathscr{X}} (\mathscr{X} \in \mathsf{B} \wedge X, Y \in \mathscr{X}) \vee X = Y = \mathbf{0} \cap \mathbf{P}\langle\iota\rangle)$

The *relation of being a relevant feature* of a given sound in an idiolect ι and with respect to a phonemic basis B will be symbolized by $\mathbf{Rf}(\iota,\mathsf{B})$. Its formal definition is the following:

13.14 $\mathbf{Rf}(\iota,\mathsf{B}) \underset{\text{df}}{=} \{Z,X \colon Z \in \mathsf{U}\mathbf{K}^* \wedge X \in \Sigma^{(\iota)} \wedge \mathsf{U}\Omega(\iota,\mathsf{B})`X \subset Z\}$

According to the above definition, Z is a relevant feature of X with respect to ι and B, in symbols: $Z\, \mathbf{Rf}(\iota,\mathsf{B})\, X$, if and only if Z is a phonetic feature (in the generalized sense), X is a proper sound in ι and the feature Z pertains to all segments belonging to elements of the phoneme $\Omega(\iota,\mathsf{B})`X$.

13.15 $\mathsf{B} \in \mathbf{PB}^{(\iota)} \wedge \overline{\overline{\mathsf{B}}} \geqslant 2 \wedge X \in \Sigma^{(\iota)} \rightarrow \mathbf{Rf}(\iota,\mathsf{B})^{\vee}X \neq \Lambda$

Proof. From the hypothesis by 13.9 it follows that $\Omega(\iota,\mathsf{B})`X \in \mathsf{B}$ and, moreover, the basis $\mathsf{B}$ contains also some other elements. From this by 13.1(iv) we infer that there is a $Z$ such that $\mathsf{U}\Omega(\iota,\mathsf{B})`X \subset Z$. Thus, by 13.14 we have $Z\, \mathbf{Rf}(\iota,\mathsf{B})\, X$ and, consequently, $\mathbf{Rf}(\iota,\mathsf{B})^{\vee}X \neq \Lambda$.

13.16 $\mathsf{B} \in \mathbf{PB}^{(\iota)} \wedge \mathscr{X} \in \mathsf{B} \wedge X, Y \in \mathscr{X} \rightarrow \mathbf{Rf}(\iota,\mathsf{B})^{\vee}X = \mathbf{Rf}(\iota,\mathsf{B})^{\vee}Y$

Proof. From the hypothesis follows $X, Y \in \Sigma^{(\iota)}$, and, by 13.13, $\Omega(\iota,\mathsf{B})`X = \Omega(\iota,\mathsf{B})`Y$. Hence $\mathsf{U}\Omega(\iota,\mathsf{B})`X = \mathsf{U}\Omega(\iota,\mathsf{B})`Y$. If, now, $Z\, \mathbf{Rf}(\iota,\mathsf{B})\, X$, then by 13.14 we have also $Z\, \mathbf{Rf}(\iota,\mathsf{B})\, Y$; and conversely.

13.17 $\mathsf{B} \in \mathbf{PB}^{(\iota)} \wedge \mathscr{X} \in \mathsf{B} \wedge X \in \mathscr{X} \rightarrow \mathbf{Rf}(\iota,\mathsf{B})\langle\mathscr{X}\rangle = \mathbf{Rf}(\iota,\mathsf{B})^{\vee}X$

Proof. If $Z \in \mathbf{Rf}(\iota,\mathsf{B})\langle\mathscr{X}\rangle$, then $Z \in \mathbf{Rf}(\iota,\mathsf{B})^{\vee}Y$, for some $Y \in \mathscr{X}$; and hence by 13.16 $Z \in \mathbf{Rf}(\iota,\mathsf{B})^{\vee}X$. Thus $\mathbf{Rf}(\iota,\mathsf{B})\langle\mathscr{X}\rangle \subset \mathbf{Rf}(\iota,\mathsf{B})^{\vee}X$. The converse inclusion is obvious.

13.18 $\mathsf{B} \in \mathbf{PB}^{(\iota)} \wedge \mathscr{X}, \mathscr{Y} \in \mathsf{B} \wedge \mathscr{X} \neq \mathscr{Y} \wedge X \in \mathscr{X} \wedge Y \in \mathscr{Y} \rightarrow$
$\rightarrow \mathbf{Rf}(\iota,\mathsf{B})^{\vee}X \neq \mathbf{Rf}(\iota,\mathsf{B})^{\vee}Y$

Proof. From the hypothesis by 13.1(iv) it follows that there exist two different and homogeneous features Z_1, Z_2 such that $\mathsf{U}\mathscr{X} \subset Z_1$ and $\mathsf{U}\mathscr{Y} \subset Z_2$. But since $X \in \mathscr{X}$ and $Y \in \mathscr{Y}$, therefore by 13.7 and

13.8 $\mathscr{X} = \Omega(\iota,\mathsf{B})`X$ and $\mathscr{Y} = \Omega(\iota,\mathsf{B})`Y$. Hence $\mathsf{U}\Omega(\iota,\mathsf{B})`X \subset Z_1$ and $\mathsf{U}\Omega(\iota,\mathsf{B})`Y \subset Z_2$. From this by 13.14 we have $Z_1 \in \mathbf{Rf}(\iota,\mathsf{B})^{\vee}X$ and $Z_2 \in \mathbf{Rf}(\iota,\mathsf{B})^{\vee}Y$. And since Z_1 and Z_2 are homogeneous features, therefore $Z_1 \notin \mathbf{Rf}(\iota,\mathsf{B})^{\vee}Y$ and $Z_2 \notin \mathbf{Rf}(\iota,\mathsf{B})^{\vee}X$, which establishes the thesis of our theorem.

13.19 $\mathsf{B} \in \mathbf{PB}^{(\iota)} \wedge \mathscr{X},\mathscr{Y} \in \mathsf{B} \wedge \mathscr{X} \neq \mathscr{Y} \longrightarrow \mathbf{Rf}(\iota,\mathsf{B})\langle\mathscr{X}\rangle \neq \mathbf{Rf}(\iota,\mathsf{B})\langle\mathscr{Y}\rangle$

Proof. From hypothesis by 13.3 follows that $\mathscr{X}$ and $\mathscr{Y}$ are non-empty sets. Let $X \in \mathscr{X}$ and $Y \in \mathscr{Y}$. Then by 13.17 $\mathbf{Rf}(\iota,\mathsf{B})\langle\mathscr{X}\rangle = \mathbf{Rf}(\iota,\mathsf{B})^{\vee}X$ and $\mathbf{Rf}(\iota,\mathsf{B})\langle\mathscr{Y}\rangle = \mathbf{Rf}(\iota,\mathsf{B})^{\vee}Y$. From this by 13.18 follows the thesis of our theorem.

The *relation of being a distinctive feature* of a given phoneme in an idiolect ι and with respect to a phonemic basis B will be symbolized by $\mathbf{Df}(\iota,\mathsf{B})$. Its formal definition is as follows:

13.20 $$\mathbf{Df}(\iota,\mathsf{B}) \underset{\mathrm{df}}{=} \{Z,\mathscr{X}: Z \in \mathbf{Rf}(\iota,\mathsf{B})\langle\mathscr{X}\rangle \wedge \bigvee_{\mathscr{Y}}\bigvee_{\mathscr{Z}}\bigvee_{V}(\mathscr{X} \in \mathsf{B} \wedge \mathscr{Z} \in \mathbf{K}^* \wedge Z,V \in \mathscr{Z} \wedge Z \neq V \wedge \mathsf{U}\mathscr{Y} \subset V)\}$$

13.21 $\mathsf{B} \in \mathbf{PB}^{(\iota)} \wedge \overline{\overline{\mathsf{B}}} \geqslant 2 \wedge \mathscr{X} \in \mathsf{B} \longrightarrow \mathbf{Df}(\iota,\mathsf{B})^{\vee}\mathscr{X} \neq \Lambda$

Proof. It follows from the hypothesis of the theorem that the basis B contains in addition to $\mathscr{X}$ also another phoneme $\mathscr{Y}$. On account of 13.1(iv) we infer from this, that there is a kind of features $\mathscr{Z}$ and features $Z,V \in \mathscr{Z}$ such that $Z \neq V$, $\mathsf{U}\mathscr{X} \subset Z$ and $\mathsf{U}\mathscr{Y} \subset V$. But since by 13.3 $\mathscr{X} \neq \Lambda$, therefore $\mathscr{X} = \Omega(\iota,\mathsf{B})`X$, for some $X \in \mathscr{X}$. Hence $\mathsf{U}\Omega(\iota,\mathsf{B})`X \subset Z$. Thus by 13.14 $Z \in \mathbf{Rf}(\iota,\mathsf{B})\langle\mathscr{X}\rangle$, whence $Z \in \mathbf{Df}(\iota,\mathsf{B})^{\vee}\mathscr{X}$ and the thesis of our theorem is established.

13.22 $\mathsf{B} \in \mathbf{PB}^{(\iota)} \wedge \mathscr{X} \in \mathsf{B} \longrightarrow \mathbf{Df}(\iota,\mathsf{B})^{\vee}\mathscr{X} \subset \mathbf{Rf}(\iota,\mathsf{B})\langle\mathscr{X}\rangle$

13.23 $\mathsf{B} \in \mathbf{PB}^{(\iota)} \wedge \mathscr{X},\mathscr{Y} \in \mathsf{B} \wedge \mathscr{X} \neq \mathscr{Y} \longrightarrow \mathbf{Df}(\iota,\mathsf{B})^{\vee}\mathscr{X} \neq \mathbf{Df}(\iota,\mathsf{B})^{\vee}\mathscr{Y}$

Proof. It follows from the hypothesis that there is a kind of features $\mathscr{Z}$ and features $X,Y \in \mathscr{Z}$ such that $X \neq Y$, $\mathsf{U}\mathscr{X} \subset X$ and $\mathsf{U}\mathscr{Y} \subset Y$. Since by 13.3 $\mathscr{X} \neq \Lambda$ and $\mathscr{Y} \neq \Lambda$, therefore $\mathscr{X} = \Omega(\iota,\mathsf{B})`X_1$, for some $X_1 \in \mathscr{X}$, and $\mathscr{Y} = \Omega(\iota,\mathsf{B})`Y_1$, for some $Y_1 \in \mathscr{Y}$. By virtue of 13.14 $X \in \mathbf{Rf}(\iota,\mathsf{B})\langle\mathscr{X}\rangle$ and $Y \in \mathbf{Rf}(\iota,\mathsf{B})\langle\mathscr{Y}\rangle$. Hence by 13.20 $X \in \mathbf{Df}(\iota,\mathsf{B})^{\vee}\mathscr{X}$ and $Y \in \mathbf{Df}(\iota,\mathsf{B})^{\vee}\mathscr{Y}$. But since X and Y are homogeneous, therefore $Y \notin \mathbf{Df}(\iota,\mathsf{B})^{\vee}\mathscr{X}$ and $X \notin \mathbf{Df}(\iota,\mathsf{B})^{\vee}\mathscr{Y}$.

The last theorem expresses one of the fundamental principles of phonology: every two different phonemes may be characterized by different systems of distinctive features. In connection with this some authors simply say that phonemes are bundles of distinctive features.

It seems that the definition of the notion of relevant feature assumed by us should be sufficient for the majority of concrete applications of this notion. However, our definition diverges from

Pilch's definition quoted above and perhaps also from more or less explicit intuitions of other linguists. In fact, our definition does not contain any condition analogous to that which Pilch associates with the word 'Mindestmaß'. In order to elucidate this problem, let us consider the following example. Let B be a phonemic basis of the idiolect ι, which contains five phonemes shown on the table below. Further, let the distinctive features (in the sense of our definition 13.20) of these phonemes be as shown in the second, third and fourth column of the table. Perhaps Pilch's intention is not to consider X as a distinctive feature of $\mathscr{X}_1$ in this situation. For, if X is excluded from the set of distinctive features of $\mathscr{X}_1$, this phoneme is still in opposition to every other phonemes: the difference between $\mathscr{X}_1$ on the one hand and $\mathscr{X}_2$ and $\mathscr{X}_3$ on the other hand being that

phonemes	*distinctive features of the kind*		
	$\mathscr{L}_1$	$\mathscr{L}_2$	$\mathscr{L}_3$
$\mathscr{X}_1$	X	Y	Z
$\mathscr{X}_2$	X'	Y'	Z
$\mathscr{X}_3$	X	Y'	Z
$\mathscr{X}_4$	X	Y	Z'
$\mathscr{X}_5$	X'	Y	Z'

between Y and Y', while the difference between $\mathscr{X}_1$ on the one hand and $\mathscr{X}_4$ and $\mathscr{X}_5$ on the other hand being that between Z and Z'. Let us notice, however, that it would be impossible to remove Y instead of X from among the distinctive features of the phoneme $\mathscr{X}_1$, since with the removal of Y the phoneme $\mathscr{X}_1$ would not be in opposition to $\mathscr{X}_3$. It may happen, however, that of two distinctive features (in the sense of our definition 13.20) of some phoneme either may be removed without affecting any oppositions.

It is by no means easy to construct a definition of the notion of a distinctive feature which would exclude from the set of distinctive features of any phoneme all 'unnecessary' (as explained above) features. For, if we take into consideration the fact (which has been indicated above) that distinctive features may be associated with a phoneme in several ways, it immediately becomes obvious that the definition of one particular relation of being a distinctive feature is insufficient and it is necessary, rather, to define the whole class of various relations, each of which may be considered as the relation of being a distinctive feature of a phoneme. Perhaps the following definition may serve:

(3) F is an *assignment of distinctive features* with phonemes in the phonemic basis B of the idiolect ι if and only if F is a binary relation fulfilling the following conditions:

(i) $\mathrm{C\!\!I}`\mathsf{F} = \mathsf{B}$

(ii) $\bigwedge_{\mathscr{X}} (\mathscr{X} \in \mathsf{B} \rightarrow \mathsf{F}^{\vee}\mathscr{X} \subset \mathbf{Rf}(\iota,\mathsf{B})\langle\mathscr{X}\rangle)$

(iii) $\bigwedge_{\mathscr{X},\mathscr{Y}} (\mathscr{X},\mathscr{Y} \in \mathsf{B} \wedge \mathscr{X} \neq \mathscr{Y} \rightarrow \bigvee_{\mathscr{Z}} \bigvee_{X,Y} (\mathscr{Z} \in \mathbf{K}^* \wedge X, Y \in \mathscr{Z} \wedge$

$\wedge X \neq Y \wedge X \in \mathsf{F}^{\vee}\mathscr{X} \wedge Y \in \mathsf{F}^{\vee}\mathscr{Y}))$

(iv) $\bigwedge_{\mathscr{X}} \bigwedge_{X} (\mathscr{X} \in \mathsf{B} \wedge X \in \mathsf{F}^{\vee}\mathscr{X} \rightarrow \bigvee_{\mathscr{Y},\mathscr{Z}} \bigvee_{Y} (\mathscr{Y} \in \mathsf{B} \wedge \mathscr{Z} \in \mathbf{K}^* \wedge X, Y \in \mathscr{Z} \wedge$

$\wedge Y \in \mathsf{F}^{\vee}\mathscr{Y} \wedge X, Y \in \mathsf{F}^{\vee}\mathscr{X} \dot{-} \mathsf{F}^{\vee}\mathscr{Y} \wedge \bigwedge_{Z,V} (Z, V \in \mathsf{F}^{\vee}\mathscr{X} \dot{-} \mathsf{F}^{\vee}\mathscr{Y} \wedge$

$\wedge Z \neq V \wedge [X,Y] \neq [Z,V] \rightarrow \bigwedge_{\mathscr{Z}_1} (\mathscr{Z}_1 \in \mathbf{K}^* \rightarrow Z \notin \mathscr{Z}_1 \vee$

$\vee V \notin \mathscr{Z}_1))))$

If F is an assignment of distinctive features with phonemes in the basis B of the idiolect ι, in the sense of the above definition, and $\mathscr{X}$ is a phoneme in B, then $\mathsf{F}^{\vee}\mathscr{X}$ is the set of all distinctive features of the phoneme $\mathscr{X}$ under assignment F. In accordance with (ii) elements of $\mathsf{F}^{\vee}\mathscr{X}$ are relevant features of sounds belonging to $\mathscr{X}$. According to (iii) the assignment F has the property that every two different phonemes $\mathscr{X}$ and $\mathscr{Y}$ form an opposition, this opposition finding its expression in certain homogeneous and different elements of the sets $\mathsf{F}^{\vee}\mathscr{X}$ and $\mathsf{F}^{\vee}\mathscr{Y}$. Point (iv) is the most essential part of the definition (3). It is (iv) that requires all 'unnecessary' features to be removed from among distinctive features of every phoneme. To be more precise, this postulate requires every distinctive feature of a given phoneme to be the only basis for the opposition to at least one other phoneme.

The notion of phonemic form of sound, which has been defined in 13.7, will be presently employed in the definition of the notion of phonemic structure of a phonetic chain. If x is a complete phonetic chain, by the *phonemic structure* of this chain with respect to ι and the phonemic basis B we shall mean the following sequence of phonemes:

$$\Omega(\iota,\mathsf{B})`\varphi_1^{\iota}(x), \quad \Omega(\iota,\mathsf{B})`\varphi_2^{\iota}(x), \ldots, \quad \Omega(\iota,\mathsf{B})`\varphi_n^{\iota}(x),$$

where $n = \lambda_x^{\iota}$. This sequence will be denoted by $\Phi^{\iota,\mathsf{B}}(x)$, and the successive terms of it by

$$\Phi^{\iota,\mathsf{B}}(x), \quad \Phi_2^{\iota,\mathsf{B}}(x), \ldots, \quad \Phi_n^{\iota,\mathsf{B}}(x).$$

The formal definition of the sequence $\Phi^{\iota,\mathsf{B}}(x)$ is as follows:

13.24 $$\Phi^{\iota,\mathsf{B}}(x) \underset{\mathrm{df}}{=} \Omega(\iota,\mathsf{B})/\varphi^{\iota}(x)$$

The next formulas are corollaries from the above definition.

13.25 $x \in \mathbf{cch}^{(\iota)} \wedge \mathsf{B} \in \mathbf{PB}^{(\iota)} \longrightarrow \mathrm{D}`\Phi^{\iota,\mathsf{B}}(x) \subset \mathsf{B} \cup [[\mathbf{0} \cap \mathbf{P}\langle\iota\rangle]]$

13.26 $x \in \mathbf{cch}^{(\iota)} \wedge \mathsf{B} \in \mathbf{PB}^{(\iota)} \longrightarrow \mathrm{Cl}`\Phi^{\iota,\mathsf{B}}(x) = \{n : n \leqslant \lambda^{\iota}_{x}\}$

13.27 $x \in \mathbf{cch}^{(\iota)} \wedge \mathsf{B} \in \mathbf{PB}^{(\iota)} \longrightarrow \Phi^{\iota,\mathsf{B}}(x) \in \mathrm{fnc}$

13.28 $\Phi^{\iota,\mathsf{B}}_{n}(x) \underset{\mathrm{df}}{=} \Phi^{\iota,\mathsf{B}}(x)`n$

13.29 $x \in \mathbf{cch}^{(\iota)} \wedge \mathsf{B} \in \mathbf{PB}^{(\iota)} \wedge n \leqslant \lambda^{\iota}_{x} \longrightarrow \Phi^{\iota,\mathsf{B}}_{n}(x) \in \mathsf{B} \cup [[\mathbf{0} \cap \mathbf{P}\langle\iota\rangle]]$

13.30 $x \in \mathbf{cch}^{(\iota)} \wedge \mathsf{B} \in \mathbf{PB}^{(\iota)} \wedge n \leqslant \lambda^{\iota}_{x} \longrightarrow \Phi^{\iota,\mathsf{B}}_{n}(x) = \Omega(\iota,\mathsf{B})`\varphi^{\iota}_{n}(x)$

13.31 $u \in \mathbf{Ut}\langle\iota\rangle \wedge \mathsf{B} \in \mathbf{PB}^{(\iota)} \longrightarrow \Phi^{\iota,\mathsf{B}}_{1}(u) = [\mathbf{0} \cap \mathbf{P}\langle\iota\rangle]$

13.32 $u \in \mathbf{Ut}\langle\iota\rangle \wedge \mathsf{B} \in \mathbf{PB}^{(\iota)} \wedge n = \lambda^{\iota}_{u} \longrightarrow \Phi^{\iota,\mathsf{B}}_{n}(u) = [\mathbf{0} \cap \mathbf{P}\langle\iota\rangle]$

13.33 $x \in \mathbf{cch}^{(\iota)} \wedge \mathsf{B} \in \mathbf{PB}^{(\iota)} \wedge n,m \leqslant \lambda^{\iota}_{x} \longrightarrow (\vartheta^{\iota}_{n}(x)\, \mathbf{E}\, \vartheta^{\iota}_{m}(x) \longrightarrow$
$\longrightarrow \Phi^{\iota,\mathsf{B}}_{n}(x) = \Phi^{\iota,\mathsf{B}}_{m}(x))$

13.34 $x,y \in \mathbf{cch}^{(\iota)} \wedge \mathsf{B} \in \mathbf{PB}^{(\iota)} \longrightarrow (x\, \mathbf{E}\, y \longrightarrow \Phi^{\iota,\mathsf{B}}(x) = \Phi^{\iota,\mathsf{B}}(y))$

By means of the notion of phonemic structure we may easily define the notion of a phonological system of an idiolect. Phonological systems are ordered pairs with the set of phonemes as the first element and the set of phonemic structures of all phrases as the second. Therefore the definition of this notion will be largely analogous to the definition of phonic or phonetic system. This is, however, only a partial analogy, since idiolects may have several different phonemic bases and thereby several different phonological systems. Therefore, it is not the phonological system of an idiolect ι which should be defined here, but the class of phonological systems of the idiolect ι.

13.35 By a *phonological system* of an idiolect ι we mean every ordered pair of the form

$$\langle \mathsf{B}, \Phi^{\iota,\mathsf{B}}\langle \mathbf{Phr}\langle\iota\rangle\rangle\rangle$$

where B is a phonemic basis of the idiolect ι.

Let us point out also that having accepted (3) as the definition of the notion of distinctive feature of phoneme, phonological systems should rather be defined as ordered triples of the form

$$\langle \mathsf{B}, \mathsf{F}, \Phi^{\iota,\mathsf{B}}\langle \mathbf{Phr}\langle\iota\rangle\rangle\rangle$$

where F is an assignment of distinctive features to phonemes in the basis B.

Before we conclude, let us return to the above theorems on the notion of phonemic structure of phonetic chain. Let us point out that the sign of implication used in the consequents of 13.33 and 13.34 cannot be replaced by the sign of equivalence. We do not want to say, by any means, that the propositions resulting from such substitution are false. What we mean is, merely, that these propositions are not theorems of our system. This is, however, understandable considering the possible existence of (at least in certain idiolects) non-identical free variants. The only disquieting fact is that everything seems to indicate that neither is the proposition below a thesis of our system:

$$(\mathbf{H}_2) \quad x,y \in \mathbf{cch}^{(\iota)} \wedge \mathsf{B} \in \mathbf{PB}^{(\iota)} \wedge \Phi^{\iota,\mathsf{B}}(x) = \Phi^{\iota,\mathsf{B}}(y) \rightarrow \overline{\rightarrow} \bigwedge_{i} (i \leqslant \lambda_x^{\iota} \rightarrow \varphi_i^{\iota}(x)\, \mathbf{Fv}_{\iota}^{\mathsf{1}}\, \varphi_i^{\iota}(y))$$

Thus, the phonemic structure of a phonetic chain may not unequivocally determine the sounding of this chain and, what is more, the possible existence of non-identical free variants is not solely responsible for this situation.

In order to realize more profoundly the importance of the above fact, it should be noticed, that as a result, our theory does not guarantee that there is only one way (up to free variants) of reading a phonemic transcription. (Phonemic transcription consists in the one–one assignment of signs with particular phonemes in the given phonemic basis and in describing phonemic structures of utterances of the given idiolect by means of these signs). This circumstance in the eyes of linguist may seem to be a considerable shortcoming in our theory. The following is what Harris wrote on this subject from the point of view of his theory:

'The occurrence of a phoneme represents the occurrence of some member of its class of segments, each member being environmentally defined. Whenever the phoneme appears we can always tell from the environment which segment member of the phoneme would occur in that position (i.e. we can always pronounce phonemic writing). Conversely since complete overlapping is avoided, whenever we are given a segment in an environment we can always tell in which phoneme it is included (i.e. we can always write phonemically whatever we hear). Phonemic writing is therefore a one–one representation of what was set up in chapter 4 (and 6) as being descriptively relevant (i.e. contrastive, not substitutable) in speech.' [1]

And again in another place the postulate 'to write differently any two utterances which are different in segments' is defined by Harris simply as 'a basic consideration of phonemics'.[2]

[1] Z. S. Harris [7], p. 72. [2] Z. S. Harris [7] p. 62, footnote 10.

Of course Harris explains in detail that he is concerned with the one–one nature of phonemic representation of speech up to free variants:

'If the phonemic representation of speech is described as being one–one, this does not mean that if a particular sound x is associated with a phoneme Y, then when we are given the phoneme Y we associate with it the original particular sound x. The one–one correspondence means only that if a particular sound x in a given position is associated with a phoneme Y (or represented by the symbol Y), then when we are given the phoneme Y we will associate with it, in the stated position, some sound x', x'', which is substitutable for the original x (i.e. has the same distribution as x). In the stated position, the symbol Y is used for any sound which is substitutable for x, x', etc.' [1]

As may be seen from the above, (*a*) the postulate of phonemic representation of speech as being one–one (up to free variants) is one of the leading ideas of Harris' theory, and Harris himself is convinced that (*b*) his theory guarantees such one–one correspondence. And since, as has been stated above, our theory does not give such guarantee (since the proposition (H_2) is not its theorem), it would follow that our theory is not an adequate reconstruction of Harris' theory. It would certainly be so on the assumption that Harris' conviction expressed in (*b*) were right. But at this point some doubts may arise, since Harris did not even try to justify his conviction, and what is more, such justification on the grounds of his theory seems to be altogether impossible.

In order to make the above statement more clear and convincing, let us consider the following theoretical example.

Let B be a phonemic base of a given idiolect comprising among others the four following phonemes: $\mathcal{X}_1$, $\mathcal{X}_2$, $\mathcal{X}_3$, $\mathcal{X}_4$. Let us further assume that

$$\mathcal{X}_1 = [X_1, Y_1], \qquad \mathcal{X}_2 = [X_2, Y_2],$$
$$\mathcal{X}_3 = [X_3, Y_3], \qquad \mathcal{X}_4 = [X_4, Y_4],$$

where $X_i \, \mathbf{Cm}_\iota \, Y_i$, for all $i \in [1, 2, 3, 4]$. Does this situation exclude the existence (in the given idiolect) of phrases x, y having the following phonetic structures, respectively:

$$X_1, X_2, X_3, X_4$$
$$Y_1, Y_2, Y_3, Y_4.$$

In our opinion neither Harris' theory nor our own exclude such a possibility. Needless to say that if the above described situation did

[1] Z. S. Harris [7], p. 5.

occur, we would have two ways of reading (pronouncing) the following phonemic structure:

$$\mathcal{X}_1, \mathcal{X}_2, \mathcal{X}_3, \mathcal{X}_4.$$

Of course, the above example is purely theoretical. What is more, we are unable to present an analogous example from any concrete language. It is even possible that nobody will ever be able to find such an example. Thus, although not being a thesis of our system of phonology, the proposition (H_2) may in spite of this be empirically true. In this situation nothing stands in the way of accepting (H_2) as an empirical hypothesis. This hypothesis could be called the *second fundamental hypothesis of phonology*. Of course, it should be verified by empirical examination of all existing concrete languages.

Should, however, this hypothesis prove to be false, then we should be obliged to modify our definition of the concept of a phonemic basis. The modification could—roughly speaking—consist of the addition of a further postulate, namely that of 'one–one representation', to the definition. This definition would then be somewhat complicated, but the truth of the hypothesis (H_2) would be guaranteed: the hypothesis would then be a theorem of our system.

Chapter 14

FINAL REMARKS

The system of theoretical phonology reconstructed in the present work does not embrace the whole of Harris' phonological theory. There are two things absent from our system: the theory of junctures and the theory of suprasegmental elements of utterance. The reason of our omitting them is that both of them are still immature and they require a more full elaboration by linguists themselves. In their present state they are not fit for logical analysis and formal treatment. It is not inconceivable that the conceptual apparatus which has been worked out in this work may be helpful for further linguistic elaboration of both these sections of theoretical phonology. This concerns particularly the theory of junctures; the theory of suprasegmental elements seems to be far more difficult for exact treatment.

We are aware that not all sections of our theory are equally satisfactory. Thus, for instance, our conception of compound phonetic features, which may seem slightly artificial, may arouse various doubts among linguists. But even this conception has its justified place in our system. From the theoretical point of view the indispensableness of this or a related conception is unquestionable if unit-length segments are understood as the result of 'linking' of certain elementary segments.

What are the principal results of this work? We consider the following can be listed: the submission of the set of primitive notions which suffice to define almost all other notions of phonology, the submission of axiomatic characterization of these notions, arrangement of conceptual apparatus of phonology, analysis and definition of the notion of a unit-length segment, precise formulation of the principles of distribution and above all analysis of the notion of a phoneme and formulation and discussion of fundamental hypotheses of phonology.

REFERENCES

[1] Batóg, T.: *Logiczna rekonstrukcja pojęcia fonemu* (A Logical Reconstruction of the Concept of Phoneme). Studia Logica XI (1961), 139–83.

[2] Batóg, T.: *Critical Remarks on Greenberg's Axiomatic Phonology*. Studia Logica XII (1961), 195–205.

[3] Batóg, T.: *A Contribution to Axiomatic Phonology*. Studia Logica XIII (1962), 67–80.

[4] Bloch, B.: *A Set of Postulates for Phonemic Analysis*. Language 24 (1948), 3–46.

[5] Bloomfield, L.: *A Set of Postulates for the Science of Language*. Language 2 (1926), 153–64.

[6] Greenberg, J. H.: *An Axiomatization of the Phonologic Aspect of Language*. Symposium on Sociological Theory, ed. L. Gross, Evanston—New York 1959, 437–80.

[7] Harris, Z. S.: *Structural Linguistics*. Chicago 1960. (First edition under the title: *Methods in Structural Linguistics*, Chicago 1951.)

[8] Hockett, C. F.: *A Course in Modern Linguistics*. New York 1958.

[9] Hockett, C. F.: *A Manual of Phonology*. Baltimore 1955.

[10] Jassem, W.: *Fonetyka języka angielskiego* (The Phonetics of English). Warszawa 1954.

[11] Jassem, W.: *Węzłowe zagadnienia fonematyki* (The Main Problems of Phonemics). Bulletin de la Société Polonaise de Linguistique XV (1956), 13–30.

[12] Jassem, W.: *Próba funkcjonalnej definicji wyrazu* (A Functional Definition of a Word). Bulletin de la Société Polonaise de Linguistique XIX (1960), 35–49.

[13] Jones, D.: *The Phoneme: Its Nature and Use*. Cambridge 1950.

[14] Kanger, S.: *The Notion of a Phoneme*. Statistical Methods in Linguistics, No. 3 (1964), 43–8.

[15] Kleene, S. C.: *Introduction to Metamathematics*. Amsterdam 1952.

[16] Kuratowski, K.: *Introduction to Set Theory and Topology*. Oxford 1961.

[17] Marcus, S.: *Un model matematic al fonemului* (A Mathematical Model of Phoneme). Studii şi Cercetări Matematice XIV (1963), 405–21.

[18] Mostowski, A.: *Logika matematyczna* (Mathematical Logic). Warszawa–Wrocław 1948.

[19] Pike, K. L.: *Phonemics: A Technique for Reducing Languages to Writing*. Ann Arbor 1947.

[20] Pilch, H.: *Phonemtheorie*. I. Teil. Basel 1964.

[21] de Saussure, F.: *Cours de linguistique générale*. Lausanne–Paris 1916.

[22] Suppes, P.: *Axiomatic Set Theory*. Princeton, N.J. 1960.

[23] Tarski, A.: *Appendix E* in: Woodger, J. H.: *The Axiomatic Method in Biology*. Cambridge 1937, 161–72.

[24] Tarski, A.: *Introduction to Logic and to the Methodology of Deductive Sciences*. 2nd ed. New York 1946.

Index